AWAKEN, CHILDREN!

Dialogues With
Sri Sri Mata Amritanandamayi

VOLUME III

Adaptation & Translation

SWAMI AMRITASVARUPANANDA

MATA AMRITANANDAMAYI CENTERS
San Ramon, California

AWAKEN, CHILDREN!
Volume III

PUBLISHED BY:
Mata Amritanandamayi Center
P.O. Box 613
San Ramon, CA 94583-0613
Tel: (510) 537-9417

FIRST PRINTING April 1991
SECOND PRINTING November 1994

ALSO AVAILABLE FROM:
Mata Amritanandamayi Mission Trust
Amritapuri P.O., Kollam Dt., Keralam
INDIA 690525

ISBN 1-879410-54-0
LIBRARY OF CONGRESS CATALOG CARD NUMBER: 91-118937

This Book Is Humbly Offered At The

LOTUS FEET OF HER HOLINESS
SRI SRI MATA AMRITANANDAMAYI

The Resplendent Luminary Immanent
In the Hearts Of All Beings

Vandêham-saccidânandam-bhâvâtîtam-jagatgurum |
Nityam-pûrnam-nirâkâram-nirgunam-svâtmasamsthitam | |

I prostrate to the Universal Teacher, Who is Satchidananda (Pure Being-Knowledge-Absolute Bliss), Who is beyond all differences, Who is eternal, all-full, attributeless, formless and ever-centered in the Self.

Saptasâgaraparyantam-tîrthasnânaphalam-tu-yat |
Gurupâdapayôvindôh-sahasrâmśêna-tatphalam | |

Whatever merit is acquired by one, through pilgrimmages and from bathing in the Sacred Waters extending to the seven seas, cannot be equal to even one thousandth part of the merit derived from partaking the water with which the Guru's Feet are washed.

GURU GITA
Verses 157, 87

ACKNOWLEDGMENTS

My heartfelt gratitude is due to Professor M. Ramakrishnan Nair, the compiler of *Mata Amritanandamayi Sambhashanangal*, the Holy Mother's conversations in Malayalam. The present book, *Awaken, Children!* is a faithful translation of the same, interspersed with some additional materials which were recorded by me. I would like to thank my spiritual sisters Sabari and Remadevi who edited and typed the text, Brahmacharin Nealu who did the typesetting, and all of the Holy Mother's children who took part in producing the book.

TABLE OF CONTENTS

CONTENTS

CONTENTS

SONGS

PREFACE

Dear brothers and sisters, herein is contained a direct translation of Holy Mother's *divya upadesha* (Divine advice) into the English language. The tremendous blessing that is bestowed by presenting the Mother's teaching to the English speaking world is not yet fully realized. Now it is left to the reader to sanctify his or her life by a careful reading of the material and a whole-hearted practice of it in daily life.

Several points should be remembered in order that this translation is approached with right understanding. First of all, these conversations have occurred between the Mother and Indian householders and renunciates in the cultural context of India. Also the Mother's advice is given according to the level of understanding of each person to whom she is speaking. Often a word-for-word English translation falls short of conveying the totality of what the Mother has expressed through her mother tongue, Malayalam. One must consider these factors when contemplating her words to achieve deeper insight.

Secondly, the Mother's use of language is direct and earthy. Her words convey an immediacy and intensity of purpose to transmit the Essential, particularly when speaking to *sadhaks* (spiritual aspirants). For instance, when it comes time to bring a point across to a renunciate, the Mother does not mince words. Thus we can understand her expression, "Worldly pleasure is equal to dog excreta," to be sound advice to one whose sole aim is God-Realization.

In a separate conversation with a householder, the Mother's advice takes on an entirely different tone. "Mother does not say that you must give up all desires. You can enjoy them, but do not think that this life is for that only." Keep in mind that in the Mother's language, the word 'world' literally means 'That which is seen' as opposed to the invisible Reality or God. Knowing this will be of great help in interpreting her use of the word 'worldly.' When the Mother contrasts that which is spiritual to that which is worldly, she refers to the attitude with which actions are done. Spiritual actions are those actions which lead one to God through selflessness and purity. Worldly actions are those actions which lead one away from God, performed as they are in a spirit of selfishness.

Finally, the Mother speaks to us from the exalted state of *sahaja samadhi*, the natural state of abidance of a Self-Realised Master in the Absolute Reality. The challenge in translating is to render the Mother's transcendental vision into English for the layman. The vital ingredient in this process is the contemplative mind of the reader. Abandoning all superficiality, may our mind and intellect become subtle and assimilate the eternal Wisdom of the Mother's words. Firmly established in their practice, may we all revel in the direct experience of the Supreme Absolute without delay.

INTRODUCTION

To express the inexpressible, the subtlest of all experiences from "where speech along with the mind returns, unable to reach There," silence alone is the language, the language of the Self. A Perfect Master (*Satguru*) can teach his disciples through silence, provided that the disciples have the proper ears and heart to hear and assimilate the teachings of the Guru.

Our most beloved and revered Mother Amritanandamayi, who is ever established in that Supreme State of Silence, the Silence of Eternal Bliss and Peace, speaks only because we are not subtle enough to understand the meaning and depth of the spiritual message which She conveys through Her Silence. In other words, it is compassion, compassion alone, which prompts Her to speak to Her children about the indescribable state of Perfection.

The Mother's compassion towards Her children, who play with the toys of sense objects in the muddy fields of the world, is vast, deep and infinite like the ocean. In order to make us taste, enjoy and experience the bliss of Immortality, the Mother continuously feeds us with Her nectarous words. But we children are stubborn and impatient. We do not turn to Her to have a sip of that Ambrosia. Whereas, She, the Mother is extremely patient, ready to wait and wait and wait, until we develop a real thirst for It. A loving and affectionate Mother, She still waits at the doorway of our hearts, constantly knocking, hoping that we will open it some day to welcome Her and allow Her to dwell therein forever. The Mother's arms are outstretched. Simply fall into them. In Her all-embracing and all-consuming love, She will take us, carry us and bathe us in the never-ending stream of bliss and make us rest in Her arms, not for a while, but forever and ever.

We try to listen to the Mother's words but do not hear the Sound from the depths. We were trying to listen to Her through the previous two volumes; we listened but did not really hear it. Therefore, another opportunity to hear the constant ringing of Her call, both from within and without, is volume three of *Awaken, Children!*

Swami Amritasvarupananda

WINTER IN THE TROPICS of South India was drawing to a close as the cool early morning gave way more quickly to the late-rising sun. In these early months of 1984 the Ashram consisted of a small temple, a classroom also used for meditation, huts of thatched coconut leaves, and the building which housed the family of the Holy Mother. The Arabian Sea was a short walk to the west, splashing its waves onto the shore, unceasingly beckoning the fishermen to challenge its waters. The long, wooden boats that braved this sea recalled ancient times. To the east, the *kayal*, a system of backwaters, was lined with the tall, wooden skeletal frames which held the large fishing nets for night-fishing. This fishing village had been the Mother's ancestral home, and now it had become a home for many spiritual seekers and devotees, whether they were residents or not, for "home" is where the Mother is.

Monday, 27 February 1984

A seven day discourse on the *Srimad Bhagavad Gita* was being conducted in the Ashram. Many householder devotees and inquisitive young men and women who were very eager to learn participated. This was a time when they could all stay with the Holy Mother while leading a life of seclusion and perform spiritual practices in Her Divine Presence. During special occasions like this they found peace and acquired enough mental balance in order to continue their daily activities in the outside world with mindfulness. Daily meditation on the seashore with the Mother, chanting with Her the *Lalita Sahasranama* (the Thousand Names of the Divine Mother), attending classes on different scriptural texts taught by the residents in the light of the Mother's teachings were inspiring experiences for the devotees and something they will never forget in all their lives. On certain days, the Mother, with her own hands would serve lunch to all the devotees. The personal *darshan* (audience with a holy person) that each devotee received and the answers which the Mother gave to the different queries put forth by the devotees added even more splendor to those glorious days, thus creating an indelible impression on them.

Today was the final day of the discourse, which began on the twenty-first of the month. Just after the morning session of classes and meditation, the Mother was lying down on the sand behind the temple. Her head rested on the lap of a young girl and her feet was placed on the lap of another girl. A group of ladies sat attentively around the Holy Mother. They were longing to hear whatever she had to say, for they had always yearned for a rare moment like this, to be with the Mother in an informal situation. Not only they, but all of Mother's devotees wait for and cherish these precious moments. The Mother was in bliss, laughing and cracking jokes. The women also seemed very joyful, probably reflecting a fraction of the radiant bliss which overflowed from the Mother.

One lady: Amma, could you please give us some instructions about marriage and married life?

Amma: (smilingly) What has happened, daughter? Are
you in a dilemma? Never leave *mon* alone. *(mon* means
"son," here referring to the husband. The Mother will
often address her children as *mon*, "son," or *mol*,
"daughter.")

(As all have burst into laughter) Daughter, marriage
and married life, in fact, are another way to attain God-
Realization, although many are not aware of it. For the
attainment of this goal, both the husband and the wife
need a certain amount of understanding about leading a
married life coupled with spirituality. Patience, love and
forgiveness are the three qualities that are needed to
maintain a good relationship. In most cases, neither the
husband nor the wife will have these qualities. Such relationships will always end up in a tragedy. Doubting
each other's love, they will always quarrel. A silly, insignificant incident or sometimes even a single word is
enough to make them lose their mental balance. They
will always blame each other but never try to find a solution for the misunderstandings and conflicts. As a result, they suffer and also cause their children to suffer.

Parents should always set an example for their children in words and deeds. They are their children's first
teachers. Remember that by fighting and arguing with
each other in front of your children, you are setting a
bad example and spoiling their future as well. If you
cannot straighten out your own difficulties, that is your
problem, but why should you create problems in your
children's lives too?

Children, life is not a joke; it is a serious affair which you should handle with the utmost care and alertness. After one has acted thoughtlessly, there is no sense in worrying and shedding tears about it; therefore, try not to act foolishly.

Question: Amma, please suggest a solution.

Amma: Suggesting a solution is easy, but living up to it is much more difficult and important. There should be a sincere effort from your end. It is not difficult if you really want to lead a happy life. Thoughtless words, indiscriminative actions, anger and impatience will always create problems. Why should we consciously jump into problems knowing that to do so will only create sorrow and suffering?

Anyhow, in order to solve a problem, either the husband or the wife should have a certain amount of patience. When Mother says "patience," love and forgiveness are also implied. Real patience comes only when there is love and forgiveness.

Suppose you have a weakness of getting angry easily. Now, what you should do is this. Once you become normal again, go and sit in the family shrine room if you have one, or sit in solitude; then regret and repent your own anger and sincerely pray to your Beloved Deity or to Mother Nature, seeking help to get rid of it. Try to make your own mind aware of the bad outcome of anger. When you are angry at someone, you lose all your mental balance. Your discriminative power completely stops functioning. You say whatever comes into your mind and you act accordingly. You may even utter crude words at your own wife or children, or your own father or mother. Once you lose your discrimination you may even kill someone. By acting and thinking with anger you lose a lot of good energy. Become aware of this great truth, that these negative feelings will only pave the way for your own destruction, and sincerely try to put forth effort to overcome them.

WHICH IS THE PLACE
WHERE MOTHER IS NOT?

At this time a devotee came to write down Mother's words. Seeing him coming, the Mother smiled brightly.

Amma: Here comes the novelist. (All laugh.) (Turning to the devotee) Son, you will give a speech today.
Devotee: Mother, please don't ask me to speak.
Amma: Son, if you are Kali's son, Mother will make you speak today.
Devotee: The *vasana* (tendency) to show off as if I am great will come if I speak.
Amma: That will not happen if you speak in Mother's presence.
Devotee: Mother is just saying that. This is how Mother plays tricks on everyone.
Amma: (in a very stern voice) No, it will not happen in that way. You will not feel egoistic if you speak, having been told by Mother to speak.
Devotee: Anyhow, I do not feel like speaking.
Amma: But you speak daily in the college, don't you?

Devotee: (not speaking aloud, but thinking to himself)
That is how I earn my livelihood. But I cannot speak in
Mother's presence.

The Mother smiled mischievously and mysteriously.
Fixing her eyes skyward, she replied,

Amma: If so, which is the place where Mother is not?

The devotee was tongue-tied. He was a scholar and a
college professor and thus was stunned to hear the
Mother speaking out what he was thinking; she had
read his mind. The other devotees rejoiced, understanding the depth of the Mother's words. Even though the
scholar wanted to say, "But Mother, I don't see you
when I lecture in the college," he couldn't. Instead, he
fell at the Mother's feet and agreed to speak that day. He
said, "Obedience — unconditional obedience — is the
only way in the Mother's presence, because she is omniscient and omnipresent."

For the rest of the day the devotees who had heard
this exchange between the Mother and the scholar
shared this incident with whomever they met, quoting
the Mother's statement, "Which is the place where
Mother is not?" In fact, one could say that those words
were literally echoing in the atmosphere.

KNOW KALI IN PRINCIPLE

Everyone was resting after lunch. Though the sun's rays were very strong, it seemed that the people hardly felt it. Maybe the Holy Mother's presence made them feel cool and relaxed. It was always true that whenever they visited the Ashram, the devotees would forget everything about the world outside, and would even become oblivious to the immediate surroundings and circumstances while they were in the Mother's presence. They were not bothered by the lack of bodily comforts. The Holy Mother was sitting on the cot in her hut. Taking this as a good opportunity, some devotees, both men and women, gathered around her.

Amma: The children need only their mother.

Devotees: Mother, we are all plunged in the quagmire of worldliness. These are the only occasions we get to cleanse the body and mind. Mother, it is your duty to clean us up.

Amma: Good, Mother likes this attitude. Children, it is good that you are so frank and direct in your questioning. However, to wash away the mind, the child should stand still without resisting. What if the child struggles and runs away while the Mother tries to scrub away the mud which has dried and become hard due to a prolonged period of accumulated dirt? Obey the Mother and allow her to remove it.

Another devotee: Amma, we have heard that when you visited the houses of some devotees you removed and brought here the pictures of *Bhadra Kali* (the fierce as-

pect of the Divine Mother). We also learned that you instructed that householders should not worship the fierce
forms (of gods and goddesses). Therefore, we expected
you to take the picture of Kali from our house as well.
But you did not take it when you came to our house.
Amma, why didn't you?

Amma: Children, you worship while knowing and understanding the *tattwa* (essential principle) behind it.
There is no harm in that. Your attitude is that Kali is
Brahmamayi (the nature of the Absolute Pure Being),
Parashakti (the Supreme Power), and that She is Everything. Whereas, many worship Kali considering Her
only as a fierce goddess who kills the enemies. Those
who worship Her in that manner will have the same fi-
ery nature. Quarrels and conflicts will occur in such
houses, which will cause harm to them who worship in
that way. In fact, that is the wrong conception and the
wrong way to worship Her. There is no harm if one
worships while understanding the essential principle or
tattwa.

The devotee who asked the question was truly surprised because he had never disclosed to the Mother
what the attitude was in which he worshipped Kali. He
had instilled the same faith and idea in the minds of his
wife and children; and therefore, when he heard the
Mother address "children" instead of "son," he realized
that she knew all about their manner of worship. He
was amazed.

THE MOTHER AND GOD IN ONE

As the puzzled devotee sat dumbfounded and inspired, a *brahmacharin*, out of his excitement, said,

"Mother is Kali, sometimes very fierce, but that is only when we are disobedient and arrogant. At other times, she is as loving as the Mother who gave birth to us. Mother has instructed the *brahmacharins* to fast on Saturdays. The *brahmacharins* do not have any work to do on that day, Only *japa* and *dhyana* (repetition of mantra and meditation). But Mother herself will prepare rice and curry for everyone and serve it by noon. Mother will not agree if someone says 'no' to the food. Mother has more love on that day." (All burst into laughter, the Mother as well.)

Amma: Whatever it is, Mother is the one who gave birth, isn't she? How can Mother bear it when the children sit without eating? Mother will become restless by eleven o'clock. Mother herself will go and cook all the food. There is another intention and meaning in cooking and bringing the food by Mother herself on that day of fasting. Mother wants to make the *brahmacharins* experience that if, having dedicated everything to God, one sits for God alone, then God will bring everything to him. Now Mother does it. Later God Himself will bring and give everything to them.

Devotee: (Looking skyward, as if searching) Who is that God? Where is that God? I cannot see Him. (Again looking at the Mother, in a humble tone). Oh, oh, now I have found Him. Here He sits. (He prostrates at the Mother's feet. All burst into laughter.)

One householder devotee: Mother cannot bear it when the *brahmacharins* fast because she says, "Is not Mother the one who gave birth to them?" If this is the case, then she would be everyone's biological mother, wouldn't she? Yet, she doesn't show the same compassion to others as well, does she? How many people suffer!

Amma: (Smilingly) Oh, about that Mother will say that the *brahmacharins* who stay here are those who have come giving up all material pleasures with the attitude, "Mother alone is the refuge." Mother acts towards them accordingly. Whereas, the other children who lead a worldly life are not like this. They live egotistically, believing in their own power and ability, without taking refuge in God. Thus they experience sorrow caused by this. God gives the fruit (result) according to each one's attitude. Otherwise, God does not have any partiality at all. Let the others take refuge in God, relinquishing everything else; then God will also pay attention to their matters directly. The Lord lets those who have the egotistic attitude, "we are sufficient enough to look after our own matters," live in their own way. This does not mean that Mother has no love for them. Mother's love is equal towards everyone, but each one experiences it according to how they receive it in their heart.

One devotee: Here in this village many of the natives do not favor Mother or the Ashram.

Amma: They have faith in God. They will go to temples. Theirs is *kamya bhakti* (a lower type of devotion in which the devotee prays and worships the Lord in order to have his desires and wishes fulfilled). They do not know *tattwattile bhakti* (devotional practices performed while knowing and understanding the essential principles). They do not have the right understanding to know God through the essential principles. How can we blame them?

At this point Sugunanandan, the Holy Mother's father, came into the hut where she was sitting with the devotees. Seeing him, the Mother called out in a loud voice, "What, Sankara?" (Sometimes the Mother simply calls people by that name. Sankara is also a synonym for Lord Shiva.) And then she laughed like an innocent little girl. Sugunanandan grinned and patting his belly said, "Years ago Ammachi had told us, 'I have my devotees in distant places. They will come and join us here.' Now everything is slowly getting straightened out. (Rejoicing, enjoying himself) Oh my, all the things we have seen!"

Something very interesting had occurred in the meantime. As the conversation between the Mother and the householder devotees had been going on, one little girl said, "After meeting Mother we have no fear at all. We have Mother with us." Immediately after the girl had finished saying this, somebody pointed his finger up towards the roof of the hut. Everybody looked up and saw a snake hanging with its head downwards from the main wooden beam. It was swinging back and forth.

The rest of its body was coiled around the beam. The children who were in the hut, particularly the little girl "who had no fear at all," jumped out of the hut, crying loudly. The Holy Mother coolly remained seated on the cot, smiling and gazing at the snake. Seeing the Mother sitting there unmoved, the children felt a bit more coura-geous. They all came back to the hut, but feeling scared, they sat very close to the Holy Mother.

Amma: The main beam is the spine. The snake is the serpent power. (Referring to the snake) He resides here with me.

The snake slowly crawled into the thatched roof made of coconut palm leaves and disappeared.

One devotee: Among the Gods and Goddesses, Kali is the only one who didn't marry. Eternal virgin, *yogini* (one who is established in eternal union with Shiva, the Pure Consciousness), eternally celibate! That is why Kali is very dear to me.

Amma: (Laughing) Whom should Kali marry? Who can marry Her? Shouldn't there be two people in order to marry? Where is that second person? How could Kali's marriage happen? Kali is neither man nor woman. She is both. She is Pure Consciousness as well as Primordial Nature. (In a voice filled with *Shakti)* She fills both out-side and inside. Kali is the compassionate Mother of the devotee who longs to see Her as well as the fierce *Bha-dra Kali,* who kills the ego of the egotistical one. Kali is everything. Kali is here and there, up and down, inside and outside, above and below... Kali!... Kali!... Kali!...

The Holy Mother stood up. The call became louder and louder. It even went beyond the highest pitch. At the top of her voice, she called out, "KALI!" The sound was seemingly endless. It reverberated and echoed all around. The atmosphere shook as if the hut was going to come down. It seemed that each and every atom repeated, responded and resounded to the call, "Kali!...Kali!...Kali!..." The atmosphere was charged with vibrant spiritual energy. The devotees stood still. They were struck with awe. There was pin-drop silence. The call slowly ceased. The Mother's body became still. All her hairs stood on end (like goose bumps). Her eyes rolled back and her breath stopped. She held a Divine *mudra* (gesture) in her right hand and her left hand was tightly gripped in a fist. There was a Divine glow on her face. A benign smile lit her countenance. All eyes were fixed on her radiant face. Five, ten, fifteen minutes. The *brahmacharins* started singing *bhajans* (devotional songs) in praise of Kali, *Om Bhadra Kaliye...*

> O Bhadra Kali, O Goddess who ever gives refuge
> Enchantress and Mother, bless me
> O Goddess who killed the demon Chamunda,
> Please lovingly protect Thy people,
> Giving them delight.
>
> We bow to Thy Lotus Feet
> Which are adorned with gold anklets,

O Chandika, O Beautiful One, O Great Dancer
Bless us with Thy glance of grace.

O valiant Bhairavi,
Who has severed the head of the demon Darika,
We sing Thy praises, seeking Thy Feet,
Hail, Ocean of Grace, we bow down to Thee.

Seconds and minutes went by. Half an hour passed.
Brahmacharin Pai chanted some Sanskrit verses from
the *Saundarya Lahari* glorifying and describing the divine form of the Mother:

United with Shakti, Shiva is endowed
With the power to create the universe.
Otherwise, He is incapable even of movement.
Therefore, who except those endowed
With great merits acquired in the past
Can be fortunate enough
To salute or praise Thee, Mother Divine,
Who art the adored of even
Hari, Hara and Virinchi?

After thirty-five minutes had passed, the Holy Mother
slowly brought down her uplifted right hand which held
the Divine gesture. She slowly and gently moved her lips
as if uttering something. The Mother tried to move from
where she was standing, but her steps faltered. Fortu-
nately, Gayatri, who was standing just by her side, gently
supported her from behind and made her lie down on
the cot. Thirty more minutes passed and the Mother re-

gained her normal state of awareness. She sat down but still could not speak for some time. A few more minutes passed; it was now three o'clock. The Mother asked for something to drink. Gayatri brought *kanji* (hot rice gruel) of which the Mother took a few sips and then handed it back. The Holy Mother now seemed her usual self.

One devotee remarked, "Amma, you can switch on and off from this world whenever you want," to which she replied, "There is no switching on and off; it is always on."

Devotee: Amma, what is the meaning and significance of all the different *devatas* (demi-gods)?
Amma: Children, when viewed from *saguna* (the state of names and forms), the different realms of *devatas* (subtle beings), this, that and everything is there in existence. After having thought about how to control nature in a way that is not harmful to human beings, the ancient *rishis* (sages) made the *sankalpa* (pure resolve) to create all these different *devatas*. There are essential principles in all of them. They have a purpose and a benefit. We should not abuse them without knowing the real matter. The *rishis* were not mere dullards.
Question: The *rishis* by their *sankalpa* created the *devatas* in order to prevent any harm from nature. Did that help to remove the harm thereafter?
Amma: It seems that son wants to put all the blame on the shoulders of the saints and sages. If you suffer, whose fault is it? Is it the *rishis* who committed the mis-

take? No, it is not. It is the evil actions of the people
which created the disharmony in nature. The people became greedy and selfish; they wanted more and more.
They were never satisfied. "More...more...more..." was
their slogan. In their greediness and selfishness to
achieve and possess more, they started doing all kinds of
wicked and crooked actions. They totally polluted Nature. These *devatas* are nothing but Nature Herself. The
people exploited Her. They did nothing to please Her.
Steeped in selfishness, they became completely blind. In
that darkness they forgot that it was from Her that they
had received everything and that without Her blessing
they would lose everything. Now it has happened that
She has withdrawn Her blessings. It is now the urgent
duty of all human beings to please Nature by performing
selfless actions endowed with mutual love, faith and sincerity. When this is done, then She will bless you back
with endless resources. Simply blaming the *rishis* without knowing or understanding the logic behind their
deeds is meaningless. Such an attitude is not good for
an intelligent human being to have.

The Holy Mother continued,

Amma: Changes will go on occurring as the population
increases. These changes can be both good and bad.
Suppose there are ten children in a house. Nine out of
these ten children will have devotion in the *Kali Yuga*
(the dark age of materialism). Only one will be spoiled.
But that one will be a person who "eats up" the other

nine. A real demon! The children will have the same mother and father but will be of two different natures.

As the *Kali Yuga* ascends to its peak, devotion will also ascend to its peak. Ninety-nine out of a hundred people will have devotion.

Question: It is said that all the four *yugas* (ages or periods of time) will continue to come and go in a cycle.

Amma: Children, looked at from one standpoint, all four *yugas*, *Krita*, *Treta*, *Dwapara*, and *Kali*, exist in us at the same time. The *yugas* are dependent on one's nature.

In the Krita Yuga (also known as *Satya Yuga*) there was only Truth, one hundred percent. This was the Golden Age. People in this age were completely selfless, living amongst each other with faith and mutual understanding, abiding by higher values. Perfect harmony existed between humans and nature in such a way that there was one hundred percent yield for crops sown. People would simply sow the seeds and then would have no need to return to the field until the time for the harvest. No fertilizers had to be used and no weeds interfered with the growth.

The *Treta Yuga* gave way to a twenty-five percent loss of truth; dharma declined. The once-perfect harmony between human beings and nature diminished so that some care was required for tending the crops. The yield decreased to seventy-five percent. In the *Dwapara Yuga* there was further decrease to a fifty percent loss of Truth. Tending of the crops required active cultivation with manure for fertilizer, irrigation, and removal of

weeds. Even then, only a fifty percent yield was pro-
duced. Just as there was a diminishing yield in harvest,
the human qualities of selflessness, faith, mutual understanding and abidance in higher values, also decreased
proportionately in these two *yugas*.

Now in the *Kali Yuga* there is no Truth, no *dharma*
(righteousness). Complete selfishness prevails among
people. The harmonic relationship between human beings and nature has disappeared so that no matter how
hard people have to work, production is always insuffi-
cient for our needs. It is said that in the *Kali Yuga*, the
father will "eat" the son and the son will "eat" the father. This means that all the family bonds and ties will
crumble into pieces. The relationships like father and
mother will all end up in utter meaninglessness. Oh,
what an age! What things are being uttered by five year
old children in this age! Such useless chatter! In the
olden days even twenty-five year old people would not
say such things. It is certainly the sporting play of the
Kali Yuga. From now on the child will be speaking even
as it comes forth from the mother's womb. The growth
of the body will diminish as crooked-mindedness will increase in the *Kali Yuga*. How tall human beings used to
be before! From now on as each year passes by, the
height of human beings will become shorter and
shorter.

BHAVA DARSHAN

Question: We have never heard of other *Mahatmas* having *Bhava Darshan* like you. Amma, can't you also do
spiritual activities without *Bhava Darshan?*

Amma: Children, some will ask why things here are not like there, why things that are seen here are not seen there, and so on and so forth. Let us take our ancient history. Was Krishna like Rama? Was Buddha in any way like them? Was Jesus Christ like Nabi? It seems that each of their ways was different, even though they all taught the same principles. Should it be said that here Mother must act like them? *Bhava Darshan* can be considered as Mother's special way of acting. How many people have received peace and tranquility through this? That is the most important thing, isn't it? Ninety-nine percent of the people who come here are those who love *Bhava Darshan*.

BRAHMAN, THE ABSOLUTE PRIMORDIAL NATURE, AND CREATION

The Mother had been describing the Age of Kali when a devotee raised the question about *Bhava Darshan*. The discussion about the Age of Kali once again came up as the Mother finished speaking about *Bhava Darshan*.

One devotee: Mother has described the evil effects of the Age of Kali, hasn't she? I would say that all the problems and troubles arose because God has carelessly created the world; otherwise, how could things become so bad?

Mother laughed loudly and through the laughter she said,

Amma: Even before creation that Fellow (Lord Shiva) had related what was inevitable. And even after that, He gave the necessary instructions about how one should live here in this world.

Question: What do you mean, Mother?

Amma: Before creation, Shakti (the Primordial Nature, Cosmic Energy) heard an ethereal voice. It said, "There is only sorrow in creation. You should not try to do it." It was the voice of Shiva (Pure Consciousness). Shakti replied, "No, it needs to be done." Thus even before creation, Shiva gave hints to Shakti regarding the essential principle. It was only after that, that permission was granted to create.

After creation, He, the Pure Consciousness aspect, moved away. He went and hid in the depths. In reality, He has nothing to do with all these things happening around us. Later, Shakti went running to Him, complaining, "I have no peace. Look here, the children are scolding Me. They blame Me for everything. Nobody takes care of Me."

Shiva said, "Hadn't I told you at that very same time that it was going to be like this and that you should not pursue that (creation)? Now you create an uproar, having pursued that. Aren't you the one who is responsible for all this that has happened? There was no problem when it was I alone, was there?"

Humorously, the Holy Mother further related,

Amma: Sometimes when the longing of the children here in the Ashram declines, Mother cannot bear it. She will feel inexpressible pain. At these times Mother will tell her children, "Alas! At that very moment itself that Fellow (Shiva) had told me not to depart from Him and bother with all this. Look here, now I am suffering." (All burst into laughter.)

The Mother continued,

Amma: At that very moment He, that Man, had reminded me of all this. Now at this last moment, how can I go and complain to Him? He will ask, "Hadn't I warned you about this earlier?" (laughing and rejoicing, enjoying herself).

Though jokingly put, these "crazy utterances" are profound and have great philosophical depth. Of course, everything is a joke for her, or a hide-and-seek game.

Like a little girl the Holy Mother sat, leaning on the back of a woman devotee. It was quite a sight to see the devotee's joy, as if she had attained heaven. After a short pause, the Mother continued.

Amma: Children, what Mother has stated might sound like something worldly, but there are also spiritual principles in it. God instructs, prescribes, warns and reminds. He speaks through the scriptures and *Mahatmas* (*great souls*), sometimes from within, and other times through an experience. But we do not care about what God teaches. We go on creating and sustaining desires; we never destroy them. Creation and sustenance of desires will only push us again and again into sorrow. And then when sorrow comes, we rush towards God, panting and crying aloud. He is untouched by all this. He is not responsible for it.

That which is called *Brahman* is established in That Truth forever. Never will It change. That never has any involvement in all these external things. That is Truth. In fact, does anything exist when we are in deep sleep? No, there is nothing like wife or child, you or I, happiness or sorrow. Only when we wake up from that state of deep sleep do feelings and ideas come, e.g., "that is my wife, this is my child, that is the backwaters, this is my house," etc. Just as we are relieved from pain when we take a pain-killing drug, in deep sleep nothing of this world exists. This can be said to be somewhat similar to the state known as *Brahman*, i.e., nothing of this world exists for us. Deep sleep can be considered analogous to a slight glimpse of the experience of *Brahman*. In that state, there is neither bondage or pain, nor body or mind. That which exists is "That" alone. *Brahman* always remains as *Brahman*.

The difference between deep sleep and the state of *Brahman* is that in the former latent tendencies are there in the dormant state which will start functioning as soon as one wakes up; whereas, in the latter, all *vasanas* completely end. Their roots are destroyed.

What we call "real," i.e., the world, is not something non-existent. *Mithya* only means ever-changing, not "it doesn't exist at all." The world is unsteady or unstable. Every moment it undergoes change. It is impermanent. An impermanent object cannot give us permanent happiness, can it? External appearance changes, but that which causes it to appear is changeless. That is *Atman*, the substratum upon which all changes occur.

Suppose we sow some grain. It grows up, yields and ripens. Human beings then eat it and, after digestion, throw out the waste as excreta, which again fertilizes the grass, which cows and other animals eat, and the transformation process continues. Thus change goes on and on. The forms are different but there is no difference in the basic principle. It is only from the seed that the tree comes forth and it is only from the tree that the seed springs forth. This itself is That and That itself is This. There is no two, but only One.

LIFE AFTER DEATH

Question: Mother, if only the souls of the dead take birth again, then how has the population increased? And how then can the theory of life after death be true?
Amma: Son, couldn't there have been more individual souls in the previous age than in the present? Is there any scarcity of souls in God's creation?

That ten people take birth when ten people die is not what the theory of life after death says. There are billions and billions of *jivas* (souls), which include trees, creepers, insects, worms, birds, animals and so on. Any one of these can take birth as a human being. When a human being dies, he would not necessarily take birth as a human being again. He or she might take birth as a cat or a dog or as anything else. According to each one's *karma phala* (fruit of action), billions and billions of *jivas* in nature will accept any *janma* (birth) in the continuous cycle of birth, death and rebirth. All creatures of this world are evolving. Before the end of a particular lifetime each creature evolves and reaches a certain level. In some cases, downfall will also occur. The next birth, whether it will be a higher birth or a lower birth, is determined by the evolution or degeneration of that particular soul. It all depends on the mental, physical and intellectual actions which one performs. Therefore, there is no difficulty in having an increase or decrease of population.

PURIFICATION OF DEPARTED SOULS

Question: Mother, for what purpose are the rites of purification of departed souls?

Amma: The souls can evolve and enter into higher planes, owing to the effect of the after-death rites or ceremonies. Some souls after death will come to a standstill. When a certain limit is reached where they can neither see nor hear anything, they neither enter the plane of *Paramatman* (Supreme Self) nor do they enter the world of *jivatman* (individual self). They stand in between that which vibrates and that which does not vibrate. When the purificatory rituals are performed by those thinking of the departed ones, the latter again take birth after having received purification. This is what happened in the case of Subhagan (the Mother's brother). Having remained in the Ashram atmosphere for three years after his death, Subhagan was born again as Shivan through Kasturi, (the Mother's sister). Even before it occurred, Mother had mentioned that it would happen in this way. The *jiva* which leaves the body remains in the atmosphere in the shape of a balloon. This will take another body or be pushed into one according to the actions performed and the gravity of its unfulfilled desires.

Question: Will one take birth immediately after death?

Amma: No, it won't necessarily happen immediately. In the shape of a balloon the soul will remain as if neither on the earth nor in the skies. There is an aura around us. This works exactly like a tape recorder. All our words and deeds will be recorded by this. This air-like thing cannot remain in our body after death. Round in shape like a balloon, this travels through the atmosphere. It will select and take birth in a body befitting or suitable for its desires and attachments in its previous birth. Some *jivas* take birth on the earth only after two or three years.

It is enough if you tell such things only to those who have faith. Otherwise, there are people who would walk around saying that these are all mere stories. They do not know anything about it.

This aura which surrounds each human being will become darker and darker as we become more selfish, wicked and ego-centric. This will pull us back down onto this earth, making us suffer again and again. However, if we cultivate and develop good actions and good thoughts, the same aura will become golden in color, which will help us evolve to the higher planes of consciousness.

Question: What leaves one body and enters into another when one takes another life during rebirth?

Amma: Children, there is only one *Atman* (Divine Self), not many. That *Atman* is all-pervading. It neither dies nor does it take birth. Therefore, the *Atman* can neither leave one body nor can it enter into another one. The *Atman* fills everywhere. Where can it come from and to where can it go?

It is the mind which goes from one body to another. What we call *jiva* is only the mind. This *jiva* will have a form like an illusory appearance. This will be just like waves. Attached to this will be the subtle body with all the inherited tendencies from the previous birth. Usually around a tree or such other thing, an aura can be seen surrounding it. While one is meditating, this aura can be seen around the face just like a layer of air, but not touching the skin. This aura will leave the body and go along with the *jiva* when we die.

Doesn't air exist in both the form of a breeze and a whirlwind? There is special power in a whirlwind, isn't there? Both are one, yet we can tell a difference between them. Even though the *jiva* is of the *Atman*, it does not merge with the *Atman*. The mind will remain separate due to its impurity. There is also a view that a pure mind without *vasanas* (vicious tendencies) is *Atman* itself. Then it is not the mind, but *Atman*, the Self.

Question: Mother, is this world real or apparent?

Amma: Children, it is apparent, and at the same time, not apparent. Shouldn't it be eternal if it is Truth or real? Do the dog and the cat exist for us in deep sleep? No, that is why it is said that the mind creates everything. The world of objects manifests only when the mind functions. At other times, no world, no objects. That is why it is said that the world is apparent, not real. Through *sadhana* when the mind is eliminated, the world of plurality also disappears. In that state there is nothing but Brahman; even the world is Brahman. In the state of Realization everything is filled with Supreme Consciousness. Therefore, One who has attained this state beholds only Reality everywhere.

Until then, the apparent world is still present. When Eternity is experienced, the changing world stops deluding you. It is a state where you become constantly established in the changeless *Atman*. Children, do not think that the world will disappear completely when you become Realized. If that were the case, it would have disappeared when the first person attained Realization.

Question: Who takes it as is and not apparent?

Amma: Those who are deluded by it will take it as "real." Those not deluded by it won't have such feelings at all. They will always remain in themselves alone. They will perceive the Self through the Self.

Question: Amma, it is easy for you to say such things; you are beyond all these dualities. But what about the ordinary human beings who are attached and caught up in the worldly pleasures and objects?

Amma: Son, who told you that it is the worldly objects which have caught you up? It is the other way around. It is you who have caught them up. These objects themselves have no power to attract you or to catch you. You have tightly embraced them and you do not want to let them go. Then you cry aloud beating your chest saying, "Oh, what can I do, these bondages, these relationships, my wife. My car has been stolen, my house is falling down," and so on and so forth. None of the objects called you to them waving their hands. It is you who developed the attraction towards them.

There is a proverb in Malayalam, "You want to get something sitting on a higher elevation, but you do not want to let go of the thing kept in your armpit." This thing kept in your armpit represents the objects of the world. You are tightly embracing them. If you want to obtain something on a higher level, i.e., eternal happiness, the only thing that you have to do is to loosen your arm a little, and it (the objects of the world) will fall away. But you want both; you want to keep the pleasures of the world and also have spiritual bliss. No, that is impossible. Therefore, slowly let the worldly pleasures fall off your bosom. Lift your hands and arms fully and the thing under your arm will fall down and you will have the object above.

Question: Amma, my question is, who is affected by *maya* when everything is *Brahman?*

Amma: Son, *maya* has not affected anyone; it is you who have embraced it. The illusory world has no power to delude you. It is you who have gone after it due to your accumulated tendencies. You look at things through the glasses of your *vasanas.* You weigh things and stamp them as good and bad according to your likes and dislikes.

Everything is *Brahman,* that is right. But have you realized That? It is like a blind person saying that there is light everywhere. Why do you talk unnecessarily about something which you have no idea about at all? You constantly experience the world and its objects, but you talk about something which you have never experienced.

For a person who has gone beyond *maya,* everything is *Brahman* since he constantly experiences It. But for a person who lives in *maya* it is not so. He has everything around him. Thus, he must put forth a deliberate attempt to come out of it. He should try to convince himself that the world and the pleasure-giving objects are flickering and dream-like.

Suppose you have a dream in which you see that you have accumulated a lot of wealth and have become a multi-millionaire. Then, in due course, name and fame follow and you are elected Prime Minister or President of the country. While you are dreaming, the dream is real, but when you wake up, it no longer has reality. Exactly in the same way, this (empirical world) is all a dream created by the thoughts and the mind, a long dream. *Atman* or the Self has nothing to do with it. It simply illumines everything, just as the sun illumines the whole world. The sun cannot but shine. In the same way, the nature of the Self is light; it cannot but illumine.

Just as you come to realize that the dream is unreal when you wake up, you will realize that the world is unreal when you wake up to God-consciousness.

Question: *Sadhana* need not be performed to wake up from a dream. We will wake up automatically. Similarly, *sadhana* is not needed to remove *maya*, is it?

Amma: Son, who told you that one wakes up from a dream without doing anything? In the dream state we dream that we are doing many things. We wake up as a continuation of the actions that we perform in the dream state. One cannot say that actions performed in the dream did not cause us to wake up. In the same way, dwelling in this diverse world in the midst of changing objects is a long dream. Although this world is a dream, we are so identified with it that we do not feel it as a dream. We believe that it is true. Therefore, *sadhana* is needed to wake up to God from this waking-state dream.

Although we are of the nature of the ever-free, eternal *Atman*, at present our understanding is that we are bound and limited. To remove this feeling of bondage and limitation, *sadhana* is necessary.

Little children will take excreta in their own hands. They will try to catch hold of fire or walk into a pond or river. Will grown-up people do this? No. Therefore, discrimination is needed for each one to grow according to their own inherited tendencies. One should move forward adhering to the instructions given by wise people. There is no use in disputing and arguing unnecessarily. Doubting is an aspect of the mind. You should use your discriminative powers to stop this doubting nature of the mind. Only when doubts come to an end will the light of God enter into one's heart.

Doubts will not end fully until the attainment of Self-Realization. One will not have the power to go beyond doubts until then. There will not be any doubts once you know what should be known.

THE NATURE OF THE MIND

Question: Mother, even if these are the facts, almost all people feel that life in the world is happy, don't they?

Amma: That is no wonder. That feeling is there in all creatures. Even a pig which lives in dirty mud thinks that life is very happy and that its abode, the muddy waters, is the best dwelling place on earth and that its ugly body is the most beautiful one of all.

There were once two astrologers who were very close friends. One day they wanted to know about their next births, what they would become. They made certain astrological calculations and found that one of them would take birth as an elephant and the other as an earthworm. The second man, who was going to become an earthworm, felt very sad and depressed. Seeing his friend's desperate mood, the first astrologer, who was to become an elephant, tried to console him. But it was of no avail. Finally, the would-be earthworm astrologer requested of the would-be elephant astrologer, "My dear friend, you alone can save me from this ill-fate. In your next birth search for me and once you find me be kind enough to trample me under your foot. For if you kill me, I might get a better body by getting rid of the dirty body of an earthworm." The would-be elephant astrologer said that he was only too happy to render this great service to his friend.

Years went by. Both the astrologers died, one after the other. As foretold, the first astrologer reincarnated into the body of an elephant and the other one, the body of an earthworm. But both of them forgot about their previous births. Luckily, one day the astrologer who took birth as an elephant remembered his previous birth and the promise that he had given to his friend. Immediately he went in search of his friend who had reincarnated into the body of an earthworm. In between lumps of clay, in ploughed fields, in loosened soil, under the trees, in muddy places and between dried cracks in the ground, he searched and searched. This went on for several days. At last when he lifted up a big rock, lo and behold, there lay his dear earthworm friend. The elephant astrologer was very happy to find his friend, who was now living with his wife and children under the rock. As the elephant raised his front foot to fulfill his promise to trample the earthworm, there arose a hue and cry. The earthworm shouted at the elephant, "Hey, demon, what are you trying to do? Are you going to kill me and my beautiful wife and children? Are you going to destroy my fancy house? Stop it! How cruel you are!"

Children, that is what every creature on this earth feels. Everything depends on one's understanding. What we do not like can be equal to ambrosia for someone else. What we like may be equal to poison for another person. There is no object in this world which can give happiness to everyone. In other words, there is no object in this world which has happiness as its nature. One person is very fond of watching T.V., but another person will get a terrible headache if he happens to look at the T.V. screen. There are people who enjoy smoking more than anything, but there are others who will cough if they merely see someone smoking. In this way, likes and dislikes differ from person to person.

People are drowning in pleasurable objects. Just as a pig which lives in the dirty mud thinks that it is the happiest place, human beings also think that living in the midst of worldly pleasures is heavenly. All pleasures of the world, whatever they are, end up in sorrow. Real bliss will be had only when we discriminate between the eternal and the non-eternal.

It was time for the discourse to begin. The Mother got up from her seat; otherwise, nobody would go to listen to the speech. The Holy Mother went to the hut and the devotees sat in the tent and listened to the discourse.

There were two pigeons which always sat on top of the meditation hall, on the roof of the Mother's hut or somewhere closeby whenever the Mother sang *bhajans* or conversed with the devotees sitting outside. This time too they were seen on top of the meditation hall. These

pigeons would not move from the place until the singing or the conversation was over. They would sit there
unmoving as if listening to her. Sometimes these pigeons would come very close to the Mother if she was
alone. Many times devotees and residents would see
them sitting right in front of the Holy Mother when she
sat in solitude. The Mother once hinted that they were
two devoted souls.

The discourse went on until six o'clock. At six-thirty
the evening *bhajan* started. The Mother, the *brahmacharins*, and a few householder devotees who could sing, sat
inside the Vedanta Vidyalaya (a small hall like a classroom meant for teaching Vedanta to the *brahmacharins*),
while the others sat in the tent specially made for these
events. The Mother sang *Vedanta Venalilude...*

> Now where is the truth of the Gita
> That proclaims that Thou wilt help
> A traveler to Brahman all alone?
>
> Even though I am swimming
> Through the forest-like way
> For a peaceful soul, for the attainment of Thee,
> My mind is filled with sorrow.
> O Friend of the miserable,
> My heart forever burns for something,
> I know not what.
> Hast Thou not the intent
> To remove all my sorrows?

O Mother, O Bhagavati Devi,
Don't you know that without my merging
Into Thy mind-enchanting Being
There is no peace?

The devotees became totally absorbed in the singing and their hearts overflowed with joy. Some persons shed tears while others sat with eyes closed and palms joined trying to imbibe the bliss and become more absorbed in the *kirtan*. The Holy Mother always sang with eyes closed to set an example for the *brahmacharins* and other devotees. The Mother always reminds us,

"While singing the Divine Name, you should always keep the eyes closed; otherwise, the eyes, persuaded by the mind and tempted by the objects, will run after them. Children, behold the inner Light; it cannot be seen if you look at the external light."

28 February 1984

The seven-day discourse ended yesterday. It had been a busy week. The Mother hardly had any rest. All of the three *Devi Bhavas* during the seven-day discourse were so very crowded that the Holy Mother had to sit for *darshan* from six-thirty in the evening until five or six the next morning. Besides that, she received the devotees in the daytime as well. Even though the Mother does not care about taking a rest, sometimes her body suffers due to the lack of it. Of course, her mind is always unaffected. This is quite obvious from her ever-cheerful mood even when her body is tired.

Quite often she says, "Mother is happy when her children are happy. Mother's health and wealth are her children." If there are devotees to see her, she will not remain in her room in the name of rest or privacy unless there is a good reason. If somebody asks her to take some rest when her body is too tired, the Mother would reply,

"The purpose of this body and of Mother's whole life is to serve her children. Mother's only wish is that her hands should always be on someone's shoulders, consoling and caressing them and wiping their tears, even while breathing her last."

Every glance the Mother gives exudes compassion. Every movement she makes is an unforgettable visual delight. Every word she utters showers and embraces one with the bliss of immortality. Her deeds are a living witness to all the religious dictums of the world.

Not all who came to attend and participate in the discourse had gone. Some people planned to go after today's *Devi Bhava darshan*.

The Mother came to the hut by nine o'clock, but it seemed that she was not well. Even though she took her usual seat on the cot, the Mother did not speak very much. Some people left, having offered their salutations to her. Others simply sat there silently as the Mother did not speak. Gayatri said, "Mother is not well. She didn't sleep last night. The whole night she was rolling on the floor. There is a terrible pain in her throat and she feels some giddiness too. If you devotees pray, she might take some rest." There were pimples all over her body. A woman devotee suggested, "Why don't we all go out. Let Mother take a rest today. Only if her body is well enough and healthy can she continue to bless us for a longer period of time."

There is no need to say that the others all agreed to this suggestion. Everybody got up to leave the hut, but suddenly the Holy Mother exclaimed,

Amma: No, no, don't go, children. Mother knows that you will feel very sad if you cannot see her after coming here. Do not think about Mother's sickness. It has been taken from different people. Mother suffers for thirty or forty minutes, or maybe a day, what they have had to suffer for thirty or forty years. Mother is only happy to do this. Who will do it for her children except Mother? Nonetheless, whatever is accepted willingly can only be exhausted by experiencing it. Mother does not care about herself. Each and every drop of Mother's blood, each and every particle of her energy is for her children. But she wants to see you growing, my children; she wants to see you growing spiritually. Children, you will only become weak-minded if you think, "Mother is tired", or "Mother is sick...", or things like that.

Her words were touching. Hearing them, some devotees silently shed tears. One devotee couldn't contain his grief and said,

Devotee: Mother, why should you suffer like this for us? Why can't you give some of your physical suffering to us? Since we are your children, isn't it our duty to repay you, if we could, for the great sacrifice that you are making for us?

Full of love in her eyes, the Holy Mother heartfeltly laughed at the innocence of the devotee and replied,

Amma: No, son, neither can you repay nor can you endure even an infinitesimal fraction of the suffering that this body undergoes. Son, this innocence is good.

In a few minutes the atmosphere completely changed. The Holy Mother began receiving people one by one. Her mood was as cheerful as ever. There was singing which the devotees participated in, forgetting everything. After each song there was a meditative silence. Now and then the Mother also sang a song. At one point, the Mother sang a song which depicted Kali's fierce form, *Kurirul Pole...*

> Who is this One with such awesome form,
> Dark as the darkest night,
> Swaying like a host of blue flowers
> On the waters of a lake of blood?
>
> Who is this One, dancing on the battleground,
> Splattered with blood of all sides,
> Masking Her Gorgeous Form
> Even as She is clad only in all-pervasive ether?

Who is this One with three eyes,
Blazing as incandescent fire,
The One with disheveled hair
Appearing like a streak of dark rain clouds?

Why does the earth tremble
Bearing the brunt of Her mighty gait?
Oh! This frolic-some damsel is none
But the Beloved of Shiva who carries the trident.

If a devotee happened to have his or her head resting on the Mother's lap while having *darshan* as the Mother sang, that devotee received a longer *darshan*, truly enjoying the experience of bliss, since the Mother went into *samadhi* (equipoised state of Oneness with God) several times during the singing and was totally oblivious to the external surroundings.

Mother left the hut by twelve o'clock. At three o'clock she again came and sat in the coconut grove. Naturally, the devotees were also attracted to that spot. Now she was completely well. The pimples had disappeared, and she was quite normal. For a short while the Mother sat still and silent, fixing her eyes somewhere, indiscernible as to whether she gazed at the sky or beyond to infinitude. She seemed to be all alone in her own world. Then turning her attention from wherever it was, she called the name of a young man sitting far behind the others and said, "Son, your mother wants to see you. Go home immediately." The Mother then turned to another devotee who was sitting near her and inquired,

"Son, are you leaving now?" He replied, "Yes, Mother." "If so, then take this son with you to his house along the way," said the Mother.

By that time, the young man who was asked to return home came up to the Mother. Looking at him and pointing to the other person, the Holy Mother said, "This son here has a car. He will give you a ride. Don't worry. Everything will be all right." Both of them bowed down at the Mother's feet. She gave sacred ash to the young man that she was sending home but not to the other devotee. The young man seemed to be a little worried, seeing the mysterious way in which the Mother acted towards him. The Mother again smiled at him and said, "You look worried, son. Why be afraid? Mother is here for you, isn't she?" Both devotees then left.

Without speaking another word, the Mother sat in meditation for about ten or fifteen minutes. She opened her eyes and smiled at the devotees and said to them, "That son's mother is a heart patient. She suddenly had an attack. His father is out at work and he was here. There is nobody at home, but there is no problem now; she is all right." She stopped there as if she did not want to disclose the rest.

A woman devotee who could not control her excitement asked in a loud voice, "But Mother, how is it possible that you know all that about them? The young man's house is fifty kilometers away from here. Nobody came from there to inform you." The Mother giggled and said, "Mother had to go there, because she prayed so innocently. It is her..." The Holy Mother stopped abruptly and said, "Now, let us stop discussing it. All those things just happen. Let us talk about something else."

There was a short pause, after which, a *sadhak* (spiritual aspirant) asked,

Sadhak: Mother, is a vow of silence necessary for a *sadhu (monk)?*"

Amma: Silence is good. *Mauna* (vow of silence) will come spontaneously when we become introspective. Silence will help to prevent unnecessary dissipation of energy. We lose a lot of energy through talking. Most of the time our topic is something unimportant and silly. We discuss things about a film star or a movie, a football or baseball player, or maybe we recall an ornament or piece of jewelry that we lost two years ago, or perhaps we gossip about the neighbor or the woman we saw on the road last week. Does it make any sense to talk of such trivial things? By finding fault with others and criticizing them, we lose a lot of energy. Do we benefit at all from this?

If you want to feel the difference, keep silence for a few days, say five days, and talk on the sixth day. When you begin speaking again, you will clearly feel that you have lost something which you had acquired.

Question: Mother, you say that observing silence will help to conserve energy. But what about the thoughts that arise in the mind?

Amma: There will arise bigger and smaller ripples in a dam in which water remains blocked and conserved.

But the water will not flow out; it will remain in the dam. Similarly, thoughts will arise in one's mind even while one is observing silence, but since they do not get expressed through speech and action, a major portion of the energy will be conserved. This means that there will be relatively less dissipation of energy. Therefore, observing a vow of silence is good for those who really want to attain the goal.

Question: Mother, could you please give some instructions about how one should begin that observance?

Amma: Start with an hour, then two, three...and slowly try to do it for half a day, then for a whole day. Thus you can slowly and steadily increase the time for as many days as you wish. It all depends on your determination and *lakshya bodha* (intent on the goal). If you are really determined, you can even take a vow of forty-one days silence. However, do not start with forty-one days in the very beginning. One whole day or even a few hours will do at first. Slowly you can increase it to forty-one or more days if you wish. Our habit is to talk; therefore, the mind will compel and tempt us to speak unnecessarily. In fact, real *mauna* means to speak moderately with very good control over your mind. But as our natural tendency is to speak unnecessarily without any control, we need to keep complete silence so as to train the mind properly.

One will feel discouraged if one tries to start with forty-one days in the beginning. One should proceed by getting the taste and by enjoying it little by little. The mind should become conducive or favorable by itself.

Do not force it. Even then, it may become necessary to force two or three days in the beginning. Thereafter, one should take silence according to the taste that one gets from it. Having observed silence for a day, when we are about to speak on the next day, the mind will say, "Silence, silence." *Abhyasa* (constant practice) will guide you. Also, for the length of time that we maintain silence we will be able to chant our mantra.

Let everything happen as destined by God. But we must do *sadhana* (spiritual practice). It is useless and meaningless to blame destiny for anything and everything that happens in our life. In a certain way, that is nothing but foolishness. Act properly and sincerely, and then if something goes wrong, consider it as fate. It is the fruit of your own actions; so be at peace. But still you must work in the present to make your future happy and blissful.

Children, speak less, and only when it is absolutely necessary. When you do say a word, say it very carefully because a seeker or a devotee should not utter meaningless things, even if only a single word.

Question: Mother, what is the right attitude to have?

Amma: If somebody gets angry, you should carefully try to prevent your mind from getting disturbed or unsteady. Some people will say, "I have not done anything wrong, and yet he scolded me. Therefore, I got angry." You should consider it as, "Those scoldings might have been meant for me, even if I did not do anything wrong." Then you should pray, "O Lord, whatever mistakes I may make, please remove them right at that very moment. O Lord, please point out my errors. O Lord, entrust me with Your work; please do not let me sit idle. O Lord, let it be Your work so that I can do it, whatever it may be, remembering You. O Lord, please let others point out my faults to bestow on me the right under-standing, and let me not hate them or get angry with them, no matter whether they point out my faults in a harmful or a gentle way." This should be the prayer of a devotee or a true seeker.

We are trying to learn how to see God, or the Pure Essence, in everything and everybody and not the de-mon in them, even in the wicked. If you see the demon in others, the very same negative forces will swallow you up and you yourself will become a demon in the end. Children, that is not our way. Hate evil, not the evil-doer. If somebody is egotistic or selfish, hate egotism or selfishness, not the person. We can do this if we really try. If the son is a drunkard or a drug-addict, the parents will hate his drinking habit or his addiction to drugs but they will still love their son. In fact, such children are of-ten especially loved by the parents. In the same way, try to love others, even if they are bad. The right attitude is, right understanding of a particular situation in life, us-ing proper discrimination, and then wisely putting it into application.

AIR-CONDITION THE MIND

The Holy Mother continued,

Amma: Do not walk around complaining that certain people got angry with you and that they criticized and scolded you. Let them give a lecture criticizing and teasing you. You just keep quiet. All the things that they have said about you will revert back to them. When you react or retaliate, that means you have accepted it, and then they will fabricate even more things about you and you will also do the same about them. There is no way to settle that kind of argument, and the end-result is utter humiliation, anger, hatred, revenge, and the like. Son, why do you engage in such self-destructive processes? Observe silence, keep quiet. Do not accept what others say about you. Or, if you want to accept it, receive it as God's gift. If you are very adamant and determined to accept it only as a demonic challenge, no one can save you from the final disaster, not even God.

Suppose somebody gives you a television as a present. What will happen if you do not accept it? No doubt he will take it back and keep it in his own home. In a similar manner, if you do not accept a word said or an act done against you by someone else, he will have to take it back. That is all there is to it.

Spiritual life is meant for renunciates. They will experience and enjoy bliss even if they lie in the trash. The mind should be air-conditioned, not the external world. If a person who has no peace of mind tries to sleep in a

house with air-conditioning, will sleep come to him? No,
it won't. How many incidents are there where people
committed suicide even while living in air-conditioned
houses. Having made enough money, people lie down
on majestic beds in palatial buildings, but only if they
have peace of mind will they get any sleep. Therefore,
children, it is quite clear that it is not the external objects which give one comfort and happiness. If that were
so, people with immense wealth should be able to lead
peaceful lives. But this is not seen to be true, and they
are often the most worried ones. If they want to sleep,
they will need to take sleeping pills or an injection. Even
to enjoy worldly pleasures properly, one must have a
tranquil mind. Therefore, children, the mind should be
air-conditioned. A person with an air-conditioned mind
will have only bliss at all times and places. That is what
we have to strive for. Therefore, it is not wealth or any
other thing that gives bliss. The real giver of bliss is the
mind.

TO ELIMINATE MENTAL AGONY

Question: What should be done to eliminate mental
agony?
Amma: Children, if one's mind is obsessed with diffi-
culties, one should tell God. However, people do not do
this. Instead, one person will complain to another; this
person will discuss his problems with that one. A wife
will tell her husband, and the husband will confide in
his wife. Children will rely on their friends or parents,

and elderly parents will talk with their children. There-fore, God will think, "All right, they remove their diffi-culties by telling each other, don't they? No one takes refuge in Me. Then why should I care about them? They themselves are enough for each other." But the fact is, our burden doubles when it happens in this way, when we simply tell others and do not rely on God.

We should pray to God in this manner, "O Lord, please bestow upon me the power to proceed intelli-gently and with proper discrimination in every circum-stance. Let me not forget You in any situation. O Lord, both in happiness and in sorrow, grant me the boon to remember You without fail." We should always have a positive attitude towards life. Optimism is a great factor for eliminating agony from life.

Take, for example, the life of Pumtanam (a great devotee of Lord Krishna who lived in Kerala about four hundred years ago). His devotion to Lord Sri Krishna was very deep. He was righteous, *sattvic* (full of good-ness), simple and humble. Yet he had to face many diffi-culties. His only child died. His wife thought that he was crazy and became antagonistic toward him. Once he was attacked by a band of robbers as he was going to Guruvayur, (a famous temple dedicated to Lord Krishna). He had to undergo many difficulties, but still his devo-tion was unshakable. All the difficulties were the Lord's tests. Do you know the verse he sang when his only child died? "Do I need another child when *Unnikrishna* (Baby Krishna) sports in my heart?" His life was quite a tragedy from a worldly point of view, but he was always blissful. Do you know how and why? The answer is the previously mentioned verse which he himself sang. Once you enshrine the Lord within, there is only bliss, not just within but without as well. Real bliss will come to you, not the mere reflection (i.e., the so-called happiness we derive from external objects is merely a "reflection"). But to attain that bliss, you have to give up the so-called "happiness."

This is the case even in a worldly sense. In order to get more pleasure, you spend a lot of money on a T.V. Once you buy it, you automatically give up your radio. Why? Because now you get more comfort, more happiness from the T.V. and less from the radio, so the radio is relinquished. In the same way, the happiness of spiritual bliss is the highest and most everlasting. Therefore, it is very expensive, and in order to attain that, you need to give up the lower and less pleasure-giving things.

Sorrow and happiness are relative. When there is more happiness and less unhappiness we call it a happy moment, and when there is more unhappiness and less happiness, a sad moment. Still, you are not completely happy because sorrow will come again. All your efforts to eliminate sorrow will end in futility. It is unavoidable and inevitable. Therefore, be aware that this is the nature of life, and accept it. Try to go beyond it. Welcome both happiness and sorrow equally.

Question: How can we go beyond it when we are bound by all these relationships and objects of the world?

Amma: What a pity! These inert, silly, trivial things have bound you. But in fact, son, it is not the things which have bound you. On the contrary, it is your mind which has entered into that bondage. The objects have no power to bind you. Human beings, who are supposed to control the objects, are now being controlled by them. This is the cause of all our problems.

Again, let us take the same Pumtanam's life as an example. Children, you know how his only child died, don't you? It happened when they were celebrating the child's third birthday. It was late at night and everybody was in a hurry to go to bed. The house was filled with guests and relatives. All of a sudden, a strong wind blew and put out all the kerosene lamps. When the wind subsided, they lighted the lamps again. It was at that time that they realized that the child was missing. They searched everywhere but could not find the child. At last, one person had an intuition and proceeded to remove the mats heaped in a corner. There lay the child, dead. Somebody had inadvertently thrown all the mats over to where the child had been sleeping unnoticed. Think of the tragedy!

This devotee, Pumtanam, was very sad. He expressed it, but he could overcome it easily. Why? That is what spirituality teaches, to overcome any grievous situation. Of course, it was a great tragedy, maybe the greatest for this family. You may think, "But it was a child...the poor little thing." Yet this devotee clearly realized that it was nothing at all but a play, a play of his Beloved Krishna. Krishna here represents the Highest Truth.

Anyhow, the body will die, today or tomorrow; it is un-avoidable, inevitable. Will this change if we go on la-menting? No, it won't. Just as it is the nature of the river to flow, the sun to shine and the wind to blow, so birth and death, happiness and sorrow, success and failure are all part of the nature of life. But the True Self, Krishna or Rama or Jesus, never dies. That is what en-livens the body. "When that Universal Self is playing or sporting within me in the form of Krishna, why should I grieve?" The Self never dies nor takes birth. This is what the devotee Pumtanam meant when he sang the verse.

The ocean is the Supreme Self, *Satchidananda*. The waves are the *jivas*, the individual souls. The ocean never changes; it remains as the substratum of all the waves that arise in it. What is a wave, after all? It is only water. One wave comes and disappears. Another one comes and that also disappears. Yet another one rises up in another place and in another shape. But what are all these? They are nothing but the waters of the ocean in different shapes and forms. The waves appear and disappear, re-appear and disappear again, but the water remains the same; it never changes. So waves are noth-ing but the same water in a different shape and in a dif-ferent place. In the same way, the Supreme Self mani-fests as *jivas* in different forms and different shapes. The forms and shapes appear and disappear, but the essen-tial principle, the substratum, that is, the Divine Self, re-mains forever unchanged, just like the ocean.

Question: Amma, that has made it very clear. So, what Amma says is that complete surrender to the Supreme Will is the only way to eradicate all the difficulties of life?

Amma: That is right, son. At least we should try to develop the awareness that everything that happens around us is His Will. As this awareness becomes stronger and stronger, our attitude also will change.

The Lord will take note if we have any selfishness, attachments or aversions. He will not come close if there is even a little bit of selfishness. The Lord will go far away.

We should always pray to the Lord, "O Lord, I am an ignorant one. Though I am Your child, the *vasanas* (latent tendencies) keep me away from You. O Lord, be kind enough to remove these *vasanas*. Though on the level of the Supreme my real nature is of Thy Self, in this empirical world I remain as the child of my parents. O Lord, may my ignorance be removed. It is said that I am Thy child, but I do not know that. Free Your child from this prison." Thus, one has to supplicate with longing and cry to the Lord.

To live in peace, one must get rid of all mental conflicts and see only the good in people. We become mentally weak when we look at the faults. We raise our level when we see the goodness. Whoever it may be, when we say that that person is bad, we have already become bad ourselves. Let ninety-nine percent of another person be wrong, yet we should see the one single percent of good in him. Then our own level will be raised. We will lower ourselves if we see the wrong in him. We should always pray, "O Lord, make my eyes see only the good in everyone. Give me the strength to serve the world selflessly." We can have peace of mind only through such an attitude of self-surrender. Thus slowly you should try to become a good servant of God.

What this world needs are servants, not leaders. Everyone's wish is to become a leader. We have enough leaders who are not real leaders. Let us become a real servant instead. That is the only way to become a real leader.

THE SIGNS OF A RENUNCIATE AND A DEVOTEE

Question: How should one maintain the constant remembrance of God?

Amma: Children, Mother knows that it is difficult for you who live in the midst of material pleasures and with family ties, to remember God constantly. But when you become aware that you are not remembering Him, immediately repent, "O Lord, I have forgotten you for this much time. I have forgotten to chant Your Divine Name for this length of time. O Lord, please forgive me. Please bestow upon me the mental strength to cherish Your Form within and Your Name on my lips constantly and incessantly. O Lord, please do not let me waste time like this. Let the desire to behold Thy Form burn within me." Having repented and prayed thus, immediately start repeating the *mantra*. Again you might forget it. Don't worry, go on applying the same technique of repentance and prayer whenever you realize that you have not been chanting the *mantra* for a long time. Slowly in due course, you will develop the power to remember Him incessantly.

A true seeker or a devotee who has dedicated his whole life to the realization of the Self, should constantly try to fix his mind on the Self or on some aspect of God. Just as a young man and a young woman who have fallen in love will think constantly of each other, just as a chaste wife will always think of her dear husband and just as a man who is of the same character will think of his wife, we should think of God. The young man's mind will always be on his beloved. "Is she at the college now? Which sari is she wearing today? Now she might be sitting in the classroom. Though her body is there, her heart will be with me. Will we marry and lead a happy family life?" With such thoughts in his mind, he will constantly be thinking of her. Wherever he may be, he will have a special enthusiasm and joy of his own. He will always find a special beauty and happiness in letting his mind revel and wander in thinking about her. He will dive deeper and deeper into the world of thoughts about her.

In some other case, the husband may be away from the wife in a very distant place. As for the wife, her husband is as dear to her as her own life. Whatever activity she might be engaged in, she will be thinking of him. A *sadhak* should be like this. His mind should always abide in God's world. He merely performs actions, that's all, but his mind is fixed on God. If one proceeds

in this way, he will reach There at the end. In the inner-
most recesses of one's heart there always exists a constant longing to realize God. He cries only to attain Him
and merge with Him. Nothing lower than complete absorption in the Lord will satisfy him. Reveling in the
world of inner beauty, that is, the Lord's immeasurable
beauty, he will always remain inwardly drawn. None of
the worldly objects will have any appeal to him. Such
things will fail to entice or excite him. Such a devotee
can be heard crying, "O Lord, when are You going to
come to me? Will you grant Thy vision to me and make
me one with You or would You abandon me!" Or if it is
a person who follows the path of knowledge, his prayers
would be, "O Self that shines in and through every object in the world, O Omniscient, Omnipotent and all-
pervading One, when are You going to reveal Your glory
and splendor to me? When am I going to realize and become one with my own Self, casting away all the limitations of the body, mind and intellect?" This is how real
sadhaks pray. Children, these are the signs of a
renunciate and a devotee.

NOT MERE DEVOTION
BUT REAL LOVE SHOULD BE THERE

It was a Tuesday, *Bhava Darshan* day. At five o'clock
in the afternoon the Mother got up and went to her
room. She came back and sat for the *bhajan* at 5:30
p.m. As usual, the Mother soared to the heights of supreme devotion and deep into her own Self as she sang
Bhramarame Manasa...

O hummingbird of my mind
Searching for pure nectar
You wander and become exhausted.

The grove of blossomed trees,
Bereft of sorrow, resides blissfully
On the banks of the river of devotion.
O Mind, do not be desperate,
For your Mother will come
To the pure heart one day.

O Shakti,
Thou art the spring of intelligence for the wise,
Removing all sorrows through knowledge;
I offer all my sorrows to Thee
In whom everything exists.

When is that day, O Mother,
When Thou wilt come?
Art Thou going to come
When all of my energy is dissipated?
O Mother, do not do that!
Won't Thou shower Thy grace upon me?
Who else is there except Thee
As my sole support?

29 February 1984

Last night the *Devi Bhava Darshan* went until three-thirty in the morning. As it was her daily practice, the Mother went around to make sure that all the devotees had a mat and a place to sleep. It was nearly five o'clock when she went to bed.

At ten o'clock in the morning, the young man who had been told by the Holy Mother to return to his home immediately the day before, showed up at the Ashram with his middle-aged mother. There were a few other devotees present. The young man's mother was almost in tears even as she entered the Ashram premises. Seeing them standing in front of the temple, Brahmacharin Balu approached them and asked the young man, "What happened yesterday? Mother did not disclose it, but we all guessed that something mysterious had occurred. Could you tell me what it was, if you don't mind?"

The young man smiled, but at the same time he could not control his emotions. Pulling out a handkerchief from his pocket, he wiped the tears which filled his eyes, and then in a very soft and gentle voice, he remarked, "That was quite an experience. To put it in one sentence, Mother saved my mother's life and gave her a second birth, or maybe you can also say that the Mother extended my mother's life span."

The young man once again wiped away his tears. His mother was also crying. Through her tears, she said, "My child, the fact that I am still alive is quite unbelievable to me. Yesterday I was literally dead. (Referring to her son) He was here and my husband was at work. I am a heart patient. I was supposed to take a pill prescribed by the doctor every morning. I knew that there was only one more pill left. I thought that I could ask my husband to buy more when he came home from work. But unfortunately, I forgot to take my medicine yesterday. Every time I remembered it I had some work to do. And then after lunch, due to tiredness, I slept for about an hour and a half. It was three when I got up; therefore, I went to the kitchen to cook some light refreshment for my husband before he came home from work. It was quarter-past three. As I blew into the oven in order to light the fire, I had an excruciating pain in my heart. It was so severe that it passed like lightning through my whole body and I felt that my heart was going to burst out. I knew that I was going to die. Suddenly, I thought about my son, who was here at the Ashram at the time. I prayed to the Holy Mother, `O Mother, if I survive for a few more hours, I might be able to see my son before breathing my last breath. Mother, will you please send him to me?' In a few seconds I fell unconscious. I don't know how much time had passed, but I slowly opened my eyes and looked around. 'I am still alive,' I thought. Suddenly, I smelled the fragrance which Mother always has around her. It was then that I beheld an unbelievable sight. The Holy Mother herself was sitting right beside me, gazing at me. She sweetly smiled at me, and rubbing my chest, she said, 'Don't worry, you are all right, daughter.' Then I saw another amazing sight. I saw the Mother holding an empty glass in her right hand and in her left hand, the pill bottle, which was always kept in a closet in our bedroom. I couldn't believe my eyes. Seeing my astounded state, the Mother soothed my forehead and said, 'Yes, daughter, you took the medicine. Be at peace. Your son will be home in an hour.' Saying thus, she placed the glass and the bottle down on the floor beside me and disappeared, after smiling at me once again. Yes, it was true, I could feel the taste of the medicine in my mouth. I was still lying down. I jumped up, ran out of the house and up to the front entrance gate. There was no trace of her. Like a mad-woman I ran to the backyard, and not finding her there, I again went into the house and searched through all the rooms calling out, `Amma, Amma!'

"Slowly coming back to my normal consciousness, I went into the kitchen once again to make sure that the glass and the drug bottle were still there, for maybe it was all a hallucination. To my astonishment, I saw a lotus petal also lying there. I rubbed my eyes and pulled my eyelids wide apart in order to make sure that what I saw was true. While looking at the things again, I smelled the familiar aroma which the Mother always carried around her; it permeated everywhere as if to clear my doubts. The fragrance filled each and every room of the house. I took the glass, the pill bottle and the lotus petal and went into the *puja* room (shrine room). There I placed everything in front of Mother's picture and cried, embracing her picture tightly to my chest. I was still in the *puja* room when my son came home.

"When my son found me, he seemed very much worried. In a broken voice, he inquired, 'What happened to you, Mother? Is everything all right? Where is father? Is he all right?' Now everything was clear to me. Mother, before she left, had told me that my son would come in an hour. He came before that. First I consoled him, reassuring him that everything was all right. Slowly, when he calmed down, I narrated to him everything that had happened. He listened to the whole story with wide-open eyes and a wide-open mouth. When the whole story was over, he spoke, but very softly as of in a soliloquy, more to himself than to me, 'Mother, so that was it. Now I know, Mother, the reason you sent me home.' The next moment he burst into tears, calling aloud, 'Amma!'"

She paused for a while; and then she opened her purse, and very carefully, reverentially and devotedly took out a lotus petal. Showing it to Balu, she said, "This is the petal...," but before she could finish the sentence, she was overcome with emotion.

It was a few minutes after eleven o'clock. Looking up towards Mother's room, they saw the Mother herself coming down. Both the mother and the son ran towards the Holy Mother, and falling at her feet, they shed tears of gratitude. Slowly and gently lifting them up, the Mother affectionately put them both on her shoulders. Like little children they went on crying. Rubbing and patting their backs and whispering into their ears, "Makkale, makkale, (Children, children), don't cry." The Holy Mother consoled them with all the love and care of a real Mother.

No one understood exactly what was happening on the previous day when the Mother had all of a sudden told the young man to return to his home . The Holy Mother herself did not disclose it. This was nothing new as it was her nature to remain humble always . The revelation of the whole mystery made the devotees very happy for this miracle to have happened.

By eleven-thirty the sunny weather became hot. Accompanied by all the devotees, the Holy Mother walked up to the edge of the backwaters and sat down. The coconut trees and other plants which grew there provided enough shade for everyone as a gentle breeze offered a cooling effect. The Holy Mother fixed her eyes on the water for a few seconds and enjoyed the fish swimming and playing therein. Then she turned around and looked at the devotees, who were thirsting to hear something from her. Recollecting the days she had spent in a God-intoxicated mood, the Holy Mother revealed, "This open ground served Mother a lot during those days. Ah, the time which I spent dancing and singing in bliss is incomparable..." Suddenly, she went into *samadhi*. Tears of bliss rolled down her cheeks. With her eyes fixed somewhere in a boundless dimension, she sat as still as a statue for quite some time.

Slowly coming down, the Mother again related,

Amma: It is always very difficult to remember those days. It will steal away all my external consciousness. The sweetness and bliss bestowed by desireless devotion is something unique. Though *advaita* (the state of non-duality) is the Ultimate Truth, Mother sometimes feels that it is all meaningless and would like to remain like a child in front of God. There are people who preach the *advaita* philosophy, but this will not help much to progress spiritually, even though it does give a certain amount of intellectual understanding. For people to have a glimpse and a taste of spiritual life, devotion and love for the Supreme is absolutely necessary. Not mere devotion, but real love should be there.

One devotee: Mother, how can one make that differentiation? What do you mean by "mere devotion" and what is "real love?"

Amma: Son, devotion can sometimes be like a mere performance of one's duty. For example, in this village, in almost all the houses you can see people chanting and singing every day at dusk, reading the *Bhagavata* and the *Ramayana* and other holy books when they get the time, and so forth. But are they doing it with intense love and longing to see the Lord? There are many people who simply do it as a duty. For them it is just a custom or a rule set forth by their father or grandfather. For the sake of family name they keep the custom of singing the Divine Name at twilight. But if we look into the kitchen or the other side of the house, we will find them saying loudly, "Hey lady, take this or take that from here to the other side," even while they sing, "*Hare Rama Hara Rama, Rama Rama Hare Hare, Hare Krishna Hare Krishna, Krishna Krishna Hare Hare.*" This is the type of *bhakti* (devotion) that we ordinarily see. Most of the time, the goal will be fulfillment of desires. Such people have some devotion to God, but they consider Him to be a mere agent to fulfill their wishes. If their wishes are not fulfilled, then they think that there is no God or that the Deity in the temple is powerless. They have no awareness about the essential principle behind it. They do not think that seeking God, serving God, loving God, and eventually merging in Him is very important. This lack of understanding makes them ignorant of real spirituality and thus they continue to do their own manner of devotional practices.

But devotion supported by real love for Him is different. It is another type of love which is selfless and constant. That love is an intense longing to merge into and totally identify with Love. Real love has an unquenchable thirst to become one with the beloved. In such love there is the factor of discrimination, e.g., "Why are we here in this world? Is there a God? If there is one, I want to see Him, experience Him and become one with Him. I find this world to be unsatisfactory; therefore, let me try to seek and find the Source of all, if there is one." Then endowed with determination, the seeker starts his inquiry immediately, without delay. When such love comes, knowledge also arises. Love is there in any path, whatever it may be. Therefore, love is known both as *jnana* (knowledge) as well as *bhakti* (devotion). *Lakshya bodha* (intent on the goal) is needed. To whom am I calling? For what purpose? Constant remembrance of the goal that has to be realized is needed. That is known as *lakshya bodha*.

For what am I studying? Is it to become an engineer or a doctor or something else? Having decided or fixed a goal of what to become, one studies with determination. But while studying, one forgets about the end-result and concentrates fully on the subject to be learned. This is the sign of the sincere student. Would any student learn anything without contemplating seriously about it? If somebody does that (neglects contemplation), then he is not a good student. First, think and decide what you want to become, then study to attain that. Knowledge *(jnana)* is needed behind action. The awareness of what I am working towards should also be there. So then, love, knowledge, devotion and intent on the goal *(lakshya bodha)* can arise. The student studies, and when the desire to score first rank comes, he will then dedicate all his time for that. There is love in dedication.

In the same way, a real devotee or seeker depends entirely on God and gets absorbed completely. By doing this, he becomes a deserving person to attain his goal. We work sincerely when we have the attitude, "I must attain God." To put up a show or pretense in front of others is not the type of devotion that we want. We should work with determination till we reach the goal. The goal is the fruit. That is Self-realization. If it is to be attained, we must forget about the fruit while working for it; otherwise, our concentration will be divided and real benefit will not be obtained. For that love is needed.

The Lord says that we should act without desiring anything. Children, only then will concentration come. There should be one-pointedness when we call God. We should converse with God, asking, "O Krishna, or O Devi, You stop there. You listen to this before You go. Where did You go, leaving me all alone? Are You trying to get away from me? No, I won't let You go," and so on and so forth. This is how you should ask.

Just as we ask our friends, we should ask Him, "Where did You go? Kanna (Krishna) why don't You come near me? Why are You not speaking? Are You a mere statue? No, that is not what I heard about You. It is You who gives us power, isn't that true? Why do You simply remain standing? Take me." Like this, you should imagine yourself talking to your Beloved Deity.

VAIRAGYA (DETACHMENT)

Question: How does one find peace and tranquility?
Amma: To attain peace and tranquility, our false way of thinking must first be changed. At present, we think that peace comes from the outside. This false conception makes us search for peace outside, in the objects of the world. But, in fact, real peace comes from within. The eternal fountain of peace is inside you. This truth should be understood first; then you can begin to work towards it.

To attain that peace, we should give solitude to the mind. Solitude does not simply mean to sit in an isolated, lovely place filled with natural scenery. Such a surrounding is only a small factor in helping us to gain real solitude. Real solitude is solitude of the mind; it means one-pointedness of the mind. Even a beautiful place will not give you peace of mind if the mind is agitated. Therefore, we should try to make the mind quiet by slowly controlling, gradually restraining it from running after anything and everything. In the beginning you should make a deliberate attempt to subdue the mind. Then, in due course, it will become effortless.

Do not mingle too much with people. Human beings have a tendency to foolishly develop attachment to another person, especially if they are around him for some length of time and it is someone they like. You meet a stranger in a bus stop or railway station. He comes near you and tells you, "I don't know why, but I feel a spontaneous love for you. You are really something special!", or some such flattery like this. Not only does our ego get puffed up, but we also quickly develop an attachment to the person. You "love" him. Why? Because he praised you. Then one day he criticizes you for something. The moment he does that, you turn against him, you hate him, you get angry with him and sometimes you may even want to kill him. Your love is gone and hatred takes over in its place. Any peace you had is now gone, and tranquility has long since flown the coop. Why does all this happen? Because of the agitation of the mind.

The same is the case with a pleasure-giving object. You see an object. You develop an attachment to it. You want to somehow acquire it; therefore, you work hard and earn enough money to get it. But at the last moment, your hard-earned money is stolen by a thief. Disappointment and anger come because you could not fulfill your desire. Your desire is obstructed. You could not get the thing which you had become attached to. You get angry with your wife, your children and whomever you happen to meet. Again, your peace is gone. Thus this peace comes and goes. It never remains with you. Why?

Because of your likes and dislikes. Therefore, try to be detached by keeping your mind away from the things that want to gush into it.

Whatever sorrow comes, take refuge in God. Tell Him, "O Lord, one person scolded me unnecessarily. I am very sad." Do not tell another person about it. Tell God instead, "O Lord, is it because I did something wrong? Or, Lord, is it You who made him do that? If so, then I have no problem because only if I have attachment would I become angry, wouldn't I? No, I don't have that. I don't have any attachment to the words or thoughts which other people utter. You are the one real nature of my Self. When I have to deal with others, I should depend solely on You and not on others, shouldn't I?"

Would we turn around and bark at a dog which barks at us as it stands by the side of the road? No, we wouldn't. If we did, then we would also be like a dog, wouldn't we? We have a world of our own with a culture and behavior befitting human beings. In the same way, each object or person has its or his own nature. We will state a very high opinion about a certain object or person without having observed properly. Afterwards we will remark, "Alas, I am ruined. I should not have bought that thing," or "Oh, what the heck! He acted in such an obnoxious way." It was we who had first given the object or the person a "big certificate" or a high opinion, and afterwards we regretfully realize the real nature of that person or object. As a result, we hate or condemn what we first admired. We should pursue our path, accepting and considering other persons and objects as having their own nature and not expect them to be otherwise. Do not pause to question or criticize their behavior. We are much more a dog than a dog itself if we turn around to question without understanding the proper nature of things.

Question: But this is difficult. How can we remain silent?

Amma: Those who have intent on the goal *(lakshya bodha)* will remain silent. They will always be alert and vigilant.

Some students, even when they are riding in a bus, will go on studying. They will neither play football nor go to the movies. They will not be seen wasting away their time gossiping or chit-chatting. Even if they sleep, they set the alarm before sleeping. They will get up early in the morning and study their lessons. A *sadhak* only needs one thousandth of the dedication and concentration of a student who studies to achieve the first rank in school. He will be saved.

We strive hard for ten or twenty years just to get a job. Two years in kindergarten, ten or twelve years in school, another five years in college and after that a few months or possibly years in search of a job befitting our educational qualifications. Even though we spend time and effort in studying and searching for a job, the possibilities of obtaining a good job are slim. Use a hundreth fraction of that time for God and the whole world will come under your feet. Yes, this is possible through one-pointedness of mind.

Children, concentration of the mind, devoid of ego is the bridge towards God. *Samsara* (the ocean of transmigration) is a vast ocean. The waves of this ocean (the *vasanas*) are huge and gigantic. The bridge of concentration is the only means to cross the ocean of transmigration. Only if we set foot on the bridge and cross over can we reach God. There is no external bridge to reach God. It is an internal bridge of concentration which we ourselves have to build and cross over. It is God's or the Guru's grace which always supports and protects us from falling down during this "trans-oceanic" crossing.

How did Hanuman (the Monkey-God who was the devout servant of Lord Sri Rama) build the bridge? It was by making a bridge through His mental resolve that Hanuman reached the other side. The bridge will collapse if the ego comes while one is crossing over. The path towards God is concentration which arises in the ego-less state. It is not a bridge built with rocks, bricks and cement. Untainted, selfless and pure love is the bridge towards God. If the ego comes, beware, you will fall down.

CONCENTRATION AND LOVE

Question: Amma, you said that concentration is the bridge. You also said that it is love which is the bridge. Which one is correct?
Amma: Both. Concentration and love are one, like two sides of a coin. Love should be there if you want concentration. It is impossible to make them stand separately.

They are inseparable, just as the length and breadth of an object are inseparable.

When we have love for something, an incessant and unbroken stream of thought flows towards that object. The thoughts are only about that. Therefore, to really love we need concentration and to really concentrate we need to love the object, whatever it may be. One cannot exist without the other. A scientist who does experiments in the laboratory needs a lot of concentration. Where does this concentration come from? From his deep and intense interest in that subject. From where comes this deep interest? It is the result of intense love that one has towards his particular subject or field of study. Conversely, if one concentrates on a subject intensely, love for it will also develop.

It is experienced that there is tastelessness behind taste. What makes us feel this taste and tastelessness? These impressions are created by our own actions. We feel them because of the *vasanas* inherited from our father and forefathers. We forsake the quest for permanent spiritual bliss as we pursue worldly pleasures. Having abandoned sweet pudding, we go after crow droppings. Remembrance of God and repetition of the *mantra* is necessary in order to escape from this bondage to worldly pleasures. As we walk we should try to chant our *mantra* once with each step, repeating it over and over again, step by step. Thus while walking, we can remember God as we chant His Holy Name.

You should repeat your *mantra* even while lying down. Embracing the pillow you should imagine that it is God. You should have the strong faith and conviction that God is always with you and will certainly appear before you if you call with longing. Try not to commit any mistakes and try not to get angry with anyone. Immediately when you get up in the morning, you should think of God and pray, "O Mind, you should only turn towards the right path. Travel towards God's world. Do not go towards the empirical plane."

BOW DOWN TO ANYTHING
AND EVERYTHING

The Holy Mother continued,

Amma: Children, you should develop an attitude of bowing down to anything and everything. Keep the plate of food in front of you and bow down to the food before eating and bow down to the plate after eating. An attitude to prostrate to anything at any time should come. In this way, an awareness, "for what am I doing this," will arise. Thus we should build up good character. Prostrate to the cloth you will wear. Bow down to the water with which you will take a shower. During these occasions of bowing down, you will have a pure resolve to see the same consciousness in everything whether with form or without. While doing so, you are in fact remembering God. While taking a shower, imagine that you are doing so with the Lord. Even if you are on the toilet, imagine that you are talking to Him. Do not waste any time. Simply do it. Constant remembrance of God, irrespective of time and place, is real devotion. If you practice in this manner, He will come; He must come. God will come and play with you. Imagine that you are talking to Him while performing any action, whatever it is.

Thus, as your imagination and resolve become stronger and stronger, you can slowly feel His presence, both inside and outside. The vague presence in the beginning will culminate into a constant experience in due course, because of your incessant practice.

Question: Amma, what does the statement, "God is the servant of everyone," mean?

Amma: He is not the Servant of an egotistic person but of a humble one. Humility is God's nature. He is the Servant of everyone. In fact, He is the Universal Servant. But it is a bit difficult to catch this Servant. In order to catch Him, you must drive away the many masters of lust, greed, anger, and other negative qualities to which you are a slave at present. This Great Servant, the Lord, likes to serve only one master, and he should be a great master who is victorious over all these demi-masters. To him the Lord will become a Servant.

Nowadays everybody wants to become a leader. No one wants to become a servant. In reality, the world is badly in need of servants, not leaders. A real servant is a real leader. A real leader is one who really serves the people without ego and ego-centric desires. In fact, greatness is not in dress, and lordship is not in acquiring wealth. Real greatness lies in humility and simplicity.

The friendship of God, the Servant, can be gained only if the ego and false pride are removed. At present we sit with the pride of a chieftain. Our attitude should become like that of a servant. We should become more humble than anything else. We should remove the ego and then He will come running to us. There is no other way to attain God. The agony caused by the longing to see God is not sorrow; it is bliss. The state that we attain by calling and crying to God is equal to the bliss that the *yogi* experiences in *samadhi.* Some people would say that crying for God is a mental weakness. Let them say that. To cry for God is to gain the highest. Anyway, crying for God is far superior than crying for trivial and fleeting worldly pleasures. The happiness which we get from the objects of the world lasts only for a few seconds; whereas, the happiness experienced from God and the thought of Him is everlasting. That 'weakness' is sufficient for us.

The Holy Mother is a living example of the Servant to all who come to her. Forever established in that Truth, she comes to dwell in our midst, on the physical plane, to guide us in our spiritual growth. Sometimes, however, it is difficult for her to stay down on this level of existence. Suddenly she went into a state of rapture. Her right hand formed itself into a divine *mudra.* Rotating the fingers of her right hand in the air, the Mother uttered her favorite *mantra,* "Shiva, Shiva..." Again, she sat motionless for some time. The devotees gazed at her countenance and silently waited for her to come down to the normal plane of awareness.

One of the women devotees sang from *Sri Lalitambike:*

O Mother, this jiva might have passed
Through several hundreds of other bodies
Before coming to this birth.
This time, by Thy Grace,
I have this human form.
O Mother, let me offer this human birth
Which is very rare to obtain
At Thy Holy Lotus Feet.

The Holy Mother once again uttered the Divine *mantra*, "Shiva, Shiva..." and slowly opened her eyes.

DEVOTION, THE BEGINNING AND END

One devotee: Amma, some say that devotion is only the first step. What do you say about this?
Amma: Son, aren't all the big scholarly books written with the same alphabet that we used when we learned in the beginning to write? Without learning the vowels, how can one learn the consonants? (In the Malayalam language, children are taught the vowels first and then the consonants.) How can someone who has not learned "Ka, Kha," (first consonants in Malayalam) write big scholarly books? All great works are written with these consonants, "Ka, Kha." The alphabet is used in all words. These letters are important for us in order to write anything. The alphabet is the substratum of writing. If a building is built without making the foundation strong, it will collapse. This is necessary until the end, even after reaching There. Without the alphabet nothing

is possible (to write). The same is the case in spirituality. Devotion is not a mental weakness; neither is it only the first step, but something like the substratum for attaining the goal. Victory is ours if *bhakti* is obtained. It is both the beginning and the end.

THE GLORY OF TEMPLES

Question: Mother, is it necessary to go to temples and give money there?

Amma: Children, human beings are living on the physical plane. They do not have any time to focus and unite their thoughts. They are always restless. There will always be problems in a village where there is not at least one temple. It is said that one should not sleep overnight in a village where there is no temple. Due to lack of faith and lack of fear in a Supreme Power or Governor, the people in a village with no temple will do wicked things. Where there is a temple, people will take refuge in it. The concentrated prayers of the people and the worship performed in it create a special feeling of divinity and peace in the village atmosphere. The power of their concentration will always remain there. This, in turn, will give peace and tranquility to the villagers themselves. This was all introduced by the *rishis* with great foresight. Again children, due to the lack of self-surrender and obedience to a higher principle, there will always be chaos and confusion in a village without a temple.

We light lamps in temples and burn firecrackers during festivals. All these things have their benefits. Don't say that these rituals are superfluous. Let human beings offer at least ten paise (about half a cent) at the temple in the name of God, so as to not spend their entire wealth in eating and excreting like animals. How much money are we wasting on movies and other things?

People think that it is a shame to go to temples. "Do not offer any money there. If we say anything there, does God hear it?" These are the questions they ask. So what. Society has degenerated due to this faithlessness and arrogance. This reflects on all our lives.

Children, God does not need money. All the wealth in the world is His alone. What could we give Him?

We are always selfish. What will happen if we try to teach the world without learning ourselves? Children, if we are unable to withstand the problems of life, won't we become weak and unsteady? At least we can let a little of our selfishness lessen by going to temples to offer and dedicate our attachments in the name of a higher principle.

Atmospheric purification will occur by burning camphor, lighting oil lamps and performing similar actions. Worship performed externally is also helpful for this. At the same time, what God likes the most is *manasa puja* (mental worship). Many of those who come here to the Ashram are people who do mental worship while sitting in their homes. More concentration is achieved through mental worship than in external worship. In reality, one's own heart is the temple, but we have not yet realized that. Therefore, we need an external temple as a reminder of the internal one.

Question: Mother, is it necessary to worship trees, snakes and things like that?

Amma: Everything in God's creation has a purpose and a benefit, whatever it is. There is a use for everything, whether it is a dog, a cat or a hen. No matter whether it is an animal or a plant, there is a purpose behind its creation. Even if human beings do not have any use for something, other creatures do. The harmony of nature depends on all things which have been created. Take, for example, the changes in weather patterns that have now occurred. Because trees have been needlessly cut down, we do not get the proper rainfall during the monsoon season. Furthermore, the temperature has increased, hasn't it? It is the trees which purify the atmosphere, absorbing all the impure air exhaled by human beings. Is it wrong to mentally worship those things which do good to us? For example, some things are considered sacred, so we honor them with due reverence, that's all. Lord Krishna has told Arjuna, "Among mountains I am the Himalayas, among trees I am the great peepal tree and amongst animals, the lion." When everything is pervaded by God, which thing is not to be worshipped?

Question: Is it right to sacrifice animals during rituals?

Amma: (Laughingly) Nowadays it is those who eat meat and drink daily who protest animal sacrifice in rituals. Do they really protest non-killing? Is it really non-killing that they object to? Do they have any sincerity? Do they have any love or compassion towards animals?

Real sacrifice is the sacrifice of our animal tendencies. That is what needs to be offered in the fire of knowledge. Interpreting this wrongly, people sacrifice animals.

Killing should not be done consciously. There is no problem or trouble if one can do it with the attitude, "I am not killing." There is no sin in that case. Sin is incurred if one does it with full awareness of killing. In other words, it depends on the amount of attachment and detachment that one has while doing the act of killing. It is difficult for an ordinary human being to be detached while doing such an act.

Soldiers kill many people in a war, don't they? But they do not have any sin because by doing so they are discharging their duty. They perform it with the thought and awareness that it is for the benefit of the nation and the people. Therefore, they do not incur any sin.

Sin and sinlessness depend on the purity and intention of the goal which is to be attained. For achieving big things we will have to sacrifice small things. To plant teakwood trees we will have to destroy many small plants and weeds during the process of preparing and ploughing the field for them. But we do not care. We mercilessly pull those plants out and burn them. Why? Because teakwood trees are much more significant and useful as far as society is concerned. Therefore, we give more importance to the teakwood trees and much less importance to the other plants. We consider it as a good cause, a higher cause. Similarly, to attain a higher goal, renunciation of smaller things is a must.

Simply for taste, to appease their hunger, to fill their bellies, people kill thousands of animals daily. What compassion they have! Mother is neither justifying nor siding with animal sacrifice. Whichever way you look at it, it is not good to kill animals in the name of religion. If there are people who protest animal sacrifice, they should refrain from killing animals and eating meat, at least, to set an example.

It is quite certain that the atmosphere will be purified if *homas* (rituals, sacrifices) are performed. There are certain times when both the atmosphere and nature become polluted and disharmonious. It is said that *yagnas* (sacrifices) and *homas* should be conducted during such times. These sacrifices will help set nature on the right track and purify the atmosphere. It is the duty of human beings to serve and take care of nature, which, in turn, will supply us with all the necessary things.

FAITH AND SADHANA

The Holy Mother got up and walked towards the side of the kitchen. The Mother's visits to the kitchen were always unexpected. At times the *brahmacharinis* (women aspirants) and the other women devotees who were in charge of cooking and other household chores were not very careful about keeping the cooking vessels in an orderly fashion. The same was the case with various cooking ingredients such as spices. Today the Mother's chance visit happened. She unexpectedly entered the kitchen and found some rice wrapped up in a newspaper, lying on a shelf. The *brahmacharini* who had cooked lunch had inadvertently placed the rice on the newspaper, forgetting to place it back into the rice sack after she poured the measured amount into the cooking vessel. The Holy Mother immediately summoned the *brahmacharini* and said,

Amma: Is this the way to do things? It is external discipline and attention which leads to internal alertness. A spiritual seeker should learn to do things in an orderly way. At present the mind is in total disorder. We have to regain and restore the lost order and harmony of our mind first. Once that has been regained, the mind becomes conducive enough to contemplate upon the Supreme Self. To attain that inner harmony we should begin with external orderliness and cleanliness.

Children, do not consider anything as insignificant or unimportant. Even a needle has its own place. We should develop the proper eyes to see it and a mind to place each and every object where it should be placed. Neither a higher place nor a lower place should be given to it. This should be the attitude of a true seeker. Forgetfulness and inadvertence are not the proper attributes for a spiritual aspirant.

The Mother then took the rice from the shelf and put it back in the sack herself. She looked around once again and then walked out of the kitchen. It was time for the evening *bhajan*, so the Mother went to the temple verandah where the usual evening *bhajan* was be-

ing conducted. She took her seat and the singing began
in a few seconds. The Holy Mother sang, *Shiva Shiva
Hara Hara...*

> O Auspicious One,
> The Destroyer, whose loincloth is the clouds,
> The beautiful One playing the damaru (drum)
> Who holds the trident in His hands
> Bestowing fearlessness and boons,
> Who wears ash on His limbs
> and has matted locks,
> Who bears the crescent moon on His forehead,
> Who has eyes full of compassion,
> Wearing snakes as a garland
> And a necklace of skulls.
> O Auspicious One, the Great God...

The devotees, singing the response to the Mother's
lead singing, felt truly inspired by the powerful melody
of this song to Lord Shiva, the personification of Supreme
Consciousness. Following this came the haunting tune
of *Kasturi Tilikam*, which especially delighted them as
devotees often identified their devotion to the Mother
with the devotion of the *gopis (milkmaids)* to Lord Krishna.

> Krishna puts the vermilion mark on his forehead
> And wears the Kaustubha gem on His chest,
> From Krishna's nostril hangs a pearl ring,
> With bracelets around His wrists
> He holds a flute in His hands,

Sandalwood paste adorns all his limbs,
A pearl necklace hangs round his neck.
Victory to Krishna,
Who is surrounded by the milkmaids,
Who is the Crest Jewel of the cowherds!

About devotional singing, the Mother says, "When great souls sing, they radiate tremendous amounts of energy. They can make people forget about the world and worldly bondages. Their mere presence will fill people's hearts with love and devotion for God. Peace and tranquility will take the place of restlessness and other negative tendencies. Concentration will come spontaneously. It becomes effortless. Even if people do not put forth any conscious attempt to acquire any spiritual energy, they will get it from that presence. For example, suppose we visit a place where perfume is manufactured. Even if we simply walk around without doing anything, we can still smell the fragrance on our body when we return home. In the same way, a *Mahatma's* (great soul) presence transmits spiritual energy to those who come to visit him."

This statement of the Holy Mother is what is truly experienced by the devotees when she sings. An onlooker will see people bursting into tears or spontaneously gliding into meditation, enjoying the unconditional bliss of supreme devotion while the Mother sings.

Bhajans continued until eight-thirty. After the *arati* (waving burning camphor in front of the Deity as the

conclusion of worship) the *brahmacharins* went to meditate in the meditation hall. The Holy Mother roamed
around in the coconut grove for some time. She was in
a state of rapture at the end of the *bhajan*. She might
have been wanting to be alone. Having revelled in her
own plane of consciousness for some time, the Mother
came back and sat on the sand at the southern side of
the temple. Somebody tried to spread a mat for the
Mother to sit on. She smilingly commented, "A mat!
For this crazy Kali who used to lie in mud and dirt.
Spread it out for yourselves, children."

At this time a few other devotees who were sitting
here and there came and sat near the Holy Mother. One
of them asked,

Question: Mother, one devotee says that there is not
much importance in *sadhana* and that it is enough to
have faith in Mother.

Amma: Son, a person who has faith in Mother will perform *sadhana* as Mother instructs. Such a person will
live without erring even a little bit. Will your disease be
cured if you only believe the doctor but do not take the
medicine? Not only that, faith will gain strength and
steadiness only if *sadhana* brings experience. Otherwise,
faith will slip into irresoluteness. You cannot progress
without *sadhana*. Can't you see even *jivanmuktas* (those
who have achieved Liberation while tenanting the body)
doing meditation and *japa* (repetition of the mantra) to
set an example? No progress will accrue to him who
simply sits, saying, "Faith will save me," without doing

anything. Unquestioning obedience is what is meant by faith and devotion. Whatever the Guru says, one should obey unconditionally. Do not ask any questions. Do not doubt the Guru. One should unconditionally obey the Guru, whatever he says, whether it is doing service to the Guru, service to society, *japa, dhyana* (meditation) or anything else. The *Satguru* instructs that which suits each person.

KANVASHRAMA

14 March 1984

Kanvashrama is a beautiful piece of land, an ashram, in a place called Varkala near Quilon. It is believed that a great sage named Kanva did penance there for a long time, hence the name, Kanvashrama. One can feel an extraordinary sanctity and peace here.

This place is owned by a Dutch devotee named De Reede, known by his spiritual name, Hamsa. Very much devoted to the Mother, Hamsa often invites the Mother to his ashram. As it is a place suitable to do *sadhana*, the Mother agreed to come with her spiritual children to his ashram and spend a few days there.

Accepting the invitation of Hamsa, the Mother decided to go to Kanvashram for a three-day trip from this day, the fourteenth of March, to the seventeenth. Everyone was getting ready to go. As usual, everything needed for the three-day stay at Kanvashram was taken, including food supplies and cooking utensils. This was the usual practice whenever the Mother went there. The *brahmacharins* had to prepare their own food. Furthermore, the Mother would not allow them to take food or drink from tea shops or restaurants. The Holy Mother says,

"In the beginning a *sadhak* should not eat anything from tea shops or restaurants. While using each and every ingredient, the shopkeeper's only thought will be how to make more profit. When making tea, he will think, 'Is this much tea dust necessary? Is this much milk needed? Why can't the sugar be reduced?' In this way, he will only have thoughts to reduce the quantity used in order to gain more profit. The vibrations of those thoughts will affect the *sadhak* .

"There was a *sannyasin* (renunciate) who was not at all interested in reading newspapers. One day an intense desire to read the newspaper sprang up in him. Afterwards he started dreaming about newspapers and about the news. When enquiries were made, it was discovered that the servant was reading the newspaper while cooking. His attention was not on the cooking but on reading the newspaper. The thought waves of the cook affected the *sannyasin*."

The van to drive the Mother and the *brahmacharins to Kanvashrama* arrived on the newly constructed seaside road. One by one, the *brahmacharins* proceeded into the van, each one carrying a cloth bag on his shoulder and a vessel or some other parcel in his hands. The Mother also took a big aluminum cooking pot. Even though devotees requested her not to carry it, she would not listen to them. The Holy Mother related, "Your Mother used to carry pots and more pots full of rice gruel on her head to and from distant places. Mother is used to it." Then, like a little child, she said, "I won't give this to anybody who asks. It is mine."

The van was filled. There were nearly twenty-five people. The Mother was always very careful to take each and every thing necessary whenever there was a trip. During such times she would become exactly like a mother who was taking care of a big family and looking after the needs of each member. Before the van moved, Mother inquired, "Children, did you take everything that is needed, as Mother instructed?" "Yes, Mother," replied Gayatri.

By one o'clock the van slowly moved south along the seaside road. Once again the Holy Mother's mood changed to that of an innocent child. Pointing to the different spots and things which she saw by the oceanside, the Mother started explaining what they were and how she knew those places.

Sometimes she simply gazed at the sea and sat silently like one lost to this world. After a few minutes the Mother started singing loudly, *Sundarini Vayo...*

> Please come, O Beautiful One
> Consort of Shiva, please come
> O Auspicious One, please come
> Please come, O Endless one.

O Vamakshi, Consort of Lord Shiva,
O Kamakshi, who radiates brilliance everywhere,
To those who look upon Thee
As their dear relative,
Thou art their very own.
O Mother, please remain
As the spring of my inspiration.

Being both of one and of many forms,
Thou art the Light of the Absolute.
Dost Thou not know my heart well?
Will Thou not come before me, even as I ask?

It seemed that the Mother wanted to sing all alone. Therefore, the children did not sing in response. They felt that it would not be appropriate to mix their voices with hers. Tears of supreme bliss rolled down the Mother's cheeks and she was slowly transported to another world. Watching her radiant form, a college professor whispered into Brahmacharin Balu's ears, "Look at her; what a wondrous and mysterious personality this is. A few minutes ago she was like a little child and look at her now! What a vast difference. Everything is her *leela* (play). We mortal human beings fail to understand such Divine personalities with our limited intellect, and thus we judge them incorrectly. By her Grace alone can we understand her. There is no other way. Human effort can only take us up to a certain extent; beyond that, Grace alone is the light and the vehicle which comes to us."

At this point an English sentence accidentally slipped out of one educated *brahmacharin's* mouth. The sentence was, "Eleven boys makes a football team." Immediately when he finished the sentence, the Mother said, "It should be 'boys make.'" The astounded *brahmacharins* and other devotees looked at each other. In the eyes of others the Mother has studied only up to the fourth grade. But such occasions are not rare when she reveals a little of her omniscience. The Holy Mother's keen observation of even the silly and seemingly insignificant mistakes of her children is quite obvious from this incident.

Once in 1982 a devotee from the West came to see the Holy Mother. Ralph M. Dickson was his name. This American became a staunch devotee of the Holy Mother from the very first sight of her. He wanted to clear some of his doubts by asking some questions during *Devi Bhava*. But unfortunately, when he came up to the Mother, there was no interpreter near her. Even then, Ralph, due to his faith mixed with excitement, related to Mother the questions he wanted to ask. Later while conversing with Nealu, Ralph exclaimed, "I heard that the Mother studied only up to the fourth grade and that she did not speak English at all, but she spoke to me in English! I had no problem conversing with her. She understood whatever I said and I understood everything that she told me." When we asked the Mother about this, she replied, "That happened because of the faith and devotion of that son."

The van proceeded along the lovely oceanside road. All of a sudden, the Holy Mother said aloud, "Oh, I am thirsty. Give me some tea." She seemed like a small child crying for milk. The van stopped in front of a small tea shop. The Mother coolly stated, "Those who want tea can drink some now." Almost all the house-holders had tea or coffee. Some of the *brahmacharins* also drank tea or coffee as well. But when someone brought a glass for Mother, she said, "Mother doesn't feel thirsty now. Mother doesn't want any." But it seemed that the Mother took a little, and again the van drove on.

The Mother and her party reached Kanvashrama at three o'clock. The atmosphere and the surroundings gave the feeling of an ancient hermitage where saints and sages of the past with their disciples performed severe penance. This piece of land, which covered a vast area, was a forest full of cashew nut trees and various other kinds of trees, bushes, plants and creepers. There were several hills, big and small, on this isolated piece of land. Down below at the southern tip of the plot there was a beautiful pond. On the eastern side of this pond lay a dense forest which was full of poisonous snakes and jackals. To the south stretched paddy fields. Here and there in the midst of the trees and bushes one could see simple, small hermitages built with bamboo and co-conut leaves. These were meant for spiritual aspirants who wanted to do serious *sadhana*. Sometimes Mother would instruct one of her children to go and do *sadhana* in one of these hermitages.

Since Hamsa was on tour, all the other residents of the ashram, headed by Markus, a German devotee who was in charge of the ashram, came and received the Mother at the entrance. After having first gone to the temple, Mother and all the devotees gathered together in the tent made of coconut leaves with all four sides open. First Markus offered a glass of tender coconut water to the Mother, then the residents of this ashram offered their salutations to the Mother. She took a few sips and put it down. "How are you, Amma?" inquired Markus. The Holy Mother with a smile replied in English, "Good, very good." (Everyone laughed joyfully.)

Markus: It is good to hear Amma speaking English. If she learns it quickly, then we won't have to depend on interpreters. The Mother can do it if she wants. The scriptures say that *Mahatmas* can learn anything and everything if they want, whatever it may be. Isn't that so, Mother?

Amma: That is right. They only have to concentrate on that particular subject or object to understand and assimilate the essence of it. All knowledge becomes under the control of such a person. A king has all the wealth of his country and the subjects under his control. He just has to snap his fingers and the thing that he wants will be right there. But a good and wise king will not misuse his power at all. He will use it only in circumstances when it is absolutely necessary. In the same way, *Mahatmas*, who are established in the Supreme State of Pure Consciousness, are the emperors of the universe. They have everything under their command and their glance is sufficient to make others act according to their wish and will. But like a just and wise king, they never do things against the already-set laws of nature unless there arises an absolute need for it.

One brahmacharin: Mother, why do some places have a special vibration and some others a strange and different one?

Amma: Each person's thoughts, words and deeds play an important role in the differences in vibrations. Places where there exists a good and spiritual vibration are where a serious *sadhak,* a saint or a person who has performed many good and selfless actions must have lived. For example, when you visit some houses you might have a very good feeling about the atmosphere in the house as well as with its members even though that is your first visit. This will be due to the mental calibre, devotional practices and such other good things that those family members do. Whereas, in some other houses we can feel an entirely different vibration. We may even feel that we want to leave the house as quickly as possible. This again depends on the thought vibrations of the people who live there. This difference can also be felt not only due to the people who live there at present but also due to those who lived there long ago. The intensity and the time which the vibrations remain in a particular area or house will vary according to the intensity of the thoughts and actions performed by the people who lived there or who were associated with that place. This is the secret behind the feeling of a meditative mood and divine presence in places where *Mahatmas* have taken *mahasamadhi* (when a great soul leaves his body).

The vibrations in an office are entirely different from those in a house. The vibrations in a marketplace are different from those in an office. Again the vibrations in a temple or an ashram are totally different from vibrations in all the other places. While the atmosphere in a market place or a liquor shop makes one confused, chaotic and tense, the atmosphere in a temple brings peace, serenity and calm. The vibrations in a temple are much more elevating, soothing and peaceful than in an office or in a house or in a liquor shop. Why is this? It is simply because of the pure thought vibrations, mental resolve and attitude of the people who come and go in those places.

THE BLISS OF SINGING BHAJANS

The Holy Mother got up from her seat, and having come out of the hut, she called aloud, "Shiva...Shivane!" raising both her hands up and gazing skyward. She went to her room which was situated near the hut. The *brahmacharins* and other devotees had their evening hot milk diluted with water and rested for some time. It was five o'clock.

A *bhajan* program had been arranged at the famous Janardanaswami Temple in Varkala at seven-thirty in the evening preceding a dance performance. Having had a refreshing bath in the cool and rejuvenating waters of the pond down below, everyone meditated for an hour or so in the calm and serene atmosphere of the ashram. Some meditated by the side of the Vishnu Tirtha, a very shallow pond which was considered sacred. Others sat under the trees. There were a few who meditated sitting on the other side of the pond near the forest.

At quarter-past seven they all set out to the temple and arrived a few minutes before seven-thirty. The Holy Mother had also come along, but she remained in the car which was parked half a kilometer away from the temple. Gayatri, one *brahmacharin* and a couple from the same town who were devotees of the Mother also stayed back with her. Since the stage arrangements were not completed in time, *bhajans* did not begin until eight o'clock. According to the published program, the ashramites were supposed to sing for two hours. It was ten o'clock and the dance troupe wanted to start their program without any delay. They asked the *brahmacharins* to stop singing. The *bhajans* were about to be concluded anyway, but the audience became excited. People got up and shouted, "We want to hear more *bhajans*. Continue the *bhajans*. No dance." Some of them even became agitated and shouted slogans, "Dance troupe, go back. We want to hear only *bhajans!*" The frightened dancers slowly withdrew from the stage and hid in the a room until the *bhajan* ended.

It was a thrilling and wonderful sight that evening. The thousands of people who had gathered there in the temple primarily to enjoy the dance program at first felt very annoyed and irritated when they had heard the announcement about the commencement of the *bhajan* singing performed by the Mata Amritanandamayi Math. But now the same crowd did not want it to stop. The people truly experienced the bliss of the Divine Name on that day. What other factor except the Guru's grace can bring such a transformation in the minds of the people?

When everyone got back to Kanvashrama, the Holy Mother related,

Amma: When Mother heard the uproar, she thought that the people were turning against her children for singing for such a long time. But the next moment Mother became reassured, thinking that that could not happen since devotion and devotional singing were the spontaneous music of the soul. Nobody can resist the inspirational qualities of such music penetrating one's heart when it is sung with concentration and devotion. It is this natural attraction which has been proven today.

It was nearly midnight when the Holy Mother retired to her room. Before going to bed, the *brahmacharins* once again meditated in the deep silence of the night.

15 March 1984

The *brahmacharins* and the other devotees got up at an early hour of the day and did their usual chanting of the Thousand Names of Devi and then did meditation and other morning practices. The dawn at Kanvashrama was beautiful. Standing on the banks of the Vishnu Tirtha, one could see the sun rising up from the eastern horizon.

At seven o'clock the Holy Mother came and sat under the banyan tree situated on the southern side of the Vishnu Tirtha. Her hair was tied up in a knot. The golden rays of the rising sun reflected on her face and delineated more of its glory and splendor. The blissful smile which lit up her countenance seemed more luminous than the sun. Fixed on the infinite, her eyes were still and steady, without even blinking once.

The Mother sat there for a long time. It was nine o'clock and the Holy Mother was still seated under the banyan tree. Around ten o'clock, a few devotees came to have the Mother's *darshan*. They all prostrated before her and took their seats in front of the Mother in a semi-circle.

Among the devotees who came just at that time, there was a young girl named Miss D. (a fictitious name). She came with her father and her uncle. Miss D. was studying for her Bachelor's degree in philosophy. Endowed with a strong longing to know God, Miss D. was very attracted to the Holy Mother. She kept gazing at the Mother's face without paying any attention to anything that happened around her. Realizing that she was burning with inspiration, Mother commented, "Miss D. mol (Daughter Miss D.) wants to swallow Mother up." Without even the least sign of timidity, she replied, "Yes, if possible." Mother laughed loudly. Everyone joined in laughter with the Mother, even her father and her uncle, although there was a slight sign of fear on their faces, seeing and hearing their daughter's strong inclination towards spiritual life. Their fear was that she would abandon worldly life and take up spiritual life.

One after another the Mother received all those who came to see her. It was nearly twelve o'clock noon, so the Mother invited all to have lunch. The devotees took leave of her, one by one, as the Mother got up from her seat and walked down towards her cottage. Hesitatingly, Miss D. also left with her father and her uncle, having prostrated to the Mother.

Responding to the invitation from a devotee's family, the Mother visited their home that evening. She sang a few *bhajans* there and did a *puja* in their family shrine room. After the singing and the *puja*, the Mother, overflowing with compassion and love, conversed with each and every member of the family, including the servants.

Everybody returned by ten o'clock. When she reached Kanvashrama, the Mother said, "It is too early for Mother to go to bed." This was a fortuitous announcement for everyone. They were only too happy to hear that they could spend some more time with her. Everyone sat around the Holy Mother in the hut near the Mother's cottage. She looked at each one's face and smiled. Again there was a short pause. The Mother said, "Mother simply wanted to see all her children's faces."

One householder devotee: When the whole *Brahmanda* (the universe with each and every object in it) is within you, why do you want to see our external faces?

Amma: For your satisfaction. What will be your fate if Mother sits saying, "The whole universe with all of you is within me. Therefore, I don't want to see you externally." None of you will be here. A person endowed

with a very strong sense of detachment and determination to reach the goal may not need such external attention. But Mother knows that you children need that
care. You give very much importance to it, don't you?
Know that Mother does things, whatever they may be,
with a purpose. A touch, a word, a look, a smile or a
patting (on the back) is sometimes sufficient to fill her
children's heart and soul with strength, courage and
peace. At present, the source of their inspiration solely
depends on Mother's physical presence. As you progress
spiritually, you may see her within.

Now the Holy Mother continued,

Amma: But sometimes it is painful to see her children
act indiscriminately. (In a serious tone) For example,
yesterday on the way here, Mother said that those who
wanted to drink tea could do so. Except for a few everyone had something to drink. The fact is, Mother was
testing your discrimination, but most of you failed.
Mother felt a little pain seeing her children act in this
manner.

Children, to test the mental strength and discrimination of the disciple, a Guru might ask the disciple to do
many things, even things which are against spiritual life.
Sometimes the Guru himself may bring it to him or create such a circumstance. A real disciple properly dis-
criminates and accepts only the things that he needs and
rejects all the rest ruthlessly. Things that he needs
means those circumstances and objects which would

help him to progress spiritually. His sharp discrimination will help him to overcome all kinds of obstacles which might arise in this path. Positive acceptance of the Guru's words and deeds and utter obedience to him with application of his teachings in one's life are what gives the greatest amount of joy to the Guru. This, verily, is the most precious Guru *dakshina* (offering) that you can offer to the Guru.

There are all different kinds of habits developed by us. All these habits must go, one by one. You may find it hard to remove them in a short period of time; yet you must strive to get rid of them with determination. At least a willingness to give them up should be there.

Habits are the biggest impediments on our path. Our own actions are responsible for them. The diligent performance of virtuous or divine actions will help the old, bad habits to be replaced with new and good ones. This needs constant practice.

Tea and coffee contain intoxicants. They will destroy many things that help to purify the sense organs. They will awaken sensual desires. They are harmful to the body also.

The *brahmacharins and* the other devotees on this trip who had tea the other day while traveling to Kanvashrama now realized how diplomatically and unpredictably the Mother had caught them. Pricked by their guilty consciences, they remained silent.

Another devotee: Mother, why do you give so much importance to the control of food?

Amma: Children, the body is made up of food. A pure mind with pure thoughts will arise only in a pure body. To get a pure body the food that we eat should be pure and *sattvic*. The body and mind are interdependent. Whatever happens to the body will affect the mind and vice versa. Above all, to control the mind, a good control over the food that we eat is absolutely necessary. Skeptics and non-believers may label this as nonsense or illogical. "Nonsense or illogical" is the explanation or interpretation for things or phenomena which they do not understand. They view the entire spiritual science with a negative attitude. They believe only in things which they think they can prove through scientific experimentation. Then why don't they try and test this science? Skeptics claim they believe in modern science, but scientists themselves ultimately believe in spirituality. What a contradiction! It seems that their only purpose is to make blank and illogical statements. How can such people elucidate something from this real science?

The time was eleven-thirty p.m. The Holy Mother with joined palms told everyone, "Mother begs pardon from all her children for scolding them. Mother feels that all her children are not different from her. That is why she talks in this way. Children, don't take it otherwise. It is only for your own good." Saying this, the Mother got up and went to her room. Everyone went to their respective cottages, having prostrated at the places where they were seated.

16 March 1984

As usual, the *brahmacharins* and the householder devotees arose at four-thirty a.m. and performed the chanting of the *Lalita Sahasranama*. When the first rays of the sun fell on the earth, they all sat around the Vishnu Tirtha and meditated. Some took their seats under the banyan tree. It was an inspiring sight. They all seemed like young *yogis* absorbed in deep meditation. The peaceful surroundings and serenity of the atmosphere added to the sacredness of this scene. The rising sun's sparkling, golden rays and the gentle, cool morning breeze caressed them. The meditation continued until half past eight. The Holy Mother came out and sat under the banyan tree to give *darshan* to the devotees at nine-thirty. A group of spiritually inclined people were present. They conducted and participated in regular *satsangs* and other spiritual activities. They asked the Mother different questions. It is usually found to be true that people who have read and learned more are the ones who have more doubts.

Question: Mother, my mind runs away and wanders while I am trying to concentrate.
Amma: Son, it is the nature of the mind to wander. It cannot sit quiet. When we try to quiet the mind by concentrating on an object of meditation, we can see it wander even more. More thoughts will come. Beginners may get frightened and sometimes feel discouraged by these numerous thoughts which come up during medita-

tion. These thoughts and other tendencies of the mind
have always been there, but because we were engaged in
different activities we had no awareness of them. These
thoughts and other *vasanas* manifest only when we try
to withdraw the mind from all external activities and
concentrate on a single point. Constant practice coupled
with determination is the only way to conquer the mind.
Therefore, during such times, do not become frightened
or discouraged. Continue your spiritual practices with
determination.

Until now we have lived in the consciousness that
we are the body. We have traveled a long way living in
this world of plurality. All the impressions gathered
from the past experiences are there in the mind, some in
the gross mind, but the major part are in the subcon-
scious mind. They are dormant like a tree latent in the
seed. To remove all these latent tendencies from the
mind needs long term practice with patience.

Another man: Is *Raja Yoga* the best path?

Amma: Children, it is difficult to say "such and such" a
path is good and "such and such" is not a good one. All
paths are equally good if they are properly practiced with
the right understanding. Anyhow, just one path cannot
be advised for all people since people are different mentally, physically, and intellectually. The spiritual disposition inherited by the aspirant from the previous birth is
the criteria to test which path is good for a person.
Though all paths are equally good, each one works dif-
ferently in different people. Each person will have a
spontaneous feeling or inclination towards a particular

path and that will be the correct path for him. In any case, to be on the safe side, it is better to approach a *Satguru* in order to find one's path, to determine which direction one should go, to discover who is our Beloved Deity and to obtain other advice for one's spiritual growth.

Children, as far as Mother is concerned, the path of devotion is the best and the easiest since most people are predominately emotional in nature. Not only that, *bhakti marga* (path of devotion) has no complications like the other paths. There are no harmful techniques or complications involved in love. Simply love the Lord. Love is not aggressive; it is a constant flow.

It is always dangerous to do *sadhana* after reading books. Always be aware that those who write books and give speeches are not all Gurus. Try to follow the footsteps of those who have fully experienced what they say or write about.

Question: *Kundalini* will rise through the practice of *Hatha Yoga*, won't it?

Amma: Why do you think about all these complicated methods when there are easier ones? *Hatha Yoga* should be practiced under the strict guidance of a Perfect Master. You cannot simply adopt any method that you feel like. Each one will have a path which they would have followed in the previous birth. Only if that path is followed will one progress in one's practice.

If *Hatha Yoga* is practiced by oneself, it might lead to the danger of becoming more aware of the body and thus will inflate the ego. Whereas, the sole aim of spiritual practice is to get rid of this body-consciousness. Whichever is the path, it is enough to gain concentration. The concept about *kundalini* rising is a *bhavana* (creative imagination). We can have the concept about God as well. It is the same idea. Whether you follow the path of devotion or the path of *karma* or the path of *jnana*, this awakening of the *kundalini* must happen. The difference is that a devotee calls the same *kundalini shakti* as Krishna, Rama, Devi, Jesus or Buddha. Children, do your *sadhana* properly and sincerely. Do not waste your energy and time thinking, "When is the *kundalini* going to awaken? Will it rise up if I follow this path or is the other path better?"

Question: Aren't Devi and other forms a mere *sankalpa?*

Amma: Do not say this. As far as a devotee is concerned, the form of his Beloved Deity, Devi, Krishna or Rama are real. If you do not like sweet pudding, why should you say that it is not at all good or that it is useless? There are many people who relish and enjoy it. Your favorite dish might be something else and something that someone else may not like.

All the names and forms, whatever they are, are only creations of the mind for one who has gone beyond the mind. But this is not the case for one who has not reached the state of Perfection. He or she may say that all names and forms are unreal and that *Brahman* alone is true and real. However, if he has not experienced Perfection, it is meaningless for him to go around declaring the unreality of forms.

Even people who have reached Perfection will set an example by worshipping, singing and chanting the different names, and glorifying the different forms, of Gods and Goddesses. They are the only ones who truly experience the world as illusory and not at all real. Yet they will perform worship and give adoration to what the forms represent because they know that we ignorant little children cannot rise up to their level of understanding and, therefore, need a name or form to aid our spiritual growth.

To pretend we know it all and to show off our pride (which is really false pride), we may say that Devi is a *sankalpa*, that the names and forms of Gods and Goddesses are merely a state of mind and thus have no reality. What authority do we have to say such things? You may say that the saints and sages have stated this in the scriptures. But they realized the ultimate unreality of all forms through their own experience. Have you realized this? If not, keep quiet. Please do not taint and stain people's faith by your speech. The *rishis* were always afraid that they might stain this Truth through their speech. That is why they always prayed, "O Supreme Self, let my word be established in my mind; let my mind be established in my word."

Question: Mother, I do not understand. What fear? Where is the fear in this prayer? I don't see its relevance.

Amma: Son, here "Let my word be established in my mind" means "Let each and every word that I might utter while describing this Truth be established in my ex-

perience." The *rishi* prays to the Supreme Self for His
Grace to reflect in his inner experience of the *Atman* in
his speech. He is afraid that he would utter some un-
truth because whenever speech comes there is a chance
for a new interpretation. Speech is also a product of the
ego. The ego is the cause of speech which is the effect.
The ego is false; therefore, the false nature of the ego
will be reflected in the effect, speech. The *rishi* wants to
sustain the purity of the *Atman* in his speech as well.
That is why he prays that his speech should reflect his
inner experience of the Truth.

The devotees and the *brahmacharins* sat amazed,
looking at the Mother's face, wondering at her deep insight in whatever spiritual topic she talked about. One
devotee remarked, " How simple are the Mother's explanations about the most complicated and subtle philosophical truths." The Mother laughed like an innocent
child and retorted, "Hey, don't praise this crazy Kali.
Crazy Kali's children are also crazy."

Question: Does Mother have the opinion that the different names and forms of Gods and Goddesses are
real?

Amma: Children, someone who has never existed or
who has never taken birth would not be worshipped
and adored by millions of people. Nobody will celebrate
the birthday of a person who has not been born, but we
do celebrate the birthdays of Rama, Krishna, Jesus and
other Great Souls.

What Mother would like to say is that names and
forms are needed for people like us with the kind of

mental calibre that exists today. It will help our spiritual growth. Do not say that ours is the best path and all other paths are wrong. If a person's choice is tea, have it, fine and good. Let those who do not like tea drink coffee, lemonade or plain water. Why should we bother our heads about people's personal preferences? Why should we say that tea alone is good and all other drinks, bad? The purpose is to quench the thirst. Therefore, whether it is meditation on the Supreme with attributes or the Supreme without attributes, the goal is to attain perfect mental peace in any circumstance. Give up all such doubts about Gods and Goddesses and do your *sadhana*.

Anyhow, even when you meditate on the Formless, a pure creative mental resolve is needed.

Toys are needed for children to play with and for them the toys are real. Grown-ups do not need toys; they know that such things are unreal and lifeless. But the grown-ups cannot say that children should not have toys because they are not real.

Each person has a certain mental level and power of understanding. Let each person start from his own level. Do not try to thrust your ideas onto them.

Question: How can God be with form and without form at the same time?

Amma: Simply because He can become whatever He wants whenever He feels like it. God is beyond space and time. He is not bound by such limitations. Therefore, He can be both personal and impersonal. He can assume a form, but He is not the form, i.e., He is not attached to the form. When water is kept in different vessels of different shapes, it assumes the shape of each vessel. The water remains as water and does not become something else even if the shapes of the vessels differ. The water does not undergo any change even if the shapes of the vessels are different. In the same way, whatever shape, form or name He assumes, God remains as God. Let those who need *sakara* (God with a form) take that. How many can do meditation on the formless? It is not a process which is possible for all.

Question: Mother, will *Raja Yoga* cause harm?

Amma: Nowadays many books are being published on *Raja Yoga*. Several young men became mentally troubled reading such books, breathing in and out irregularly. There is no harm if such practices are performed under the guidance of a very good Master.

On the other hand, it is good to read books depicting the life and teachings of real devotees. Read as many as you can. There is no harm in that. Aberrations of the mentally troubled will go if they read such books. Such books have real glue to make us glued to God. You will never err or fall.

Question: So then, is it sufficient to have devotion alone?

Amma: Mere *bhakti* is not sufficient. Love is needed. Only then will the mind get absorption.

Question: In the light of what you said just now, it sounds to me that devotion *(bhakti)* and love *(prema)* are two different things.

Amma: Son, look, this is how it can be differentiated. Devotion is praying and supplicating to God just to satisfy one's selfish motives and desires. Such people will generally cling to temples. Even if they do go to see *Mahatmas*, they will be very keen to present before the *Mahatma* all the problems that they have. Such people have devotion, but pure love is at a minimum in their devotion. They give suggestions or instructions to God or to the *Mahatma*, such as "My Lord, this is my desire. Please fulfill it," or "I don't want that to occur. Don't make it happen." They want Him to act according to their own wishes and their own wills. They think they know more than He does. Their understanding about God or the *Mahatma* is far inferior to that of a devotee endowed with pure love, who loves God or the Guru for love's own sake. Such a person endowed with love wants nothing, not even Liberation. He simply wants to love God or the Guru, no matter what happens. To love Him is his happiness. He wants to cast off all his desires except the desire to love Him.

Therefore, *bhakti* (devotion) endowed with *prema* (love) is *prema bhakti*. *Bhakti* bereft of *prema* is mere devotion. Both a person with *prema bhakti* and a person with only *bhakti* will love the Guru or God, but the one with *prema bhakti* will give all importance to God or Guru; he has no choices, no wish or will of his own. His Guru is everything for him. He simply wants to love him, surrender to him, forgetting everything else. He wants to be consumed by the flame of the love which he has towards his Guru or Beloved Deity.

However, for the second type of *bhakti*, what is of primary importance is himself. He first wants to fulfill all his desires, then he thinks of God. As far as he is concerned, God or the Guru is like an agent to fulfill his desires.

Question: Mother, you said that an ordinary devotee's understanding about the Guru is far inferior to that of a devotee endowed with pure love. What do you mean by "understanding?"

Amma: It is not a mere intellectual understanding but understanding coupled with an unending thirst to live up to it, that is, the understanding or the knowledge that the Lord is in everything and surrendering oneself to that Supreme Will. His own limited will dissolves and disappears in the Lord's unlimited will. Then there is no "he" but only "Him." There is only acceptance and no rejection, only pure love without hatred, only desirelessness and no desire. All his desires melt and disappear, except the desire to love his Beloved in any circumstance. He fully accepts the omniscience, omnipotence and omnipresence of God or the Guru and acts accordingly. Then it is not he who is acting, but the Lord who makes him act. This is real understanding. A true devotee must have this knowledge.

Ten-thirty a.m. Nobody even thought about having their breakfast even though refreshments were available. The Mother had even urged the devotees to go and partake of some food or something to drink, but everybody preferred to stay with her. At this time, a family, husband, wife and two children, came to see the Holy Mother. This was their first visit. They went to Vallickavu first. Learning that the Mother was at Kanvashrama, they came to see her here. They all approached and offered their salutations to the Mother and sat near her. The Holy Mother very lovingly asked from where they came and whether they had eaten anything. She called Gayatri and told her to bring something for them to drink. Then the Mother turned towards their children, and calling them to her, she inquired about their names and the grades they were in, in school. The Mother then looked at the father and quite spontaneously said,

Amma: Son, the path of knowledge is not the right one for you. Yours is the path of devotion and your Beloved Deity is Mother Durga. If you abandon this path and follow the path of knowledge, listening to that man who is just a book scholar, that will obstruct your spiritual growth.

The man was dumbfounded with astonishment. It seemed that he wanted to say something, but for a short while he could not. He stared at the Mother with his mouth wide open. Then after some time when he had regained his equipoise, he silently shed tears, catching hold of the Mother's feet. The Mother slowly lifted him up and wiped his tears with her own hands. This show of love and affection made him cry again. Once again, he tried to control his tears. When he succeeded in doing so, he asked the Mother,

The man: Amma, I knew that it could not have happened without your knowledge; still I was not convinced. That is why I came to see you in person. I wanted to hear it directly from you, and you told me the same even without my telling you anything about it. You have blessed me and by your Grace I will try not to err from my path and will stick to your advice to the best of my ability. Also, Mother, forgive me for testing you. It is because of my ignorance that I wanted such proof.

The Holy Mother simply smiled and kept quiet. By that time Gayatri brought tea for all of them. The Mother herself took the glasses from the tray and gave one to each person, after having sipped a little from three of the glasses. She did this for the husband and the two children but not for the wife. Everyone noticed this strange action of the Mother and they also might have felt that the Mother was being very partial on her part to do such a thing. But to everyone's surprise, the husband burst out laughing and through his laughter he said, "Amma, please pardon me for laughing like this in front of you." When he had finished laughing, he continued,

The man: I do not mind disclosing this about my wife in front of all those who are here. I assume that all of you are Amma's devotees and therefore there is nothing wrong in relating this to you. My wife was very skeptical about Amma. She did not even want to come with me. It was only because of my insistence she came. It is not her fault. She was brought up in such a skeptical family. On our way to Kanvashrama she even teased me, saying that I was too emotional, that I was silly to come to meet this lady whom she thought was an ordinary person who had no powers at all, that everything was only my own hallucinations. She even challenged, "If your Mother is all-knowing, let her give me a hint about her omniscience. If she does that I will definitely believe her." Now the Mother responded to her skeptical mind." She had taken a sip from all the glasses except hers, letting her understand that the Mother could clearly read her mind. This was exactly the answer for all her questions.

The man was thrilled, excited and inspired that the Mother had revealed her omniscience. The Holy Mother smilingly consoled the woman, saying,

Amma: Daughter, don't worry. It is not because Mother knows everything but because she knows nothing that she acted in this way. Had she known everything she wouldn't have hurt you like this.

The lady was humbled, and she said,

Lady: No, Mother, no. Don't say that. You have given me a good lesson. Too much education spoiled my heart. Now I understand that prejudice is wrong. I know that it will go on troubling me, but if I surrender to you, you will destroy it. Please give me the strength and courage to surrender.

After saying this she silently shed tears. The Holy
Mother embraced her and patted her just as a mother
does to her child. They all spent some more time with
the Mother and then took leave of her after having offered their prostrations. Before they left the premises,
the husband, whose name was Karunakaran, told one of
the *brahmacharins* about the incident which inspired
him to come and see the Mother.

Two nights ago he had a dream in which the Mother
appeared to him and clearly said to him that he must
quit the spiritual practice that he was told to do by the
scholar who taught him the scriptures. He had heard
about the Mother and was waiting for a chance to see
her. Since he was studying the scriptures from the
scholar who had instructed him to do the *sadhana* that
he was doing, the dream did have some meaning for
him. At the same time he loved and respected the
scholar; therefore, he did not want to give too much importance to the dream. But the Mother appeared to him
again on the following night. This time she added a few
more things in her instructions to him. She said, "Son,
I have told you to quit the spiritual practice that you are
doing now. The path of knowledge is not the right one
for you; yours is the path of devotion and your Beloved
Deity is the Mother Durga. If you abandon this path
and follow the path of knowledge, listening to that man
who is just a book scholar, it will obstruct your spiritual
growth."

Karunakaran continued, "This instruction given by
the Mother in the dream was very clear and the dream
was literally true. I was a devotee of Mother Durga for

many years. I always worshipped her, but due to the influence of this scholar, I abandoned that path and pursued the path of knowledge as instructed by him. But I have missed that love and remained discontented about my spiritual practices. At the same time, I did not want to displease him. In fact, I have a certain amount of attachment towards him, but I was longing to get guidance from a Real Master. After hearing about the Holy Mother, I had the dreams. The dreams, particularly the second one, had such an impact on my mind that I wanted to come and see the Mother the very next day. Besides this, even though I do have faith in Mother, to convince my ego, I wanted her to tell me directly about the dream when I met her. She did this as well. You know the rest of the story. Even without disclosing anything about the dreams or about my *sadhana* or about the devotion that I had to Mother Durga, she repeated the very same words that she had uttered to me in the dream. Now I am happy, very happy and blissful, not only because she answered my prayers but also because of the compassion she has shown to my wife in removing her skepticism, something that has always troubled her as well as me."

The Holy Mother wanted to sing *bhajans*. She asked Sreekumar to bring the harmonium, and he went to fetch it. The Mother was still sitting under the banyan tree, now at eleven-thirty a.m. The atmosphere was very calm and peaceful. The Mother gazed at the Vishnu Tirtha. The water was still, and the Mother seemed as if

she was enjoying it. Her blissful countenance shone
with a beautiful radiance.

Sreekumar brought the harmonium. The Holy
Mother sang a few *bhajans*, first *Kodanukoti*, then *Oru
Nimishamenkilum*.

> O Truth Eternal
> Mankind has searched for Thee
> For millions and millions of years...
>
> The ancient sages, renouncing everything,
> Performed endless years of austerities
> In order to make their selves flow
> Into Thy Divine Stream through meditation.
>
> Inaccessible to all, Thy infinitesimal Flame,
> Glowing like the effulgence of the sun
> Stands still without dancing
> Even in the fiercely blowing cyclone.
>
> Flowery creepers, shrines and temples,
> All have waited for Thee for aeons and aeons,
> Yet Thou art inaccessibly distant.
>
> *Oru Nimishamukilum...*
>
> O man, who runs after
> The pleasures of the world,
> Do you have peace for even one moment?
>
> O man, without understanding the essential

And real principles of life,
Deluded by the shadow of maya
You will perish like a moth in a flame.

In the evolutionary process
You have passed though different bodies,
Insects, worms and numerous reptiles,
Innumerable birds and animals.

Thus you have evolved
Through different bodies until at last
You came out as a human being.

O man, think and discriminate,
What is the real purpose of this human birth...
No, O man, this human birth is not to be wasted
For silly and trivial worldly pleasures.
Remember, it has a right of its own.

O man, without giving up your false pride,
Your desire to acquire and possess,
Your desire to enjoy and indulge,
Without attaining That state
Of Supreme Brahman,
You cannot have peace or bliss.

These profound songs, pregnant with philosophical meaning, directly penetrated into the hearts of the devotees. They were all absorbed in deep meditation. The Holy Mother sat gazing at the vast blue sky and kept swaying from one side to the other. It was now noon. Suddenly the Mother said, "Shivane! None of my chil-

dren have had their breakfast. What a cruel Mother I
am. I forgot to give food to my children. Come on, all
of you, let us eat." She called a few *brahmacharins* aside
and instructed them to make arrangements to serve food
to everyone. As they ran, the Mother shouted, "Hurry
up, be quick. Don't delay anymore."

The Mother herself served food for everyone. The
devotees' hearts overflowed with joy and bliss. After
lunch, one by one, the devotees left after offering their
salutations to her. The Holy Mother also went to her
room.

At three-thirty a group of college students came to see
the Mother. They wanted to see the Mother and ask her
certain questions. They were all between fifteen and
twenty years old. The Mother came out of her room by
four o'clock. She was very happy to see the young boys.
They seemed to be a little perplexed when they saw the
Mother. But she went near them, and like one who was
well acquainted with them for a long time, she smilingly
invited them to come and sit in the hut.

The Mother first of all asked their names, one by
one, and the place where they each were from. They politely answered the Mother's queries. The Mother's innate naturalness impressed the students very much as
they became more relaxed.

One boy who looked a little older than the others
proudly said, "We heard about you and had a desire to
see you; thus we came together. To be frank, all of us
are not believers. Some are; others are inquisitive; there
are a few who are very skeptical." He stopped. The

Mother looked at them and smiled. Then she uttered her favorite mantra, "Shiva, Shiva," a few times with her fingers held in a divine *mudra*. The Mother once again smiled at them, and then looking at the boy who introduced everyone, she asked, "Son, under which category do you fall?" The older boy blushed, hearing the straight-forward question of the Holy Mother. That was quite unexpected for him. He was tongue-tied for a moment, then slowly he said, "Mother, my parents are your devotees. I never came to see you before, but still I have faith in you. Yet I never had an opportunity to know you directly; that is why I came now with my friends." The older boy had been a little proud when he talked at first, but now he seemed very humble.

Amma: Son, you stated that all of you were not believers and that some are inquisitive and others are very skeptical. By saying this you have not said anything new. That is the nature of the world. Not everyone can be a believer and not everyone can be skeptical. Even if everyone does turn into a believer, again each person's points of view and concepts will change. Nor can we really make everyone a believer. It is just the nature of the world to have these differences. The shapes of two leaves from the same tree are not alike. Infinite is Reality and infinite are its manifestations. It does not really matter whether you are a believer or a non-believer or a skeptic. You can be a non-believer but at the same time lead a happy and successful life if you have faith in *you*. You do not have to believe in Mother or in a God who resides up above in the sky on a golden throne. It is enough if you have faith in *you*. If you don't have faith in *you* then there is not much to gain even if you believe in God. Faith in God is to strengthen your faith in you, the faith in your own Self. This is, in other words, called Self-confidence, confidence in your own Self. If that is not there you cannot succeed in life, whatever your field may be. Self-confidence is nothing but mental balance, courage and control over your own mind to confront the problems of life. You cannot escape from the problems of life; they are inevitable, unavoidable. How are you going to face them if you do not have faith in yourself? You cannot.

A skeptic means one who doubts, one who questions anything and everything. That means he even doubts his own Self, his own existence. Such a person does not have faith in himself. He will walk around arguing, disputing and refuting, creating more doubts in his own mind and in the minds of others as well. He will be an utter failure in his life. Such a person cannot create anything; he destroys. How can such a person who has no control over his own mind be a benefactor of society? His own life will become a total mess. Spirituality and the spiritual masters teach one how to build up this faith and self-control, which are the most important factors to lead a happy life. Anyhow, Mother likes you because you personally came to learn and find out. The majority of the people are not like this. They simply criticize and interpret from a distance without coming closer and studying things properly.

The Holy Mother paused. The students sat without uttering a word. They did not know what to say or how to begin. It seemed that they were searching for words. This whole time the Holy Mother sat looking at them with a beautiful smile which lit up her ever-radiant face. At last one boy broke the silence. He spoke out but in a low voice and with a very gentle and respectful tone, "Mother, you have, in fact, answered all our questions." As if to prove his innocence, he continued,

Question: I didn't come to question you. I am neither a skeptic nor a non-believer. In fact, I have a lot of interest to know more about spirituality and spiritual life. Mother, I have always wondered about the place of reason in spirituality. You said that faith is everything. But reason is also needed, isn't it?

Amma: That is a well-thought-out question. Mother likes it. Son, reason has very little place in spirituality. It should be dropped. After all, what is reason? It is the product of your intellect. What is intellect? It is the product of the ego. The ego should be eradicated. That is the aim of all spiritual practices. Therefore, reason, being a product of the ego, must go. In the path of Self-Realization, intellect or reason is a big obstacle. Intellect always doubts. Doubt is not what is needed in spirituality. Here the entire thing depends on faith—faith in God or the Guru, faith in the Scriptures or in the Guru's word. Faith in the Guru uplifts you. Doubting the Guru will destroy you. Faith unites your diverse personality and helps you to see everything as One. Doubt cuts everything into pieces. Doubt makes you more diverse; faith makes you one and whole.

Too much reasoning is the problem today. People think that intellect is everything. But that is wrong. The world suffers because of this. People have no faith. They want to question, criticize and protest everything. They do not want to believe and surrender. They go on feeding their heads and making their hearts starve. Their heads grow and their hearts dry up.

Science needs reason. The very basis of science and scientific inventions are nothing but reason and doubt. But modern science cuts everything into pieces. It never tries to unite anything. This is how science becomes destructive. Science should be beneficial to the human race. This is possible only by using it to unite people with their minds.

Question: Mother, do you mean that reason is a useless thing?

Amma: No, son. It is not. The intellect is needed. Reason must be flexible. It should be used to support the heart, our faith, the love in us, the compassion and other higher ideals in us. This means that there should be a good balance. Too much faith or too much reason, one at the exclusion of the other, are both dangerous. For example, a devotee has faith, utter faith, in his Beloved Lord. Still, behind that faith there is reason. There is the subtle understanding that all the worldly experiences, all that happens around him, both negative and positive, good and bad, are momentary and that these things just come and go. He does not cling to the world and the worldly relationships because he knows that they are all ever-changing. He does not give unnecessary importance to anything that happens. He never craves to acquire and possess. He is not after name and fame. He smilingly receives both the happy and unhappy moments of life because he knows that they are unavoidable and that it is the nature of life. All this needs intellectual understanding. But his intellect is very subtle and he uses it to reject whatever is not needed and to accept whatever is necessary. In short, his reason helps him to penetrate into the real nature of objects, the changing nature of them and the unchanging nature of his own Self. His reason helps him to strengthen his faith in the Supreme, never to weaken it.

CONCENTRATION

Question: Amma, what is the way to gain concentration?

Amma: *Sraddha* (alertness, faith) is needed. We do not go to a particular place when we learn that it is dangerous to go there. We will proceed with alertness. We do not eat something if we find out that it is poisonous. When we find out that there are thorns in a certain place, we do not walk through that place. Our alertness keeps us from danger. Similarly, through constant contemplation the mind will become one-pointed on God when we come to know what is non-eternal and what is eternal, what binds us and what frees us. Then the mind will gradually stop wandering. When we realize that we will not get the intended benefit out of an object, then we will not depend on it, will we? When the dependence on objects cease, the mind will become fixed and concentrated on the Self. Children, we must try very hard. None of these material things give us any benefit, although we may think they do. We should contemplate and understand that they are all like poison. It is difficult for us to get concentration when we, who until now have thought that the body was eternal, try to reverse ourselves and realize that the *Atman* is eternal. Constant practice is needed. You may not get it fully in a day or two, or a month or even a year. Still, you are getting it. Little by little you are improving. You may not be aware of it. Do not stop. Try and continue.

When we travel in an airplane we may feel that the aircraft is not moving, but it is, in fact, flying. Once we reach the destination, we will know that the aircraft had been flying all the time. Likewise, during the *sadhana* period you may feel that you are not making any progress, but you are. You will know it when you reach That state. You may not know the subtle progress that you are making. Therefore, do not stop. Do not give up enthusiasm; try to sustain the spirit. Do it patiently and wait for the Guru's or God's Grace to come.

Question: What is Grace?

Amma: Children, Grace is a mysterious factor. Nobody knows when, how or where it will be bestowed. Human beings have no control over it. You can make the effort; you must. Then you wait. The deciding factor is Grace. That is in the Guru's hands, in God's hands. It is our experience that many things, for which we put forth much effort, do not materialize. That is due to lack of Grace. It is also known to us that certain things simply happen without any effort. That is the presence of Grace.

A pilot can put forth effort to fly his plane to the destination, but whether it will reach there or not depends on Grace. After all, it is a machine; anything can happen at any time. Any part can stop functioning at any moment. The pilot does not have any control over it. The airport authorities and the engineers will check everything before departure and will say "okay." But who can give the guarantee? Nobody can do that. The pilot might be an expert, but he has no control over the whole aircraft, not each and every part of it. So it is Grace which takes us to the destination, not the pilot. Of course, the pilot has a major part to play, but the deciding factor is Grace. We have heard many stories of how a plane has mysteriously escaped from a terrible crash even though the pilot had lost all control over the aircraft. There are also stories about how a plane has crashed even when the pilot did have good control and where everything was seemingly in good order. Again it is Grace which serves as the deciding factor. Therefore, put forth the necessary effort and then wait patiently.

To surrender to a Guru is the best way to attain this Grace. Obedience and faith in the Guru and his words will make us competent enough to get this Grace.

Suppose we don't know Malayalam. That means we are a child as far as that language is concerned, aren't we? To learn that language we must surrender and obey the instructions of the teacher, accepting the fact that we are a child in that subject. Only then can we learn that particular language. In the same way, those who are ignorant about spirituality should approach a Guru just like a child, accepting the fact that they do not know anything about spirituality. The biased attitude of "I know" will obstruct the flow of spiritual knowledge and Grace from the Guru. If acceptance and surrender are not present, Perfection will not be reached. It is just like a child saying, "I know this; you don't have to teach me." When this happens he rejects the true knowledge that the teacher gives. He closes himself to that knowledge. His prejudice makes him non-receptive. When we are in the presence of a genuine Master, we must accept our ignorance and surrender to the Guru completely.

Question: Mother, why is there a lot of difference between the olden days and the modern age?

Amma: In the olden days people were selfless, and now people are totally selfish. That is the reason.

Children, in the olden days people had the same needs as today. They wanted food, clothing and shelter. They also had their education. They had games, arts and sports. They had civilization. They too led a married life and had children. The difference is that their way of life was not only concentrated on the world outside but on the world inside as well. They did not live only to acquire and possess wealth but also to know God. They had self-control, inner discipline. They always tried to develop good qualities like truth, compassion, love, renunciation, and patience. They were concerned not only about their own family but also about society. Each person truly felt that he or she had a duty towards society and discharged it sincerely and whole-heartedly. But today's world is just the opposite of this. People, due to their selfishness and ego-centered nature, have turned the world into a hell. Previously, the world was like heaven. We now point our fingers at each other. We criticize and question the other's arrogance or ego-centeredness. We cannot bear the other person's ego. Children, what about our own? We never think about that. We think that our ego is not a problem but that it is the other person's ego which creates problems. What a strange attitude this is. In reality, it is our own ego which creates the problems in our own life, not the other person's. Our ego should become a burden for us; only then will we try to get rid of it. At present we think that our ego is an adornment for us. This feeling inspires us to keep it as something precious. Just as you feel that the other person's ego is unbearable to you, your ego is just as unbearable to someone else. Therefore, try to eliminate it.

In the olden days whatever work people did was considered by them as a means to attenuate their *vasanas*; even married life was for that purpose. Today people add more to the existing *vasanas* by acting arrogantly and selfishly.

It is said that the human mind will become dry and narrow as worldliness increases. A person will rise up and evolve when the mind becomes expansive. But when the mind becomes narrow, not only the mind but also the physical stature will be affected due to his selfish attitude, over-indulgence and lack of restraint. The height of human beings is quickly decreasing in comparison to the olden days. In the ancient days people were of magnificent stature and were very strong mentally and physically. In the olden days how tall were the students who would today be in the tenth grade! But now how short are even those students who are studying for the B.A. and M.A. degrees. In the future human stature will diminish. There is no broad-mindedness, only selfish, narrow-mindedness. This will cause both mental and physical disintegration.

The Holy Mother now stopped. It was five o'clock. The students seemed very happy. All of them had developed tremendous interest now. The older boy spoke again, "Mother, please forgive us if we have spoken egotistically to you. Please pardon us for our ignorance."

Another boy said, "Mother, I confess that I simply came to see you out of curiosity, but now you have opened my eyes. I will try to keep this spirit." Still another student remarked, " Mother, I really had no faith in spiritual people or spiritual life. I was very critical about them. But now you have awakened the interest in me. I will never forget these instructions which you have given today."

The Holy Mother went up to them and caressed each one of them on the forehead with much love and affection. She said, "Children, Mother is very happy to see all of you. Please come whenever you want to. You are the fragrant flowers of tomorrow. Build up good character and try to do something good for society." They all prostrated to the Mother and left.

The Mother went down the hill near the pond and roamed around all alone. In a few minutes her melodious voice filled the air with a song about Krishna, *Nilakadumbukale...*

> O blue kadamba tree,
> Have you also seen my Kanna
> Who is dark blue in complexion...

She was in an ecstatic mood. Gayatri and a few others walked down and watched the Mother from a distance. None of them went very close. The Mother walked with faltering steps, but her sonorous voice did not falter as she continued with the second verse:

> Oh, the waters on the shore
> Of the River Yamuna, have you heard
> The melodious, enchanting note
> Of my darling Krishna's flute.
>
> O animals and birds,
> Why do you look all around
> As if searching for someone?
> Like me, are you searching
> For the Beloved of the Gopis?
> Are you also in the burning fire
> Of the excruciating pain of separation
> From Him, the Stealer of Hearts?

Finally the song came to an end and the Mother lay down on the grass. She became totally oblivious to the surroundings. Gayatri and Brahmacharin Sreekumar went closer. She was totally transported to another world. Her body was still, her eyes half-closed and her face glowed with immense bliss.

The song which she had sung still seemed to echo in the atmosphere. It created a deep longing in the hearts of all those who had heard it. The time approached five-thirty with the sun slowly sinking into the western horizon. A glorious blending of golden yellow and red clouds painted the sky with brilliant colors. Their reflection in the waters of the pond created a play of dancing light and shadow. The sweet singing of a nightingale from the forest near the pond accentuated the calm and quiet mood. A gentle breeze blew from the west as if to wake her up from *samadhi*. It softly caressed the Holy Mother's form. A few strands of her curly dark hair fell on her forehead and danced in the breeze.

A few more minutes passed; it was nearly six o'clock. The Holy Mother slowly opened her eyes. She remained lying down, gazing towards the sky. Then she stretched her hands and gave a sign for Gayatri to lift her up from the ground. There she sat for a short while and then slowly stood up and proceeded to climb up the hill.

As usual there was the *bhajan* at six-thirty. The Mother was also present. At ten o'clock she again took everyone to the Vishnu Tirtha and meditated there for nearly one hour. Shortly after eleven o'clock the Mother and the entire group returned and retired to their rooms.

17 March 1984

Last night before going to bed the Mother instructed everyone that they should come and meditate by the side of the Vishnu Tirtha early the next day. Accordingly, the whole group gathered there before sunrise. The Holy Mother was already at the lake. She was sitting under the banyan tree. The *brahmacharins* and other devotees sat around the Vishnu Tirtha and meditated. The sun slowly rose from the eastern horizon. The meditation went on for about one hour and a half. Afterwards everyone came and sat around the Holy Mother who was still sitting under the banyan tree. The Mother had some bananas at her side, and she distributed them to the devotees and *brahmacharins*.

One devotee commented, "What Mother gives is the fruit of knowledge." Another devotee remarked, "The fruit of our meditation is bestowed right after its performance."

Amma: Stop saying such things. You are wasting what you have gained through unnecessary comments. Keep silence for a few minutes.

Thereafter nobody spoke for some time.

By eight o'clock some devotees from outside of Kanvashrama came to visit the Mother. The sun's rays emitted greater and greater intensity. At this time a young boy who was about fifteen years of age came with a big notebook in his hands. He was sent from a nearby spiritual institution which ran an orphanage. They had forgotten to request the Mother to write a congratulatory note in the book on the day she had visited, so now they had sent it to the Mother for her to write a message in it.

Just as a mother does to her child, the Holy Mother expressed love and affection to the boy as she conversed with him. She asked his age and his grade in school. The Mother said, "It seems that you are very mischievous. What will be the end result of all these mischievous deeds? You will end up in trouble for them, won't you? Therefore, my child, you should study diligently and grow up as a good boy. Okay?"

The boy enthusiastically nodded his head in agreement with what the Mother had said.

The boy: Amma, I would like your address.
Amma: Mother has no such thing as an address.

The Mother took the diary from the young boy and started writing on one of the pages:

> Darling Children,
>   Your happiness is Mother's health. Let Children's attitude of selfless service last forever. The compassion that we show towards the poor and needy is the real duty towards God. That is real service. God does not need anything from us. What can we give to the Ever-Full One? The

whole universe belongs to Him. The sun
does not need a wax candle. An electric
bulb does not need a kerosene lamp.
These orphaned children are equal to
God. God dwells in those who have the
attitude "I have nobody else." Eternally
blessed and blissful are those who look after them selflessly. Let Children's selfless
service be everlasting, darling Children.

A devotee wrote down the Ashram address and
handed it to the boy, saying, "Here is Amma's address."

One devotee: Is Mother's handwriting clear enough?
Another devotee: It is enough if one clearly under-
stands the meaning of what Mother has written.
Amma: It is not enough if one reads Mother's words
only with one's intellect. One should try to read them
with one's heart too.

A devotee wanted to take a picture of Mother. He
asked the Mother's permission. She said,

Amma: A *sadhak* should not permit others to take his
picture. Some of our power will be lost while each photo
is taken, just as the fetus is adversely affected if a pregnant woman is x-rayed. If Mother allows you to take her
picture, the children *(brahmacharins)* will also imitate
her in the same manner in the future. That is why
Mother does not allow people to take her picture unnec-

essarily. Concerning herself, Mother has nothing to gain or lose.

Question: Amma, what do you expect from your children?

Amma: Nothing. Mother expects nothing. If you feel that Mother expects something, it is to take you beyond all expectations. It is for you, not for me. A father or mother accepts whatever is given to them by their child, even if it is an insignificant object like a stone or a toy or a balloon. By doing so, the father and mother do not get anything; they do not expect it. Still, they accept whatever the child may give, however small or insignificant, just for the satisfaction of the child, not because they expect the child to give the toy or the balloon to them. When the child out of innocence gives the balloon to the father, he simply accepts it because he cannot reject it. When the child offers the piece of biscuit which he has played with for a long time and which is now full of sand or dirt, the mother simply takes a bite because she cannot reject the child's expression of love. The thing which the child offers is an expression of its love towards the mother. Not that she expects it from the child. In fact, she really doesn't want to eat it because it is full of dirt; still, she accepts it. True love cannot be rejected. A child's love is true because he has innocence. There are no expectations in true love. It simply flows like a river. In the same way, when you offer something to Mother, you are doing it as an expression of your love, aren't you? Mother accepts your love, your heart, not that she expects it but simply because she cannot reject it. When you offer something whole-heartedly, she cannot say "no." But she does not expect it. Whatever may be your offering, what Mother accepts is your heart.

Suppose one of her children makes a special dessert for Mother. While making it, he or she will be thinking of Mother all the time, dreaming about how Mother would like this special treat, about the way she would eat it and so on and so forth. And when that person brings this special delicacy to her, Mother cannot reject it because it is cooked in his or her love. It is his or her heart that is being offered. Who can reject pure, innocent love? Whether one accepts it or not, pure love simply flows.

Mother does what she does because she cannot do otherwise. To love is her nature, to serve is her nature. She doesn't expect anything in return. But your feeling that Mother expects you to do something will encourage you to do good things in life and to progress spiritually.

Krishna did not expect anything from the Pandavas. He did everything for them, for he could not do otherwise. That was His nature. He tried to correct the Kauravas as well. He tried to avoid the battle. He put forth all His efforts to stop it, but the Kauravas rejected Him. The Pandavas accepted Him; therefore, he was with the Pandavas. The Kauravas rejected Him, so He could not be with them.

The Mother got up from her seat to walk down the hill to the hermitage where she stayed. On the way she met a few more devotees who had just arrived. Among them again was Miss D., her father and her uncle. Mother stopped and affectionately called each one of them to her and gave *darshan*. She commenced her journey down the hill, followed by all the devotees. She caught sight of a *chakora* bird (Greek partridge) sitting on one of the branches of a cashew nut tree. The Mother suddenly came to a halt, and stretching her arms towards the bird, she blissfully called out, "Oh, oh, oh, Amma, Amma, Amma..." She then made some unfamiliar sounds. After that the Mother closed her eyes and remained still for a few seconds, holding a divine *mudra* with the fingers of her right hand. Then upon opening her eyes, the Mother waved her index finger in a circular motion for a few times in the air and uttered the familiar *mantra*, "Shiva, Shiva..."

Arriving at her hut, the Mother stepped into her room. Still enchanted by their walk with the Mother, the devotees stood in front of her hermitage for some time before dispersing to their own rooms.

Hamsa, the head of Kanvashrama, was in Madras, so he left Markus in charge of the ashram. Markus was very devoted to the Mother. Extremely happy and blissful that she was here at Kanvashrama, he went around with great enthusiasm to find out if the devotees were in need of anything.

That morning at nine-thirty everyone had their breakfast. By eleven o'clock the Holy Mother came out again. The Mother, with the whole group following her, roamed around all over the hills, singing *bhajans* every now and then, entering into *bhava samadhi* at times, talking, laughing and asking questions like an innocent child, "How did this butterfly's wings become so colorful?" or "Can you tell me how the bud opens up into a flower?" She sometimes called aloud "Shiva" or "Amma" while gazing at the sky as she walked, or stopping and looking at a flower or a butterfly. Occasionally she would sit down to relax. Thus she made everyone roam, not only over the hills but within the reveries of their minds, allowing them to forget the world outside and all their problems.

By twelve-thirty the Holy Mother returned with all the devotees. She asked the *brahmacharins* to make arrangements for lunch. After the usual chanting of the *Srimad Bhagavad Gita*, everyone started eating. Just as a mother feeds her little children, the Holy Mother fed each one a ball of rice with her own hands. After that she went to her room.

After the three days at Kanvashrama, the party was returning to Vallickavu today. Everyone packed their things ready to leave. They all gathered in front of the Mother's cottage by three o'clock.

It was the season of spring. The trees and plants bore beautiful and fragrant flowers of different colors. Though a clear and sunny day, it was not very hot. Miss D., the young college student, looked very thoughtful and sad. She was sitting in a corner on the verandah of the Mother's cottage. The girl sat all alone, with her chin resting on her palms. She was awakened by her uncle's voice, "Miss D., get up. Let us prostrate and take leave of the Mother immediately when she comes out."

She got up and stood by her father's side, fixing her eyes on the front door of the Mother's room. At about three-fifteen the door opened. The Mother announced that she would like to swim in the pond before leaving. She called all the *brahmacharinis* and asked them to come with her. Their happiness knew no bounds, for such an occasion to swim with the Mother was a rare treat indeed!

All of a sudden, Miss D., the young girl, jumped forward and tightly embraced the Holy Mother. The Mother also hugged her and lovingly inquired, "Daughter, what has happened?"

Through her tears, Miss D. replied, "Mother, I am not going back home. I cannot be away from you even for a second. Please don't abandon me, Mother." The father and uncle were shocked, as if a thunderbolt had fallen on them. They were stunned. They turned pale. It took a few moments for them to realize the gravity of the situation.

Smiling, the Mother soothed her forehead and in a very gentle tone said, "Daughter, go with your father and uncle now. Don't put them in a dilemma."

Miss D. declared in a very determined tone, "No, I won't go. I want to come with you." The girl would not let the Mother move. She did not loosen her hands, not even a little bit. The father and uncle were totally perplexed. They wanted their daughter back. At the same time their devotion to Mother stopped them from taking her by force. In a very calm and quite voice, her father said, "We will go and see the Mother at the Ashram in

Vallickavu later. Let us go home now." Miss D. said, "No!" in a very stern voice.

Her uncle said, "Don't be stubborn. Think of your mother at home. What will we tell her?"

Miss D. was unshakable. She said, "I am not going. My Mother is here."

There was no way to change her mind. She would not even move a little from the Mother's side. The father and uncle helplessly looked at the Mother. They could neither forcibly take her home nor could they leave her behind.

Finally the Mother took Miss D. down to the pond. The father and uncle waited, hoping that Mother would speak with her and change her mind. In a few minutes the whole atmosphere changed. The devotees could hear the splashing of water and through it the Mother's blissful laughter. Then everybody heard the Mother singing loudly while the girls responded to *Srishtiyum Niye...*

> Creation and Creator art Thou
> Thou art Energy and Truth
> O Goddess, O Goddess, O Goddess!
>
> Creator of the Cosmos art Thou
> Thou art the beginning and end.
>
> The essence of the individual soul art Thou
> Thou art the five elements as well.

Some of the male devotees seemed a bit sad. One of them said, "What a pity. I wish that I were a woman. I really feel unfortunate and left out."

The whole atmosphere of Kanvashrama vibrated with the Mother's divine voice. There was a large number of men and women devotees sitting farther up on the other side of the hill. All their attention was fully concentrated on the Mother's voice which emerged from the pond down below. There was not even a bit of noise which could disturb the prevailing mood. The chirping of birds and the Mother's poignant songs were the only exhilarating sounds which enlivened the whole ashram atmosphere. Everybody felt so happy and blissful, everybody except Miss D.'s father and uncle.

After bathing the Mother talked to Miss D., sitting on the concrete steps of the pond. She said, "Daughter, you should think it over again and again before you make a final decision. It is not an easy path. Don't be impatient. Go back to your home and think patiently. Look, your father and uncle are in a dilemma. You are giving them trouble. They cannot go back home without you. Your mother also will be very sad. What will be her condition when she hears that you have gone. Above all, if you leave home deserting your parents, it will bring a bad reputation for Mother and the Ashram. You can come to the Ashram and see Mother with your parents. So now you return home."

Miss D., "No, I am not going. I want to be with you." That was all she said and then she kept quiet. She was so determined and firm. She was not even slightly moved; she displayed no excitement at all. She was very relaxed and cool.

Just to play her part sincerely and properly, the Mother still tried other means. She summoned a few of the elder *brahmacharins* to talk to her. Her father and uncle were also called. A long discussion took place. Each one tried to convince Miss D. about the different aspects of the matter. She quietly sat, unmoved, as if this discussion did not concern her. Every now and then she turned to the Mother and softly said, "No, I am not going."

It was getting late. Mother had to reach the Ashram in Vallickavu that very same day. The scheduled time to leave had passed. Miss D.'s affair was still up in the air. She seemed to be a "hard nut." Finally the Mother told her uncle and father, "Don't worry, you go back home. Before proceeding to the Ashram, Mother will come to your house with daughter Miss D.."

Both the father and the uncle left.

Many things concerning Miss D. came into light later. She was very devoted even from a very young age. She had read only spiritual books. It was also her habit to do *japa* and *dhyana* regularly while at home. Several times she had told her parents, "I will take up *sannyasa*. I won't allow you to give me in marriage."

According to her own wish and will, Miss D. took philosophy as her main subject for her B.A. degree. Two days ago when she met Mother at Kanvashrama for the first time, she was completely drawn to her and decided to leave the world, accepting the Mother as her

Guru. She had the strong feeling that Mother was the incarnation of Kali, the Divine Mother. Having understood her mind, the Holy Mother did not even give Miss D. a chance to talk to her. The Mother also noticed that this girl was endowed with a very good spiritual disposition. She said, "Mother expected this when she saw her on the very first day. A girl with very good spiritual inclination. Mother knew that this would happen; that is the reason why she intentionally prevented the girl from having an opportunity to talk to Mother."

Returning home after her first visit with the Holy Mother, Miss D. prepared to leave her hearth and home and take up *sannyasa*. On the morning of the seventeenth she left home, saying that she was going to the college. She took off all her gold jewelry and left them in the house. Just with the clothes that she had on Miss D. left the house and walked towards Kanvashrama without going to the college. It was at that time that she ran into her father and uncle who were coming from another direction on their way to Kanvashrama to have the Mother's *darshan* again. They were surprised to see Miss D., and when they learned that she also wanted to see the Mother, all three proceeded to Kanvashrama together. Since Miss D.'s father and uncle were spiritually inclined, they were not against her wish to see the Mother. In fact, Miss D.'s father used to take her to classes to listen to spiritual discourses. Had they known that things would take such a sharp turn for what they considered the worse, they would not have brought her to see the Mother. Now the Holy Mother spoke to Miss D.

Amma: Daughter, external learning and education are also necessary. You can come and join the Ashram after finishing your studies. Furthermore, your father is a person who is learned in religious texts. It is not a blind devotion that he has. He knows the essential principles of religion. Therefore, it is not a problem for you to lead a spiritual life. But is your mother like that? No. She will scream and create an uproar in the house, which will make things worse. It is said that when the great Suka renounced everything and became a *sannyasin*, Vyasa, who himself was a great soul, went after him crying and calling aloud, "My son." That is the power of *maya*. So what can be said about the reactions of ordinary people? No father, even if he himself is a *sannyasin*, will allow his son to become a monk. Your mother is the one who gave birth to you, isn't she? Therefore, she will not be able to bear it if you were to leave her.

One devotee: (Intended for the Mother) The mother who gave birth is sitting here, right in the front. (All laugh, including the Mother.)

At last the van carrying the Mother and her children proceeded north. There was a lot of luggage on the carrier rack on top of the van. All the pedestrians and people who stood on the roadside looked at the extraordinarily big bundle of luggage on the top and were puzzled. As the van moved the Mother laughed and jokingly remarked aloud, "This is a trip with pots and pans. We are beggars." (Laughter)

All the while Miss D. was sitting close to the Mother. The latter was very cool and fully relaxed, acting as if nothing had happened. The others were thinking about what would happen when they reached Miss D.'s house. The girl seemed determined, but what would be the family's response?

The van stopped in front of Miss D.'s house. Everybody there knew about the incident by now since the father and uncle had gone ahead of the Mother's van. A small crowd was gathered in front of the house. Most of them were relatives, a few were neighbors and passers-by who were curious. Miss D.'s mother was crying, screaming and beating her breast. She ran out of the house and rushed towards the van, screaming and lamenting. She burst out at her daughter, who remained seated in the van, "Hey, girl, you'll go only after killing me." The father, uncle and other relatives even tried to bodily force the girl out of the van. No matter what was said or who tried to pull at her, Miss D. would not come out of the van.

Amma: The Ashram is a spiritual institution. Mother will not accept daughter without the permission of her parents.

Miss D.: Mother, are you abandoning me?

Amma: No, daughter, never. You are Mother's alone. But the public will not believe that you have chosen to take up spiritual life out of your own volition. They will say other things and even fabricate stories. Therefore, it is better if you come to the Ashram later, with the permission of your father and mother.

Miss D. remained seated in the van. She was unmoved. At last, the Mother stepped down off the van.
She asked Miss D. to come out with her. The girl obeyed.
The Mother caught hold of her hand and took her into
the house. Having entered the house, the Mother loudly
said, "All these people will say different things if I take
Miss D. now. If she is determined enough and if she is
destined to become a *sannyasini*, it will happen." Having
said this the Mother explained to Miss D. particular
statements and certain comments which people would
make about Miss D. and her family if the Mother took
her now. The family members were astounded and
amazed to hear these things which the Mother was saying because she was repeating exactly what they had
rebukingly said against her, even without missing a
single word. (We were informed of this later by a devotee who had happened to be in the house at the time.)

As the Mother came out of the house, one elderly
person related from behind, "What a wonder, this Mother.
She is a person who knows everything. Didn't you hear
her repeating all the things that we had said here, not
even missing a single word!"

The van again moved north after leaving Miss D. in
her house. One devotee asked, "Will they beat the girl
or do something else to her?" The Mother answered in a
very determined voice, "No, they will not even touch
her."

As the journey north continued, the atmosphere
changed and everyone became happy and enthusiastic.

The Mother also soared to the peak of bliss as she ecstatically sang, *Maname nara jivitam makum...*

> O mind, this human birth is like a field,
> If not cultivated properly
> It becomes dry and barren.
>
> You know neither how to sow the seeds properly
> Nor how to grow them well,
> Neither have you the wish to know.
>
> By removing the weeds and putting fertilizer,
> By taking proper care,
> You may have a good harvest.
>
> The early part of life
> Is spent in helpless cries
> And youth is spent in lustful attachment.
>
> As old age approaches
> Your strength is taken away,
> You become like a helpless worm
> Without any work, time spent
> Looking forward only to the grave.

The Mother led a few more *bhajans* as everybody responded. It seemed that they all forgot the fact that they were traveling in a van. Such was the joy and exhilaration as each person partook of the abundant flow of spiritual bliss.

When the *bhajans* were over the Holy Mother laughingly said, "When her mother created such an uproar, screaming and lamenting as she came towards the van, do you know what daughter Miss D. told Mother in a soft voice? 'Mother, these are all just pranks to show Mother. It will last only for a short time.' She is not a woman but a man. She was unmoved even when her mother was crying."

Thus while the talk went on, the van stopped in front of another house, the home of a devotee. The Mother spent a few minutes there. First of all, she went to the family shrine room and did a small *puja*. The son, who was studying for his medical degree, did not want to continue. He wanted to take *sannyasa*. The parents were against this. His sister also had the same leanings. She read only spiritual books. The parents were very worried about what would happen to the children. The Mother consoled everyone and again got into the van. She remarked,

Amma: It is really strange to see people behave in this way. They would rather give their children to the God of Death than give them to *sannyasa*. What a pity! *Kali Yuga* at its peak. What else is there to say!"

En route was another program at another devotee's house. This was not on the main road, so the van had to deviate and drive a few kilometers through the back roads. At nine o'clock the Mother's party reached the house which was in a village. The *brahmacharins* were supposed to conduct *bhajans*; therefore, the Holy Mother remained in the van. Gayatri and a few householder devotees stayed with her. The devotee in whose house the *bhajan* was being conducted somehow learned that the Mother was in the van, so he rushed over and prayed to her to come and sanctify his house by her presence. Unable to disregard the devotee's prayer, the Mother entered the house, where he received her with proper respect and led her to the shrine room. A priest was performing the *puja*, and the Mother sat, simply gazing at the worship that he did.

The time was approaching eleven o'clock as we finished having supper after the *bhajan*. Upon leaving the house, we saw a monk giving a speech in the front yard. As his talk was nearing its conclusion, it revealed that he followed the path of knowledge.

One devotee said to the Mother, "It seems that the swami did not have much esteem for the path of devotion."

The Mother answered, "No, no, do not think this. These are the things that he said." And thus the Mother started repeating all the things the swami spoke about, in the same order, from the very beginning. The devotee who had listened keenly to the swami's speech was struck with wonder. Neither he nor the others saw the Mother listening to the swami's speech at any time while they were there. To them it appeared that she was intent on watching the *puja*.

It was midnight when the Mother and the group reached Vallickavu. As soon as she alighted from the van, she loudly said, "Shiva...there is no water anywhere here." Nobody could figure out why she said this and everybody was curious. One *brahmacharin* could not contain his curiosity and asked her, "Mother, why do you say that? How do you know that? We have not reached the Ashram yet." The Mother simply smiled and said, "Nothing. Craziness, what else?"

But everyone realized the meaning of what she had said when they reached the Ashram. Each one went up to the water taps to wash their faces and feet, but there was not even a drop of water. Neither was there any water in the holding tank. For the last two days there had been no electricity either. Some wax candles were lit so that everyone could manage to get to their rooms and go to bed. By twelve-thirty the Mother also went to her room.

18 March 1984

The Holy Mother came to the steps near the front verandah of her room in the morning at seven-thirty. Her curly black hair was loose, cascading down her back, reminding one of Kali, the Divine Mother. Some residents and householder devotees were standing on the steps. The discussion was about having women aspirants in the Ashram. Some did not favor the idea.

Amma: To avoid the possible obstacles in *sadhana* it is said that men and women aspirants should not be put in the same Ashram. There is no problem if there are girls endowed with *vairagya*. Even then, one should constantly be alert about this. Since the attraction between men and women is natural, pitfalls will occur if one is not very careful. Women aspirants need manliness. Previously, Mother did not like being a woman. She used to ask the neighbors, "When am I going to become a man?" Anyhow, as far as the Ashram is concerned, Mother is here to take care. Therefore, there is nothing to worry about.

While the conversation was going on, the Mother's brother, Suresh, came and began cutting her fingernails. Her nails had grown very long. She did not care about such things. The Mother was not concerned in the least about her body. Sometimes Gayatri had to remind her about things like taking a shower, having her food and something to drink at the right time, going to bed, etc. The Mother was very careless about these personal matters, especially food and sleep. She had very little of either. As Suresh continued to carefully cut her nails, the Mother said,

Amma: *Mahatmas* will make rules for others. But they themselves do not abide by them. They are beyond all rules and regulations. Nothing binds them.

One devotee: While on the street, sometimes I feel like chanting the Divine Name aloud.

Amma: There should not be any shyness, shame or false modesty to chant the Divine Name. Call aloud the moment you feel like doing so. Do not suppress it. Let your heart break open and flow towards Him without any hindrance. Such spontaneous calls will certainly help to open the heart.

The Mother looked up and saw some children carrying bricks for the Ashram. Shivan, son of the Mother's elder sister Kasturi, was among them. The Mother raised her voice and said to them, "Shivan...carry the bricks chanting Aum...Aum...Aum." She then started talking about how to bring up young children.

Amma: If children are given proper training when they are very young, they will not err. Parents should take a personal interest for this to happen. Many children err just because of the careless upbringing by their parents. Love without discipline is not real love; it is mere attachment. Too much attachment, which is usually the case with parents for their children, especially in mothers, will spoil the child. Parents should try hard to build good character in their children. To make this possible, they themselves should have a certain amount of purity in their own character. They should set an example. A father who is a chain-smoker cannot advise his son not to smoke. By smoking himself, he actually encourages his son to do so. A father who always gets angry with the mother cannot ask his son not to get angry with his wife. A mother who always craves to see movies cannot advise her daughter not to go to movies. Parents have a great influence on their children. If the parents are morally good, their children will be also, and the reverse is true as well.

Suppose two boys walk down the street. One person may point out the boys to his friend and say, "Look at those children. I have never seen such arrogant and bad children before in my life." Then his friend might comment, "Oh, that is no wonder. Their parents are 'so and so,' aren't they? What else can we expect from the children of those people." We can also hear the opposite comments about some other boys or girls, "It is no wonder that they are so good. Their parents are so pure in character. Undoubtedly their children will be the same."

Therefore, parents should be very careful when they deal with their children. Don't give whatever they ask. They have no discrimination. If you do not use your discrimination when you fulfill their wishes, you are leading them to destruction. When you nourish their body, don't forget to nourish their minds by disciplining them properly. Give some physical work to your children as well. Let them sweat and toil a little every day. Otherwise, they will become lazy and good-for-nothing. Give them a chance to know the value of work.

Gayatri brought a glass of tea for the Mother. She waited with it in her hands as she stood behind the Mother. One householder devotee softly said, "Mother, tea. Please drink it before it turns cold." The Mother took the tea from Gayatri's hands and had just one sip and said, "That's enough." "Mother, you hardly drank it," said the devotee. "Yes, that is enough," answered the Mother. Then she continued,

Amma: People who are running an orphanage came to see Mother at Kanvashrama. They told Mother that they have more than four hundred children there. They educate and train them to do some work or other. The children can stay and continue on if they wish. Some lead a married life after leaving the orphanage. Mother asked those who run it to also teach *Vedanta* or give them some spiritual instruction every day to help them grow internally as well. This will help them to discriminate between the eternal and non-eternal. Through this, perhaps those who are orphans will not create orphan children again. They will not live like dogs. Dogs eat, drink, and procreate; they also bring up their young ones. What difference is there if this is the same case with human beings? This is not life. This is death or equal to death. Human beings are meant to discriminate; therefore, try to live the way a human being should, not like an animal.

Human beings are supposed to be highly evolved. Even animals have discipline in their lives. A lion will never eat grass. A deer or an elephant will not eat meat. They do not change their instinctual routine, but human beings will do anything indiscriminately. We misuse our freedom of choice. If we do not live up to our intended purpose of spiritual evolution and act accordingly but instead act in an indisciplined and immature way, we are undoubtedly worse than animals. If we continue to act in an indisciplined way, it will only help pave the way for our destruction.

THE WORLD CAME OUT OF WORD

19 March 1984

Early in the morning Brahmacharin Unnikrishnan was performing the daily worship in the temple, chanting the Thousand Names of the Divine Mother. A few other *brahmacharins* were also chanting along with him, making the sound very pleasant to the ears and to the heart.

Two year old Shivan, Kasturi's son, was walking around carrying a photograph of Mother Kali, which belonged to a *brahmacharin*. He had a big smile on his face. At this time the Mother came out. She was pleased to see the child carrying the picture. She told Shivan, "Son, set the photo down and prostrate in front of it." The boy immediately did so. "Son, now pray to Devi, 'Devi, please make me a *sannyasin*,'" instructed the Mother. Shivan repeated the sentence and everybody laughed. The Mother turned to the *brahmacharins* and said,

Amma: Look at this boy. See the obedience he has. He did just what Mother instructed. This is the kind of obedience and faith that an aspirant should have.

Shivan wanted a swing. He expressed his wish to the Mother in his own childlike way. He knew whom to approach. The Mother instructed one of the residents to make one for him. The Holy Mother again conversed with Shivan, "Son, you should chant 'Amme Narayana' while swinging, okay? You should also meditate sitting on the swing, agreed?" Shivan nods his head in agreement. At this time a *brahmacharin* came and whispered something.

Amma: Children, you should be very careful when you utter each word. It was from Word that the world came into being. The world exists on Word. You should talk very carefully. In the beginning there was total silence, the silence before creation, the silence of peace. In that state the cosmic mind was totally in an absorbed state. Then the Word, the first Word, broke the silence. Thus the world emerged. This creation takes place in each one of us. Each mind is a small world. We have created a world of thoughts. Thoughts become desires, and desires, in turn, keep the cycle going. Therefore, be careful when you utter a word. We go on creating many more worlds through the utterance of words.

A householder's word is like sand; whereas, a *brahmacharin's* word has glue in it. *Brahmacharins* should speak very carefully.

Now the Mother sat down and started cleaning her teeth using burnt paddy husk mixed with salt and ground pepper.

Amma: Burnt paddy husk mixed with salt and ground pepper is very good for the teeth. Toothpaste and other things came later. In the olden days people used natural

things. In those days people lived in harmony with nature and this gave them healthy minds and bodies. But
now everything is artificial. People have stopped cooperating with nature and have stopped living in tune with
nature. Therefore, nature has stopped cooperating with
human beings. They have polluted nature, so nothing is
natural anymore. Everything is poisonous and full of chemi-
cals.

In the month of April the Mother had a plan to visit
Kanya Kumari (Cape Comorin) with the devotees. One
woman devotee agreed to meet all the expenses. The
Mother rinsed her mouth and expressed this about the
possible forthcoming trip:

Amma: Ours is not a picnic. It is a spiritual trip. No
one should speak unnecessarily. Do not try to find fault
with each other during the trip. No gossip. No chit-chat.
If householder children are coming, they should observe
the routine of the *brahmacharins*. *Japa, dhyana, bhajans,*
spiritual discussions, etc., should be done punctually. Everybody should participate in all this without fail. This trip, if it
happens, is not to waste our energy by talking, sight-seeing
and shopping. It is to acquire more energy. Remember,
this travel with Mother is to stop the never-ending travel
of our minds. Mother does not make these trips for idle
reasons.

One *brahmacharin* had difficulty in accepting the
theory of an *Avatar*, that God will descend to the earth

assuming a human form to uplift righteousness, justice and truth. He asked the Mother about this.

Amma: Son, do you believe in the omnipotent, omniscient and omnipresent nature of God?

Brahmacharin: Yes, certainly I do.

Amma: If so, why have doubts in His creative nature? Such a God endowed with all those qualities is capable of doing anything if He wills and wishes. An ordinary human being endowed only with a limited body, mind and intellect cannot understand anything without the use of names and forms, let alone understand anything about God without form. In order to make human beings experience Godly qualities, God the Formless assumes a form. Godly attributes by themselves have no form, color or taste. If He remains without a form, who is going to understand Him? Who is going to draw inspiration form Him? He will remain as something impossible and fabricated. The scriptures and the statements made therein will be a far cry from any human understanding. In order to make all this concrete, God comes in a human form to serve, to love and to set an example for the world. A human form is needed; therefore, He assumes a name and a form as per the need of the age.

God is omniscient. So, why do you doubt that He can take a form and descend to earth to serve the human race and restore peace and righteousness? God is formless, but he can assume any form at any time as He wishes. It is to enact His *leela* as a human being that God takes a form. He will behave exactly like human beings, but within, He will never forget His real nature.

Sri Rama was the Incarnation of Lord Narayana; nevertheless, didn't He shed tears when Sita was kidnapped by Ravana, the demon king? Sri Krishna was killed by an arrow shot by an ordinary hunter, wasn't He? What about Jesus Christ? Wasn't He tortured and didn't He suffer like a ordinary human being? They were all *Avatars*, yet when they were in human form, they wanted to experience everything that a mortal human being experienced. That is their greatness, to choose to suffer like a mortal even though they are fully aware of their Godhood. That is the greatest, most wonderful renunciation that a *Mahatma* will do. He takes and accepts the suffering by his own will for the good of others.

In addition, you can see an obvious difference between a person who has attained Liberation through penance and a person who is born Divine, i.e., an Incarnation. An Incarnation takes thousands of people across the ocean of transmigration. He is like a huge ship which can carry thousands of passengers. A person who has attained Liberation through *sadhana* cannot do this.

An *Avatar* comes down with all the Godly powers, manifesting them on a very large scale. He will be aware of His Godly nature from the very moment of birth. Even if He does perform *sadhana*, it will only be to set an example for others. He will have infinite power and inexhaustible energy. Whereas, one who works to attain Self-Realization through *sadhana* will slowly evolve to that state. The difference is like one who is born and reared in Bombay, a native, and one who migrates there.

Brahmacharin: (With joy) Now it is clear. Now I understand that Mother is an *Avatar*.

Amma: (Laughing and rejoicing) No, no...your Mother is not an *Avatar* but a good-for-nothing crazy girl.

Brahmacharin: Yes, yes...your *leela* as a human being is really wonderful. Now, you cannot refute this. (Softly, as if in secret, he asks the Mother) Mother, please tell me, aren't you an *Avatar*? Don't play any more tricks. (Now the Mother really bursts into laughter, seeing the innocence of the *brahmacharin*.)

At this time a pigeon came flying seemingly from out of nowhere and sat near the Mother. She took some puffed rice in her hand, and the bird pecked the rice right from her palm. Like an innocent child, she looked at the bird and suddenly started shouting, "Anandoham, anandoham, anandoham." (Blissful am I, Blissful am I...) She entered into the state of *samadhi* as she sat with the puffed rice in her out-stretched right hand. All of a sudden the pigeon, as if it did not want to disturb the Mother, stopped pecking and stood silently. The pigeon turned his head from side to side and kept looking at the Mother's face. But it neither moved from the place where it was standing nor did it take another peck of puffed rice with its beak.

Minutes passed. The Mother slowly came down from her interior heights. A few more minutes passed,

and she seemed to be completely back in her normal
mood. The Mother still kept her right hand with the
puffed rice stretched out. To everybody's amazement the
pigeon once again started pecking at the remainder of
the rice. When it finished, the Mother closed her palm
and withdrew it with the words, "That's all. Now you
go." Immediately the bird flew away. The *brahmacharins*
who were present were struck with awe and wonder.
One *brahmacharin* commented, "This bird must have been
a *sadhak* or a devotee of the Holy Mother in its previous
birth." Turning to the Mother, he asked, "Amma, am I
correct?"

The Mother smiled and said, "Who knows? Maybe."
After a short pause she continued, "There are *avadhuts*
and *tapasvis* who can take any form they want. It could
be one of them who came to see all of us together."

Another *brahmacharin* retorted, "Amma, if it was to
see all of us the bird would have come to each one of
us. (All laugh.) But it did not move an inch from your
side. Not only that, it did not show even a little bit of ac-
quaintance to any one of us except you. (More laughter.)
That means you knew each other. We poor creatures
were left out. Therefore, it came to see you, Amma, not
us."

24 March 1984

Today some people from the east of Kerala came to
see the Holy Mother and visit the Ashram for the first
time. They were very inquisitive about the Ashram and

the Mother. Because they were sincere and had no pre-conceived ideas, the Mother was also very enthusiastic in replying to their queries.

Question: Mother, we are very interested in learning about the Ashram. Different people say different things. While we were coming here, we heard some people at the junction in Vallickavu talking against the Ashram. It seems that they are not believers.

Amma: Children, most of them have belief in God. They go to temples and worship. Once a month they conduct the reading of the *Bhagavata* and the *Ramayana* in their homes. But those children do not know what an Ashram is, nor do they understand *sannyasa*. They do not know anything about the inner principles of religion and spirituality. What they have are misunderstandings and misconceptions. (At this time some young men also came and took their seats.) Therefore, Mother does not blame them. The villagers say that there must be some fraud with so many foreigners coming to the Ashram. They wonder how all these people could come without any publicity given out by the Ashram. (Smilingly) Mother would say that it is God who is the thief. He is respon-sible for this fraudulence. It is that Fellow who does all this. Their question is how have we attracted people by ways other than the kind of publicity which uses paper and ink made by human beings. They only know about things which their intellect can perceive and understand. They do not know anything about the plane beyond the human intellect, nor do they want to put any effort into acquiring any knowledge about it. They use an easy method to avoid ideas about spirituality by criticizing and rejecting such ideas without finding out more about them. They cannot think of anything beyond this physical world. All their knowledge ends in their limited perception. They cannot be blamed because human nature is such.

ASHRAM, A PLACE FOR TYAGIS (RENUNCIATES)

The Holy Mother continued,

Amma: They say that it is a place of pleasure seekers. Let them come and see. Then they will understand that this is a place for *tyagis*, not *bhogis*.

These children from the West, you know how filled with pleasure were their lives there. But once they come here and surrender, they give up all their old habits and ways. They are happy and satisfied with rice gruel for food and the thatched coconut leaf huts for sleeping. Just like the other residents, they also sleep on the floor. They sincerely do their *sadhana* and are fully content. In fact theirs is real renunciation because they had everything, all material pleasures and comforts. They lived in the midst of it. If they want they can go back and enjoy it. Mother never insists that anyone follow this path. Even then, they have renounced all the pleasure-giving objects and choose to live such a hard life. You may not watch T.V. since you do not have one. Real renunciation is when you refrain from watching it when you have one.

There were times when there was nothing in the Ashram. Mother is very particular that nothing should be asked for or sought. Yet no difficulty has ever arisen so far. Mother has no doubt that everything is done by God. If you have to starve to death, that is also His Will. This is what Mother tries to teach these children here. Mother wants to set an example for the children here. Mother will not go to catch the feet of rich people. Today if Mother does not set an example, tomorrow the children here will go after rich people. Mother will bow down in front of good character, but she will not bow down in front of riches.

There are five or six *saippu makkal* (foreign children) who have come here. All of them are very wealthy, but Mother does not want their money. Mother tells them, "Deposit all your money in your own name." Do you know why? Because if they bring it here it is possible for a little selfishness to arise in their minds, that it is their money being spent. That should not be allowed to happen. The children here have asked how we will live. Mother tells them that God will take care of everything. Yes, He takes care of everything now and He will certainly do so in the future. Even if there are a hundred children here, they should live together like one family. Love and respect for each other should be the guiding factor. That is what Mother wants. Nobody should be troubled here. People will come from the outside. A share of what we have will be given to them as well. We do not see them as different. If there is nothing, we will live eating leaves. That too is beneficial. Some leaves contain a lot of vitamins. Leaves which we do not use here are used in other places, aren't they?

If there comes a situation where we have to live by eating leaves, the children who live here will be ready to do so as well. This is a place for *tyagis*. Children, only *tyagis* will be blissful. Therefore, this place is not fit for pleasure-seekers. Here there may not be enough salt, sour pickles or chillies for the food; but it cannot be otherwise. Until now they all lived eating tasty food. From now on let them live renouncing taste. This renunciation of taste will help them to acquire the Supreme Taste, the taste of the *Atman*.

Children, the people who criticize the Ashram cannot be any other way because that is their nature. The frogs croak and the crickets chirp at night. Nobody is kept awake at night saying, "I can't sleep due to this noise." That is the nature of those creatures. They are like that; they cannot be any different. In the same way, those people who criticize the Ashram cannot be contrary to their nature. Just ignore their words and pray for their souls.

Question: Amma, when we see the suffering of the world, sometimes we think that God is very cruel.

Amma: That is what everybody says. Our suffering is created by our own actions. The sole responsibility is ours. God is in no way responsible for it. It just takes a little bit of discrimination to understand this. Suppose you get angry with your wife and slap her. Afterwards you become mentally restless. You feel very sad for beating your wife; thus you suffer. From where did the anger come? It came from you, didn't it? Why did you get angry? Because she did not bring the coffee on time. Your desire to drink coffee at your accustomed time was obstructed; therefore, you got angry. The whole incident occurs only because of your attachment to coffee. The desire was not fulfilled at the right time. You lost your discrimination, your mental balance, and thus you slapped your wife. If we observe matters in this way, we can find that all our problems and sufferings are created by our own lack of discrimination and loss of mental control.

Children, God is not cruel. He is compassionate. Is there anybody who really calls on God? There is no one who says, "O Lord, I want only You." But we say, "O God, give me this, give me that." This is how we pray. We only want our desires fulfilled. We do not pray for Him to come and dwell in our hearts. We meditate and remember the things that we need to get; we do not remember God. Then we will complain, "I have been calling on God for the last sixty years. He hasn't turned to look at me even once." If only this was said after having once remembered Him for at least one minute, then there would be meaning in the complaint. Mother will put in writing that God will not give sorrow. God gives prosperity, wealth, beauty, vitality and love; He will not give sorrow. Do not ever say that He gives sorrow.

If someone prays to God with devotion for devotion's sake, he will not suffer. Mother can guarantee this. If the contrary happens, Mother is ready to prove that such a person will not suffer at all but will always be blissful. Mother makes this statement not out of ego but from her experience.

We do not call on God. We make suggestions and tell Him what things we want. "Give it to me. If You don't, I will not make this offering to You." Ours are not prayers but suggestions, demands or warnings. Try and truly call Him for at least five minutes a day. Then you will come to know that He does not give sorrow.

Children, sorrow occurs only when there is desire. Even before creation He had said, "You will always be blissful if you go through this way. Sorrow is the result if you go through the other path." Children, having disobeyed those words you went and fell into the ditch, and now you say that you were pushed into it. God had told us about both ways. It is up to us to choose. If you want eternal and everlasting bliss, the path to God is available, but you have to work hard. If you are only interested in achieving momentary happiness, then the path to the world is open to you. This too needs effort but not as much as what is needed to attain God. To become king, one should be a repository of good qualities and talents. Similarly, to become His dear one and the king of the whole universe, one should have inner purity, and this takes constant striving. But to become a mere enjoyer of the items created and owned by Him, only little effort is needed.

Question: Why are there two paths? It was enough to have the path of happiness only, wasn't it? Why did God introduce the path of sorrow?

Amma: What? Do you mean that happiness alone is enough and there is no need for sorrow? There is everything in creation. Even a small needle and a blade of grass has its own purpose. Nothing is a waste in creation. Keenly observe. It is sorrow which helps our growth. Human beings will not work and move forward if there is no sorrow. Fear of suffering and sorrow makes one work. If there were only happiness, people would not have feared anything, and this would have culminated in laziness and over-indulgence. Laziness and over-indulgence will only cause utter ruin.

It is your mind which creates sorrow, not God. There must be everything in creation, both good and bad. Having one without the other is not creation. To act understanding the place and importance of each and every object is our duty. Everything has its own place in life. Just give things their proper place, their proper due, neither more nor less, then everything will be all right.

Even if God had created a world of only goodness, human beings would have turned it into a hell through over-indulgence. Not only that, to understand and realize the greatness and beauty of goodness, the bad also is necessary, isn't it? Without anything to compare with, how can one know any particular thing? To understand and appreciate beauty, we must be able to recognize ugliness.

God has clearly given us instructions as to what is the path of bliss and what is the path of sorrow. Can't we abstain from vices, listening to His instructions?

Children, it is just like asking why God created fire which is dangerous. It was not to burn houses and kill people that God created fire. It was to cook food and use it for other beneficial matters that He created it. If we use it to harm others, is it God who should be blamed? It is we who created the bad and turned it into a hell.

There is a child and there is fire. A child can be burned by the fire. But God has given the child a mother who warns the child about the dangers of playing with fire. We cannot say that since there are many children in this world, there should not be any fire in this world. How would we cook our food? Nor can we say that there should not be any electricity in the house because it might give someone a shock. Without electricity how would we run the machines and industries? No father or mother would say, "We have a little baby, so we should not have fire in our house." If there is a fire, the God-given mother or father will take care of the child. When the child grows up he will become discriminating enough to know that fire is dangerous and will handle it carefully. Even after he is grown up, if he knowingly jumps into the fire, is it God's fault? God did not create it for him to jump into and burn himself. Since He created fire for cooking and for doing other useful things, fire in itself is not meant to be used in a harmful way. Not the thing itself but the way it is used is important. A thing in itself is not dangerous, but the way it is used can make it dangerous. Your mother has told you several times that fire is dangerous and warned you not to go near it. But if you disobey, whose fault is it?

That is why it is said that religious texts should be taught even at a very young age and that a Guru is necessary to guide us on the path. Today people do not want this at all. They think that they know everything. Nobody wants a Guru, nor does anybody want to be a disciple. As a result we are in sorrow.

What we breathe is *"soham"* (I am). Have we truly heard it and realized it, even once? How nice it would be if we really tried to hear it. The Lord is always telling us loudly, "You are That, you are That." Try to hear this; be alert and attentive. That is what you are always singing, "I am That, I am That." Try to listen to this. But nobody listens to the Lord! Strange!

Question: Why is it such that His voice cannot be heard?

Amma: It is not impossible to hear this. Children, if you sow, you reap; if you try, you get. The set rule is that one should try and hear it. If you simply sit on a chair and ask, "Why am I not hearing God's voice," without making even the least amount of effort to hear and know It, who can help you to hear that Sound?

A dog has no discrimination. We know that we should be careful when we walk in front of one. Having carelessly walked near a dog and having been bitten by it, we find fault with God.

Two of the visitors were good *bhajan* singers. The Holy Mother said to them, "Children, please sing some *bhajans.*" They sang *Matru vatsalya todenne...*

O Mother, even if you are here to protect me
With all the love and affection of a mother,
Even if I keep awake without blinking an eye,
Still there occur a number of thefts
In the home of the mind. Therefore,
O Mother, I get worried.

O Mother, the Destroyer of all afflictions,
Even though I daily make vow after vow
To continue my prayers constantly
Without any break,
O Mother, I know that it is only Your trick
If I happen to forget.

They sang the song with full devotion and love. The
Mother sat in a totally absorbed state. They continued to
sing. The next bhajan was *Pirayentu chaitu...*

O Mother, what error have I committed?
What error has Thy poor child committed?

I do not long for many things
But only for the good fortune of Thy Vision.
Why didst Thou, O Goddess and
Mother of the World,
Create obstacles even for that?

O Mother,
This unfortunate one has come seeking refuge,
This helpless, unfortunate son.
O Mother, Loving Mother,
Show compassion and save me.

My refuge, my refuge is Thy Holy Feet,
Other than Thee, refuge there is none.
Enable me to bow at Thy Lotus Feet
Bless this supplicant, O Compassionate One.

Silence prevailed for some time when the singing was over. The Mother slowly opened her eyes. In front of the Mother sat a girl who was studying for her Master's degree in philosophy. Looking at her the Mother said,

Amma: Daughter, there is a billboard advertising a jewelry shop by the road side. You will not get gold if you ask the billboard. You have to go to the shop. You won't reach the goal if you learn philosophy. *Sadhana* also is needed simultaneously. Without *sadhana*, you will start walking around saying, "I am Brahman."

Balu-mon (son Balu) has a Master's degree in philosophy. After he had been doing *sadhana* for a few years, Mother asked him to get a degree in philosophy. First *sadhana*, then philosophy. The *rishis* wrote only after experiencing. It was not the other way around. It was not mere intellectual exercise. Therefore, children, don't act or pretend as if you are *Brahman* after simply reading some books. It is not enough if we walk around talking about what the *rishis* have experienced. You should experience it for yourselves through *sadhana*. You will just go on babbling after reading books if you don't do any *sadhana*.

Mere philosophy will make your heart dry. *Bhakti* is needed. Mother never allowed these boys in the Ashram

to study the *Upanishads* in the beginning. Mother
wanted them to cultivate and develop *bhakti* first. After
some years of devotional practices, Mother permitted
them to study the *Upanishads*.

Faith is needed. One is liberated if faith comes.
Complete faith is Liberation. Only through Realization
will doubts go completely. A Guru is needed for that.

The girl: Mother, I would like to stay here in Mother's
presence for two or three days, but my parents will not
agree.

Amma: Daughter, God will definitely favor pure and innocent wishes. God will certainly help you if you have a
sincere desire. Two children, one was Brahmacharin
Sreekumar's sister and the other a child of his uncle,
used to pray every day, "O Mother, we want to stay with
you for three days. Mother, won't you fulfill this desire
of ours?" Thus the two children used to pray and cry,
looking at Mother's picture everyday. None of the family
members brought the children here, but they continued
their prayers. One day Sreekumar's father for some reason came to the Ashram with these children. His actual
plan was to return home immediately with the children.
Contrary to his plan, he had to go to Quilon urgently.
Before he left he entrusted Sreekumar to take them back
home the same day. There was a heavy downpour that
day when Sree-mon went to the ferry with these children. There was no boat to cross the river; therefore,
they came back to the Ashram. Although it was not the
rainy season, it rained the whole day so they could not
leave. They were going to go the next day, but again it

became impossible since there was a strike all over the state. Because the children were not seen for two days, relatives from their house came to fetch them on the third day. They all left on the following day, but only after staying for that evening's *Devi Bhava Darshan*. Thus those children stayed with Mother three days as they had prayed.

One day during their stay here, Mother was lying down with eyes closed as if she were sleeping. At that time she heard one of them telling the other, "Hey, Mother will hear what we pray to Her. She has heard what we have prayed sitting in our house. Yesterday Mother made it rain and today the strike." These are all proofs to show that God will hear the call of children endowed with dedication and innocence. Innocent prayers will be answered. If children say something, nature will catch it immediately and it will be fulfilled. That state should come for us also.

When a person is in the state of *jivanmukti*, he is unattached just as little children are. He might ask for something and then abandon it in no time. A *jivanmukta* will show love to all objects, but there will be no attachment to anything. He might be lying on a mattress at one moment and the next moment lying in dirty water. He may be living in a big house but will smile with full heart and accept it if he has to live in a thick forest the very next moment. In that state of *jivanmukti*, one's love for things is only apparent. When such a person expresses a desire, in reality it is giving an opportunity for others to serve him.

This state should come. Children have this state to a certain extent. That is why we feel an attraction to children and feel fascinated by their smiles and sportings. There is no *maya* in them; they are innocent and for that reason they have the power to attract. The difference between a Self-Realized Soul and a child is that a Self-Realized Soul has no trace of any *vasanas* in him. He has eliminated all *vasanas* through severe penance. In a child *vasanas* are there in the dormant state. They will slowly manifest as the child grows up. The attraction that we feel for him will also fade away as he gets older.

GURU

Question: Mother, who is a Guru? Who is a disciple?

The Mother remained silent as if she did not hear the question. Who knows why? A devotee interfered by saying,

Devotee: The answer to your question is very clear right here in Amma's presence. Amma talks and we all listen carefully. Even great scholars come to hear what she says. If one of us sits and talks, not even a child will come to listen. One who has known the Self and one who is capable of removing the ignorance of others is a Guru. One who listens with faith, sitting near the Guru, and one who surrenders completely to him in order to be disciplined is a disciple. This is the empirical plane.

This is not the plane where one experiences *sarvam brahmamayam* (everything is the Absolute). There is no Guru and no disciple once you reach there. Guru and disciple exist before you reach the goal. Isn't the attitude to think in this way, "Who is the Guru and who is the disciple," derived from someone?

The Holy Mother now spoke.

Amma: A real Guru is one who is endowed with all the Divine qualities, such as equal vision, universal love, renunciation, compassion, patience, forbearance, and endurance. He will have complete control over his mind. He will be like a huge ship which can carry thousands of passengers. His mere presence will give a feeling of protection and safety, an assurance to the disciple that he will reach the goal. Like the moon his presence will be cooling, soothing and heart-capturing, but at the same time it will also be brilliant, radiant and shining like the sun. He will be soft like a flower and hard like a diamond in his manner towards the disciple. He will be simpler than the simplest and humbler than the humblest. Even his silence will be a teaching. A real disciple is one who can imbibe the life and teachings of such a Guru and follow his footsteps faithfully. Knowing and understanding the real nature of such a Great Master, a true disciple's heart will spontaneously surrender and willingly let him discipline him.

It is not possible to proceed very far on the spiritual path without a Guru. A guide is necessary to travel in an undiscovered country. A *sadhak*, through his penances, may succeed in getting rid of his gross *vasanas* without the help of a Perfect Master, but a *Satguru's* help and Grace are a must in order to eliminate the subtle *vasanas* and to give up his individuality. There is a son who comes here. One day he openly told one of the *brahmacharins* that he had been doing spiritual practices for the last thirty-five years but never had a deep experience. He also said that he knows his problem which he stated was nothing but the hesitancy to come under the discipline of a *Satguru*. His subtle *vasanas* still remained even after thirty-five years of severe penance. He is a very sincere and hard-working son, yet no real experience occurred. This is what happens to people who cannot surrender. Once you come under a Perfect Master, then you simply obey his words and do *sadhana* without fail. If your surrender is complete and if you are determined to attain the goal, he will work with your ego, both the gross and subtle, and will take you across the ocean of transmigration. The subtle ego is very hard to break through with only your own efforts. The *Satguru's* guidance will slowly bring it out and exhaust it. A Perfect Master always works with the ego of the disciple. But he will not start until the disciple is ready for it.

Mother does not want to insist that anyone do this. If it is the Lord's will that someone should be here, let it be so. If it is to be that one should be somewhere else, let that be so. *Sadhana* will become smoother and easier if a *Satguru* is present.

THE MIND SHOULD BE MADE KASHAYA (SAFFRON)

Na-karmaṇā-na-prajayā-dhanêna |
Tyâgênaikê-amritatvam-ânasuḥ | |

"Neither through action nor progeny or wealth
But through renunciation alone one attains immortality."

(KAIVALYA UPANISHAD)

Question: Do you initiate people into *sannyasa* and give them the saffron-colored cloth to wear?

Amma: *Sannyasa!* How easily one can utter that name! But have you ever thought of the deep significance of that word? It contains the whole of spirituality. Nobody can give renunciation. It is a state that should be attained or realized. It is also a state which spontaneously flows into you. It is a state where one becomes completely natural and spontaneous. One simply flows like the river, blows like the wind and shines like the sun. It is both that which should be attained and that which should be received. To attain something, self-effort is necessary. To receive means that somebody gives it. Therefore, the state of *sannyasa* is both something that should be attained through self-effort and something that will be spontaneously and simultaneously given by the Guru (Grace).

The sole purpose of spiritual life is to renounce all that is not ours and to become what we really are. Real sannyasa is the renunciation of all desires and desire-prompted actions. In fact, it is the mind that should be made kashaya (saffron). Sannyasa is purely subjective, not objective. It is a state of the mind where one becomes completely peaceful and calm in all circumstances. In that state of renunciation, that which fills within will be expressed outwardly also.

Wearing ochre clothes externally has significance. It will help one to remember that Supreme State. It is a good reminder to make our body and mind always alert and vigilant. One who has donned kashaya will hesitate a little to commit any mistakes. It makes one remember about one's goal. The real kashaya has the color of fire. It indicates the destruction of body-consciousness and the awakening into God-consciousness. The body is burnt in the Fire of Knowledge; this is the meaning. Therefore, a sannyasin is supposed to be an embodiment of Pure Knowledge. He becomes the personification of all great qualities. He should maintain that in word and deed, in each and every action that he does. This will become spontaneous for one who has attained that state. For others it is a practice. They must make a deliberate and sincere attempt to move and act in this world in accordance with those principles until it becomes natural.

The great saints and sages of the past and others who followed in their footsteps did not give much importance to the dress and the name of sannyasa. They were the ones who made their minds kashaya. The most important thing is to know That (Brahman) through penance, not walking around in ochre clothes giving speeches after having studied the scriptures. If you do not adhere to the principles which you are teaching, it might result in other people wrongly evaluating spirituality and spiritual masters. Gurus and sages have said, "*Tapah, tapah*" (penance). It is only after experiencing it that they then said, "*Soham*," (I am That). They did not say this before the experience. How many years they did *tapas!* (Jokingly) And we, after going through only the ABC's declare, "No *sadhana*. Nothing is needed. I am That." We have renounced all those great examples set by our forefathers and now act as we like. What a great renunciation! (Laughter)

The next step is questioning, who is the Guru, who is the disciple, and so on and so forth. (More laughter) The *rishis*, living in an elevated realm, were not conscious of their physical body even when someone had severely beaten them and hacked their hands off. When they did become aware of their external condition, they returned only love and compassion to those who tortured them. Such was their establishment in that Reality. Whereas, if someone just looks at us in the wrong way we will ask with hostility, "Hey, fellow, why did you look at me like that?" The *Brahmanishtatvam* (the state of being established in *Brahman)* is gone. The *Brahman* disappears. Such people say that they are *Brahman*. And they question who is the Guru! Such a wonder! (The Mother laughs loudly.)

The young man who had asked the question "who is the Guru and who is the disciple" sat stunned. The Mother continued,

Amma: Mother doesn't want to make such statements about initiating people into *sannyasa* and declare that she will be giving the name and ochre clothes to such and such people in the future. Let them struggle and let me see how many will come out victorious, and then if it happens, let it happen, well and fine. Mother does not want to make declarations.

The Ashram is a very good battlefield. Whoever comes to this field must fight. Some will be injured and hurt; some will withdraw and run away. Mother is waiting to see how many will emerge victorious.

Question: Mother, what is needed in this age?

Amma: Undoubtedly, self-discipline. Each one of us must become aware of the urgency for it. It is not simply a need but an urgent necessity which must be practiced by every individual of the country. We go on polishing and beautifying the body and the world outside while the mind remains a mess. Do all this polishing and beautifying inside. Stop becoming tense about the external situations. Once the inside of a person is clean, then the outside automatically becomes all right. Stop giving too much importance to external objects.

All problems, both national and international, are due to lack of discipline.

Look at the *brahmins* (priestly caste) of the past. From childhood they contemplated on God. They had no bad company. It was a joint family system in those days. Everyone lived together. They worked in temples. They lived their life learning, understanding and realizing the essential principles. Their children were also full of vitality and radiance. No one could trick them or make them yield to trivial things. However, no such thing can be expected in the coming ages. Nowadays, many children who study in schools and colleges are addicted to marijuana and other drugs. It is lack of self-discipline that makes these children a slave to such dangerous things. In whatever field of life and whoever it may be, what is needed is self-discipline.

(Turning to the girl who was studying for her degree in philosophy) Daughter, whenever you get an opportunity, talk about spiritual matters with your friends. At least one person's mind might change if ten people happen to hear. That person may also become spiritual and contemplate on God.

The Holy Mother now stopped. Since it was a few minutes after one o'clock, she called one *brahmacharin* and asked him to take everybody to have lunch. The Mother got up from her seat and the visitors followed suit. She smilingly looked at them and in a begging tone said, "Children, all of you please have your lunch before going. Don't go without eating."

After saying this, she walked out, saluting everyone. Some *brahmacharins* followed her to whom she said, "Mother wants to be alone for sometime."

She walked alone on the shore of the backwaters for a while with her hands held behind her back and then later went to her room by one-thirty.

31 March 1984

Today the Holy Mother and the residents of the Ashram went to Brahmacharin Sreekumar's house. Upon invitation, the Mother occasionally visited the homes of *brahmacharins* and devotees. Such occasions were celebrated like a festival by the family members. Sreekumar's house was crowded with people, both devotees and neighbors. The Mother went around to each person, consoling and saying a few words to each one.

Children always have a very strong attraction towards the Mother. Here too, all the children from both Sreekumar's house and the neighboring houses stood around the Mother and blocked her way. As soon as she saw all the children so happily gathered together around her, the Mother also hesitated to go to the room. Sreekumar requested of the Mother, "Amma, the people are expecting the evening *bhajan* at six-thirty and it is now nearly six o'clock. Amma, will you please go to the room now and get ready?"

The Mother, like a small child, retorted, "No, I am not going. I am going to stay here with them. (Turning to the children) Yes, children?" Together in one voice, they said, "Yes, yes."

The Mother asked the children to sing a *bhajan*. Takkali, the daughter of Sreekumar's elder sister, led the song, *Amma, Amma Taye...*

> O Mother, Mother, dear Divine Mother,
> Goddess of the Universe,

Giver of food to all creatures.
Thou art the Primal Supreme Power.

Everything in the world happens
Because of Your Divine Play.

All the children responded to the lead singer. Soon the Mother was singing with them. It seemed that she was just another child playing, singing and dancing with the little ones. At one point one of them asked the Mother in a loud voice, "Amma, Amma, are you God?"

The Mother laughed aloud and looked at the child. It was a boy who was hardly five years old. The Mother embraced him and asked, "Who told you that Mother is God?" The boy, pointing to Takkali, answered, "Sheeja chechi" (Elder sister Sheeja.)

The Mother kissed him on both cheeks and replied, "You children are Mother's God."

All the devotees were enjoying the whole scene. They stood around forgetting themselves. At this time Sreekumar's grandmother, who was nearly seventy-five years old, came forward. With her hands around the Mother's waist, she spoke to her in a very sweet voice, as if to a child, "Now, dear Amma, please come to the room. Take a shower and eat something, and then come back." The elderly woman patted and caressed the Mother and repeated, "Please, come."

The Mother smiled at her. The old woman looked like another child. She was very innocent. The Mother could not reject her request. She kissed her face and walked into the room with her. As the Mother went in, she turned around and told the children, "Children, don't go. Mother will be back soon. We shall play together."

A few minutes later the Mother came out ready for the evening *bhajan*. It was not the same playful Mother; she was in a different mood. All the children surrounded her once again, but the Mother went into the family shrine room straightaway without even looking at them.

These changing moods of the Mother were always a mystery for everyone, even to those who were in close physical proximity to her. This mystery becomes more of a mystery as we spend more and more time with her. A few minutes ago she had been laughing, playing and singing with the children. She had also become a child and one could see such innocence in her. The Mother even promised the children that she would play with them when she returned. Had the old woman not come she would have gone on playing with the children. At the time she seemed so attached to the children, but now when they surrounded her, she did not even look at them. How easily she withdraws herself from a person or a thing is beyond our comprehension. Infinite are her moods.

The singing started at around seven o'clock. Gradually it ascended to its peak as the Mother poured forth devotion and inspiration through her soul-stirring songs. The atmosphere was saturated with very high devotional fervor. It reached its climax when the Mother sang *Kamesha Vamashi...*

Salutations to Shakti (Divine Energy)
The Great Goddess
Who is accessible through devotion.
Salutations to the All-Pervading One,
The One True Essence,
The Infinite and Perfect Awareness.

Protect us,
O Thou, who sits on the left thigh of Lord Shiva,
Who fulfills all desires,
Who shines through all animate
And inanimate objects.
O my Kamala (Lotus), Ruler of all...

The devotees blissfully sang with overflowing devotion. Everyone seemed to be transported to the *Devi Loka* (the world of the Devi). The Mother went on inspiring them more and more towards absorption into the Self.

The Holy Mother lost all her external consciousness and sat still. Her left hand was half-bent with its palm unfolded completely. The fingers of her right hand formed a divine *mudra*. Ecstatic tears filled her eyes and rolled down her cheeks.

Balu took over the lead singing. Rao, Venu, Pai and Sreekumar sang along with him. The devotees all responded with utter love and devotion. They went on singing the same song for a long time until the Mother came back to the normal plane of consciousness.

The *bhajan* and the *arati* ended shortly after nine-thirty. The Mother went to the eastern side of Sreekumar's house where it looked like a small *tapovanam* (a place well-suited to perform penance). She disappeared in the dark. Gayatri silently followed her. Sreekumar's father got worried but was reassured by the *brahmacharins*.

Silence prevailed everywhere. The darkness resembled Mahakali's flowing, dark, curly hair, thus creating an awesome atmosphere of reverence. Sacred are these nights for pure souls as they utilize them to fix their minds fully on the Supreme. The stars twinkled in the dark velvet sky. The devotees waited for the Mother to come back so that they could have her *darshan* before they left. By ten o'clock, the Mother emerged out of the darkness, followed by Gayatri. The latter reported that the Mother had been lying down in the sand, gazing at the sky and laughing every now and then in a strange but unique way. She also uttered certain sounds which did not resemble any familiar language. Gayatri added that it seemed to her that the Mother was talking to someone very softly.

Hidden behind the veil of *maya* is her real nature, unapproachable and impenetrable by finite human beings. When the Mother soars high to that plane of Infinite Consciousness, we mortals, for whom it is a totally strange and unfamiliar world, can only gaze at her human form with awe and wonder, unable to understand even an infinitesimal fraction of that Supreme State.

Once a *brahmacharin* said to the Mother, "Mother, my only sorrow is that I am utterly unable to understand you and your moods. How and when will I be able to understand them?" Straightaway came the reply, "Only when you become me."

AT ELEVEN SHARP

The Mother gave *darshan* to everyone. When it was ten minutes before eleven o'clock, she got up from her seat all of a sudden and announced that she wanted to go to a certain devotee's house. She seemed to be in a hurry. Without another word, the Mother walked out of the house. Everyone immediately followed her. It was very dark and the path which led to the road was extremely narrow. This did not bother her as she walked briskly and quickly to the van. Sreekumar's father ran behind her and with some effort managed to catch up with a flashlight in his hand. She entered the vehicle and asked the driver to start the motor. The puzzled driver asked, "Where to?" By that time, Gayatri, a few *brahmacharins* together with Sreekumar's father and mother had somehow managed to get into the van. The Mother replied to the driver, "To Son Madhavan Nair's house." Again the driver was in a dilemma, "I don't know who that is." Understanding where the Mother wanted to go, Sreekumar's father gave the directions to the driver, and they proceeded. The Mother seemed very restless. Though the house was not very far away, she went on urging, "Drive faster, drive faster." Everyone was surprised at the Mother showing such excitement and hurry.

In five minutes or so the van reached the front yard of the house. A man was waiting outside. Like one who has gone mad, he rushed towards the Mother, fell at her feet and cried like a little child. It was none other than Madhavan Nair. He went on exclaiming, "Compassion, compassion, what compassion, what compassion." Most affectionately, the Mother lifted him up, caressed and consoled him. The devotee together with his wife ceremoniously washed the Mother's feet and led her inside the house. As the Mother made her first step into the house, the clock struck eleven times. Madhavan Nair once again burst into tears as if he was reminded of something. The Mother went to their *puja* room and performed a small *puja*.

The *brahmacharins* sang, *Arariyunnu nin maha vaibhavam...*

Who knows Thy greatness,
O Thou who art the substratum
Of this illusory world.
Thousands and thousands of living beings
Seek Thy divine, radiant smile...
Who knows Thy greatness
O Mother, who knows...

As the nature of life
As the vitality of life itself
As the one who delights
In expressing compassion,
Existing as unlimited love,
O Devi, who art the blissful nectar of life,
Who knows...

O Thou who art worshipped by *tapasvis*,
O Thou who destroys affliction,
O Thou whose mind is inclined
To bless the ascetics,
O Thou who art ever-young,
O Thou art the beauty of the mind,
Please come, O Devi, Please come.
Who knows...

The family members could not contain their emotions. They all burst into tears, which in turn brought tears to everybody's eyes.

The events had unfolded like a divine drama. We were spectators watching it without understanding the real meaning of it. Actually, this is what had transpired:

Mr. Madhavan Nair was a devotee of the Holy Mother who was fortunate enough to be initiated by her. Twice before when the Mother had visited Sreekumar's house, he had prayed that she would come into his house as well and purify it. For some unknown reason his wish did not get fulfilled on either of those occasions. This time too, when Madhavan Nair had heard that the Mother was going to visit Sreekumar's house, he had expressed his wish to the Mother. She had agreed to come when she had the time. With great expectation and a heart full of joy, he re-arranged his *puja* room and waited the whole day for the Mother to come. "Nobody should eat today unless Mother comes," he had told his wife and children. The day passed. Night fell. He came out of the house, stood unmoving, waiting for the Mother. With a very determined voice he stated, "I will wait until eleven o'clock today. If she doesn't come..." He stopped and remained where he stood. The time slowly passed. The clock rang nine-thirty, ten, ten-thirty, ten-forty-five...At ten minutes to eleven, the devotee's heart flipped around like a fish out of water. "Won't the Mother come?" he asked himself. His longing became stronger and stronger. From the deepest corner of his heart came a whisper, "Yes, she will come. My Mother will come." At that very moment he saw the headlights of the vehicle. It came and stopped in front of his house. Madhavan Nair's emotions broke their bounds; he rushed towards the Mother and fell at her feet, crying like a child and repeating out loud, "O Amma, what compassion, what compassion..." Then when she stepped into his house, it was exactly eleven o'clock sharp! That was what happened.

1 April 1984

On a very calm and quiet morning, the sun slowly rose from the eastern horizon. Brahmacharin Unnikrishnan was performing the *puja* to the *peetham* on which the Mother sat during *Devi Bhava*. The eighty year old "Acchamma," Amma's paternal grandmother, sat in front of the temple making garlands and flower petals needed for the evening's *Devi Bhava*. The ringing of the bell from the temple mingled with the sound of the ocean waves, adding a special charm and sacredness to the silent atmosphere.

Breakfast was served at nine-thirty. It consisted of *kanji* with salt, nothing else, not even pickles. This was the usual morning food. About the food the Mother says,

Amma: Have it if you like. This is an Ashram, a place for *tyagis*, not for *bhogis*. If you want to eat good, delicious food, stay at home. Taste is good for the tongue, not for the heart. It will nourish the tongue and ruin the heart. Mother does not insist. Follow this only if you want to attain the goal. Otherwise, you can do as you like. Those who do not have *vairagya* cannot live here at the Ashram.

THE VISITORS

The Special Branch Deputy Superintendent of Police from Quilon came to the Ashram to collect information about the *Vedanta Vidyalaya* run by the Ashram and about the foreigners who stayed here. He noted down whatever was necessary. Since he was empathetic towards the Mother's activities, he liked the peaceful Ashram atmosphere very much. He wanted to see the Holy Mother and therefore waited.

A group of ten *Siddha Veda* followers (a spiritual path established by Swami Sivananda Paramahamsa, Guru of Swami Nityananda) came at noon. The group consisted of both men and women. They had attended a conference in a nearby town and had heard about the Mother at the conference venue and thus came to see her. They started cooking their own special food, a mixture of rice and green gram. Among them was a young man who walked around with an air of pride mixed with contempt.

Followed by the *Siddha Veda* people a large group of devotees from Tamil Nadu arrived. It was as if the entire Ashram premises were filled with people. There were only a few *brahmacharins* in the Ashram who had to run around to make arrangements to provide food for the devotees and to find a place to keep their luggage safely.

By three o'clock the Holy Mother finally returned from Sreekumar's house with the *brahmacharins*. Her presence showered spiritual bliss all around. Waves of enthusiasm rippled everywhere. At the same time, as if inspired by an invisible power, everyone's movements were automatically controlled. It became impossible for anyone to behave otherwise. Her mere presence enlivened the whole atmosphere with a special vibration of peace and tranquility. It was so obvious and clear that all could experience it.

The Mother straightaway went to the hut and started giving *darshan* to the large crowd of people. As it was Sunday, there were more people than usual. At Sreekumar's house she had been surrounded by adults and children until the last moment. There was not even a sign of impatience on her face as she finally ended *darshan* there at one o'clock and then went to her room.

One of the Mother's spiritual children, Gangadharan (now known as Sarvatma), once remarked, "Jesus was crucified only once, but here the Mother crucifies her body every moment for the world. This self-crucifixion of the Mother can be understood only by another one like her."

The *Siddha Veda* people stood silently observing everything. They were not standing in the *darshan* line. All of a sudden, the Mother called one of the women who came with them and asked her,

Amma: Aren't you the wife of S...? What happened to your husband when he went to the office without wearing a shirt? (The followers of Siddha Veda never wear a shirt.) Didn't he meet with some trouble there? You are not on very good terms with your husband, are you? Mother knows that there are a lot of conflicts in your family life. Maybe these family problems are God's will to make both of you get closer to your Guru.

The lady was stunned to hear the Mother speaking about so many things concerning her family affairs. This was her first meeting with the Mother; she had never met her before. She became very emotional and started to cry.

Next the Mother called the young man who seemed very proud and looked at everything with contempt. The young man was surprised when the Mother suddenly made a sign for him to come closer. He turned around and looked towards the back, thinking that the Mother was calling somebody else who was standing behind him in the queue. The Mother then called out, "No, no,

it is definitely you, son...come." The man, still unable to
come out of that surprised mood, slowly moved towards
the Mother.

She received him as she had with the others. He sat
next to the Mother, facing her. Placing her left hand on
his shoulder, the Mother with a smile on her face, gently
said,

Amma: Son, what do you want to realize? *Iswara* (God)
or *eecha* (housefly)? If it is God, then the ego should die.
Do you know the nature of an *eecha*? It flies around, sits
in decayed and rotten things, spreads all kinds of conta-
gious diseases, and finally it dies getting stuck to jaggery
syrup or molasses. In the same way, an egotistic person
will ruin himself and ruins others as well.

Therefore, you decide whether to realize God or the
ego. The ego is not an adornment to anyone, whether
he is spiritual or worldly. It always looks ugly in the eyes
of others. We ourselves should become aware of that
ugliness. Then it becomes easy to remove it. Son, here,
Mother has no differences. She accepts everyone equally.
Whether it is a person who follows the path of *Siddha
Veda* or something else, it is the same to Mother. The
ego, in any case, is the worst enemy no matter which
path one follows. That is the first thing that should be
uprooted. Mother knows that you are trying for that, but
become more aware of it and at least try not to express it
externally.

You think that yours is the only right path while you
look down on the other paths and their followers. Son,

this external show is not what is needed. Try to acquire inner beauty, then the outside will automatically be beautified.

The young man was dumbfounded. He was truly humbled. Later he remarked, "Never before have I met a person who could read my mind so clearly and specifically. She could easily deflate my ego with the same ease as pricking a balloon."

The experience of these two people appeared to be quite convincing for the whole group of *Siddha Veda* people. Now they too joined with the other devotees who were lined up to see the Mother. The Mother addressed the group,

Amma: The yoking of *jivatman* and the *Paramatman* is the goal. It is good to see that you children are doing *sadhana* according to the instructions given by your Guru. It is a rare blessing that you could dedicate everything for Self-Realization. Children, Mother is really happy to see you all together.

The lady whom Mother had called first stood shedding tears. The Mother called her once again, wiped her tears and lovingly consoled her saying,

Amma: Child, don't worry. It is all for the best. Acquire more strength to confront the impediments that might arise in your spiritual path. We cannot change situations in life, but we can change our attitude towards them. Try, Mother is with you.

The Mother then talked with the devotees who came from Tamil Nadu. They were very excited. Each one of them wanted to be in the front row.

Without even going to her room for a minute, the Mother came directly from the hut and sat in the front verandah of the temple to begin the *bhajan* at five o'clock. The singing started. The Mother soared to the heights of supreme devotion and love. Along with her, she carried the hearts of the devotees as well. The Mother and the *brahmacharins* sang *Karunya Varidhe Krishna*, a favorite for many people.

> O Krishna, Ocean of Compassion,
> The thirst for life is ever-increasing,
> There is no peace for the mind
> And alas, confusion overwhelms me.
>
> Forgiving all wrongs,
> Wipe off the sweat from my brow,
> O Kanna, I have no support
> Other than Thy Worshipful Lotus Feet.
>
> O Krishna, my throat is drying up,
> My eyes are failing, my feet are tired,
> And I am falling to the ground,
> O Krishna...

After the *bhajan*, when the *Devi Bhava* started, the *Siddha Veda* people packed up and got ready to leave the Ashram. It seemed that it was against their policy to go in for the *Devi Bhava*. But suddenly the two persons who had personal experiences with the Mother, insisted that they should go in and receive the Mother's blessings. The others had to agree, so they waited for the two to go up to the Mother during *Devi Bhava*.

The *Devi Bhava* was over by three-thirty in the morning. The Mother, as usual, went around to the devotees once again to make sure that everyone had a mat and a place to sleep. Many of them preferred to sleep on the sand. One devotee said, "Mother, this is a rare blessing and great opportunity that we get to sleep in this fine sand. We may not get this chance in the future. This place will be all filled with big buildings and houses of devotees."

The next day during a discussion about the path of *Siddha Veda*, the Mother related, "The *Siddha Veda* children came, having made the decision that none of them would go in for the *Devi Bhava*. Therefore, Mother also decided that at least one should come in. And two of them did so." (All laugh)

Devotee: Amma is the greatest trickster in the world.

Amma: Mother's tricks are not to gain anything for herself but to make you gain something. Mother plays tricks only when there is ego and selfishness. She flows to where there is innocence and surrender. Give a little space for God; a little is enough. He will flow into you. We are now completely closed, not even a hair's breadth of a crevice is there for God to peep in. To create that space as much as she can is Mother's job!

It is wonderful to watch the way Mother deals with and treats the people who come to see her at the

Ashram. She has her own unique way of being with each one. Each person's mind is an open book to the Mother.

The topic changed. Somebody asked Mother about Dattan, the leper. The Mother had licked and sucked the pus from his leprous wounds every day. It was an awful sight for everyone. One of the *brahmacharins* asked what she felt when she saw him. The Mother replied,

Amma: Mother sees him in the same way as she sees you or anybody else. He is also my child. How can a Mother feel loathing or hatred when she sees her son or daughter, however ugly or badly diseased he or she is? In fact, Mother has a lot of compassion and love for him. Mother's heart melts when she sees him.

Question: Isn't the disease the result of his actions in the previous birth?

Amma: Why do you think such things? If Mother says "Yes," then you will ask, "What kind of sin did he commit?" If Mother gives a description of that as well, then you might feel, "Then let him experience it since he had committed numerous sins in the previous birth." You yourself will develop aversion to him and consider him as a sinner. This is closing down your own heart, not allowing it to open and flow with love. If Mother gives the answer, "No," then it is against the scriptures because each one of us is experiencing the fruit of our past actions. Therefore, forget about it. The real way is to think and act with the attitude, "If it is his *karma* which makes him suffer like this, then it is my *karma* and *dharma* to love him and serve him." If you think without compassion, that is narrowing yourself down. Your path is to become more and more expansive.

A *sadhak's* heart should flow to everyone equally. He should not think about faults and failures. He should always think about victory and goodness. You might say, "This is the *sadhana* period. We are only *sadhaks*. That means a *sadhak* will err and fall, won't he?" Don't even think in that way. You should make your mind stronger and stronger to fight and win against the obstacles.

Children, let your minds open up fully and contain love with all its fragrance and beauty. Hatred and aversion will only make it look ugly. Love towards everyone gives real beauty, enhancing both the giver as well as the receiver.

Question: Mother, why do you receive Dattan at the very end?

Amma: The reason is that once Mother calls that son, the pus, blood and all the other filth from his body will be on Mother's *sari*. The germs from his wounds also will be on Mother's body as she licks all his wounds during *Devi Bhava*. It is to avoid the germs from spreading into other devotees' bodies that Mother calls him at the very end. Not only that, if Mother calls him in the beginning or in the middle, again the other devotees who have not yet come to the Mother will not be able to do so with an open heart, for they might be reacting to his leprosy. They will be benefited only if they come to Mother with fully opened hearts. Therefore, it is only for her children's sake that Mother calls him at the very end.

2 April 1984

Since morning today, the Mother had been pressing her forehead saying that she had a severe headache. Some of the newer *brahmacharins* offered her different medicines like Amritamjan and Vicks Vaporub. Somebody else asked, "Mother, shall I bring some pain killers?" The Mother smilingly rejected all these and said, "This pain doesn't just go like that. Medicine cannot heal or cure this."

The senior *brahmacharins* and other close devotees understood the meaning of what the Mother was saying. Whenever Mother took a disease from someone, whatever it was, her body had to undergo suffering. It was quite usual. This headache must have also been acquired for the same reason. However, the Mother, even though she was suffering, went on talking to the devotees about different spiritual matters.

One devotee put forth a question about the awakening of the *kundalini*.

Amma: Nowadays, talking about *kundalini* and its awakening has become a fashion. Another word which is usually used is *yoga*. They simply talk about it. Let them put forth at least a little effort to understand the real meaning of these words. The real meaning can only be known through *sadhana* and experience. Once you start getting real experience, i.e., as you go deeper into your own self, you will stop talking about it. Waves occur only when the water is shallow, not where it is deep. As you dive deeper and deeper into the subtle realms of spirituality, thought waves slowly end. There will be only silence.

After all, why should you think and worry about *kundalini* awakening and all that? Some people go around to different *sannyasins* and *gurus* asking whether their *kundalini* is awake or not. Some others try to find a *guru* who can do it with one touch. Children, do not waste your time asking such questions. Do your *sadhana* sincerely with love and devotion. There will be progress. On the other hand, if you are always worried about the awakening of *kundalini*, then your mind is split, and that will affect your spiritual growth.

One *brahmacharin* brought some rice and vegetables for the Mother on a plate, but she did not eat it. A householder devotee who was nearly sixty years old remained seated without going for lunch. The Mother noticed him and said, "Come on, Mother will feed you." She took him to the kitchen and fed him with her own hands. As he swallowed each ball of rice which the Mother herself put into his mouth, tears of inexpressible joy ran down his cheeks.

Here human intellect fails to understand the meaning in a thirty-year-old ordinary looking village girl becoming the mother of a sixty-year-old man. Any meaning the intellect gives will be either a misinterpretation or an interpretation stuffed with reasoning or logic. To find meaning we must look not on the plane of the intellect but on the plane of the experience which can only be known through the heart.

The Mother's headache continued. She wanted to be alone for a while, so she went and lay down at the southern side of the Ashram beside the backwaters. Nobody went there to disturb her.

At three-thirty arrangements were made in the library to show a film on the Mother to some devotees from the outside. With the enthusiasm and curiosity of a child, the Holy Mother also came and sat with the others. Seeing her own stout body in the movie, she called out, "Oh look, a demon," and started laughing. She remarked, "What will be my fate if I put on weight like this?" and again she laughed.

Scenes from the Mother's thirtieth birthday celebration, e.g., the chanting of the Divine Name and the performance of the *pada puja* (ceremonial washing of the holy Mother's Feet), were shown. Seeing her children sipping the sacred water with which the feet were washed, the Mother exclaimed, "What nonsense is that! Will Realization be obtained if the feet are washed and the water is drunk? Humility is what is needed."

The Mother still had the headache. Having locked the door, she lay down in the hut all alone. She again came out when it was five o'clock and she looked refreshed. The headache was gone and she was as cheerful as ever.

Just as children keep a stock of peanuts in their pockets taking them out every now and then to chew, the

Mother little by little experiences the stock of diseases which she takes from her devotees. One can see her suffering with severe pain at one time and not having any the next moment. She simply will get up and walk away as if nothing had happened.

There were some occasions when she was seen suffering a lot, even unable to sit without someone else's help. But the next moment when a devotee or an aspirant came to see her and talk to her, she would suddenly get up with as much energy as she always had and talk to that person for a long time.

At this time a devotee full of humor came. He talked very freely to the Mother. Every now and then, he cracked a joke and each time the Mother laughed with a full heart. At one point, he opened his mouth wide. He was about to imitate another person. In a split second, before he could close it, the Mother took a handful of sand and tossed it into his mouth. It was all over in a second. It was so quick. The devotee suddenly stood up and went on spitting out the sand. As he did so he expressed great joy, laughing and saying, "This is what she does to a blabber-mouth like me." Seeing him struggling with the sand in his mouth, the Mother rolled on the ground and laughed uproariously.

The devotee rinsed out his mouth and came back to where the Mother was sitting. He said to the other devotees, "What a fool I am. I should have swallowed the sand. Who knew what it was? It was *prasad*. Had I swallowed it, I might have attained Realization. We always think after the event." He sighed and stopped. Many children were gathered around the Mother to witness this scene, as were almost all of the *brahmacharins*. Since this devotee, who was close to sixty-years old, was a classically trained singer, the Mother asked him to sing a song. By vocalizing the introductory cadence to open the song, coupled with making funny gestures, he once again created an amusing scene causing everyone to laugh, including the Mother.

The evening *bhajan* started at six-thirty. The Holy Mother was also present. It was raining heavily with thunder and lightning. The haunting roar of the ocean waves beating on the sand during the storm served as a constant drone from the west. The *bhajan* continued. The Mother in her spiritually intoxicated mood swung from side to side as she sang. The sound of the dripping rain drops provided background accompaniment for the song *Amme Bhagavati Nitya Kanye Devi...*

> O Mother Divine, the Eternal Virgin,
> I bow to Thee for Thy gracious glance.
>
> O Maya, Mother of the Universe,
> O Pure Awareness-Bliss,
> O Great Goddess, I bow to Thee.
>
> O Source of all the mantras in the four Vedas,
> I bow to Thee again and again.
>
> O Thou, the Parrot in the nest of Omkara,
> I bow to Thy Holy Feet.

O Thou Who dwellest in the
Lotus face of Lord Brahma,
O Essence of the four Vedas, I bow to Thee.

All of a sudden the Mother's voice was heard above the music, "Who is that son?" The *bhajan* abruptly stopped. There was utter silence. Nobody understood why the Mother asked this question. Each one thought that he had done something wrong as the Mother again asked,

Amma: Who is that who played the wrong *talam* (beat)? Do not overburden yourself with great sin by doing so. Missing time while singing *bhajans* will bring harm. If you do not play with concentration, you will miss the *talam*. Many celestial beings and subtle beings are listening while we sing. Each instrument has a *devata* (demi-god). That *devata* will curse if we do not play the *talam* correctly.

This is another example of the discipline the Mother teaches as she uses every situation to impress upon the children how they must be ever-mindful of the actions they perform, even while playing an instrument.

They continued with the *bhajan*:

O Goddess of the world, it is just Thy play
To create the world and save it by undoing it.

O Mind of the mind, O Dearest Mother,
I am just a mere worm in Thy play.

O Thou who art merciful to the afflicted
Who doest everything without doing anything,
I bow to Thee.

O Kali of black hue,
Destroyer of the demon Mahisha,
Sankari, whose eyes are like petals of a lotus,
I bow to Thee.

O Thou who art ever young, Destroyer of sorrow,
O Thou of Great Soul, Bhaskari, I bow to Thee.

The singing continued until quarter-past-eight when the *bhajan* and the *arati* were concluded. The Mother remained on her seat leaning against the wall. Her eyes were closed as the devotees and the residents prostrated to her one by one. Still in an ecstatic mood, she continued every now and then to sing some *kirtans*. The inner bliss in which she reveled manifested itself outwardly as bursts of laughter.

After some time she lay down on the lap of a boy who was hardly seven years old. She returned to her normal mood and began patting and caressing the boy. The Mother asked him to sing. He sang *Kanna Ni Yenne*...

O Krishna, have You forgotten me?
O Thou with the color of a stormy cloud,

Have you forgotten me?
Not seeing You, my suffering increases
And my heart is unable to understand anything.

The Mother seemed very absorbed in the little boy's innocent devotion and singing. There was a beautiful smile on her face. When the boy finished the song, she asked, "Son, do you know *Manasa Vacha?*" He answered, "Yes." "Then sing," she requested. The boy could hardly sing the first four lines. He stopped and softly told the Mother, "That's all I know." The Mother went on singing the song celebrating the Divine, as both the devotees and the residents were gathered around her witnessing all the different moods she displayed.

Through my mind, speech and actions,
I remember Thee incessantly.
Why then art Thou delaying
To show Thy mercy to me, Beloved Mother?

Years have passed
But still my mind has no peace,
O darling Mother, please grant me some relief.

My mind sways like a boat caught in a storm,
O Mother, give me a little peace of mind
Lest I become a lunatic.

I am tired, Mother, it is unbearable;
I do not want such a life,
I cannot stand Your tests,
O Mother, I cannot endure it!

> I am a miserable destitute
> I have no one but You, Mother
> Please stop Your tests,
> Extend Your hand and pull me up.

All of a sudden the Holy Mother got up and went to the kitchen. It was time for supper. The Mother herself served rice gruel to all her children. When supper was over, the *brahmacharins* left the Mother in order to do their *sadhana*. Nobody wanted to leave her, but she would not let them stay around her during the times when they were supposed to perform their *sadhana*.

The silence of the night prevailed everywhere. Except for the resounding call of the ocean waves, there was no sound. The *brahmacharins* were seen meditating both in the meditation hall and on the verandah. Some of them sat outside under the coconut trees. When it was eleven o'clock the residents retired to bed, having finished that day's *sadhana*, to begin again at four-thirty the next morning.

The Ashram atmosphere was totally still. A nightin-gale was heard singing a haunting melody. After a few moments, the bird also stopped. The stars twinkled in the deep, dark velvety sky. Suddenly breaking the quiet of the night, the Mother's voice was heard from her room. She was singing, *Anandamayi Brahmamayi...*

> O Blissful One, O Absolute One,
> O Blissful One, O Absolute One,
> Whose form is of unsurpassed beauty
> O Blissful One, O Absolute One...

Her voice had an unusual touch of pathos. A few *brahmacharins* awoke upon hearing the song. They sat on the verandah of their huts and silently listened to the Mother. The song was powerful enough to make one glide into meditation effortlessly as the haunting, soulful melody unfolded..."*Aradharangal..*" (second verse of the same song):

> Crossing the six mystic centers, the yogis
> Come to know Thee, the invaluable Treasure.
> Thy Glory, O Infinite Power,
> Is only slightly revealed to them.

The ocean waves served as the background melody. The heartrending song sung by the Mother filled the atmosphere with divine fervor. The cool, gentle breeze responded to the song and reverently carried the vibrations to the far corners of this enchanted night.

The Mother stopped singing. Silence prevailed but only for a short time. It was again broken by the rhythmic jingling of the Mother's anklets. She must have been dancing, undoubtedly immersed in a blissful dance, forgetting herself and the external world, all alone in her own world beyond this one, where nobody else had access. Each of the *brahmacharins* who had woken up felt that she was dancing in his very own heart. Sad that they could not see their Beloved Mother dancing with the anklets on her feet, but visualizing and imagining in their minds how she must have been gliding the Holy Feet through rapturous steps of a mystical dance of

Devi, they remained on the verandah of the hut with their eyes fixed, looking at the Mother's room.

At last the sound of the anklets stopped. The residents waited for a few more minutes, hoping that they would hear another song or more jingling of the anklets again. But thereafter no sound came from the Mother's room, so they all went back to bed as the clock struck twelve midnight.

3 April 1984

The clock in the dining hall rang ten times. A little girl in white clothes was making sandalwood paste for the morning's *puja*. As usual Acchamma was doing her daily duty of making garlands. The eighty-year-old lady still gets up at three-thirty every morning, takes a shower in cold water, does her daily chanting of the Divine Name, sings some *bhajans* and then goes out to pluck flowers for the *puja* in the temple and for making garlands to adorn the statues and images of the Deity and for the Mother too. She is so old that she cannot even walk properly without bending over. Her determination, however, far outruns her old age.

On one side of the Ashram the *brahmacharins* were heard chanting the *Lalita Sahasranama*. The ringing of the bell while the *puja* was being performed echoed in the atmosphere. An enchanting musical note emerged from one of the huts. Markus, the hard-working devotee from Germany, was playing the flute.

This morning one of the *brahmacharins* went to the Mother's room and complained that his *vasanas* still remained even after doing *sadhana* for a long time. He blamed the Mother for not showering her Grace on him. He said that if the Mother did not remove his *vasanas* soon he would commit suicide.

Looking at him, the Mother sat without uttering a word for some time. When he cooled down a little, she called him to her and lovingly said,

Amma: Son, do you know how much energy you have wasted this morning? Mother appreciates your determination and thirst to realize God. It is fine and good that you feel the urgency, but patience is the most important thing that a *sadhak* must have to attain the goal. A true *sadhak* will not become impatient at all. Son, do you know that our forefathers, the great saints and sages of the past, did years and years of severe penance in order to realize God? They never got impatient. Had they been impatient, nothing would have been achieved. It would have been a waste of time and energy if impatience ran their lives.

Even to achieve momentary worldly goals, one needs a lot of patience coupled with self-effort. So what can be said about spiritual realization, which is the only thing which bestows ever-lasting happiness and immortality?

Suppose someone wants to go to a foreign country, say America. First of all, he must apply for a passport and then must wait patiently for it to be issued. This will not happen in a day or two, for these legal matters take time. There are many legal procedures before a passport will be issued. Once it is issued to him, he must then obtain a visa. Above all, he will have to find a person to sponsor him. All these things are time-consuming. One should not get impatient and say, "No, no, I must go to America right at this moment. Why is it not possible? I must get the visa and the sponsorship this very day. Otherwise, I will commit suicide." Thus, if one gets impatient and commits suicide a few days after submitting the applications, what will be the result? He simply dies. Nothing else will happen. It does not matter how many births one takes; if he or she is not endowed with patience, God-realization is not possible. To fulfill your wish, you should move slowly, steadily, patiently, carefully and sincerely. If everything works out properly, you will achieve your goal. If you get impatient, everything will be spoiled. You will not achieve your goal by getting impatient because you become mentally restless and scattered. By fragmenting yourself, you lose all your concentration and energy necessary to gain it. Constantly striving patiently, you can slowly make steady progress.

Son, Grace is not something which you can snatch from God or the Guru. Grace is something which spontaneously flows to the disciple. No one can say when, where or how it happens. You have no control over it. You can, and you must act. The rest depends on Grace. It just happens when the Guru feels that the disciple is fully ripe and ready. For this attainment, you need patience. You must put forth effort without thinking of the result. Then, when it is time, the Guru gives it. Do not spend time worrying about it.

Vasanas cannot be eliminated so easily. Son, how long have you been doing meditation?

The Mother paused and waited for an answer. The *brahmacharin* softly replied, "For the last two years." She inquired, "Are you doing meditation constantly? No. How many hours have you set aside to do meditation? Seven or eight hours at the most? The *brahmacharin* kept quiet. It seemed that the Mother was up to something. Again she asked, "How old are you now?" He started feeling ashamed to speak, as if he suspected something. Yet he answered, "Twenty-eight." She continued to inquire, "Have you meditated or chanted before coming to Mother?" "No," he admitted.

Amma: All right. Now look, son, you have done meditation only for two years, yet you have been in this world for twenty-six years before coming to spirituality. Now, that is only for this lifetime. Before that, nobody knows how many births you have taken and how much you have indulged. Now you are saying that all these accumulated tendencies should have gone within these two years' time. Not only that, here you are not even constantly engaged in getting rid of your *vasanas*. It may be true that you meditate for seven or eight hours a day, but what about the concentration you get? Let us say that you will get one minute of concentration when you sit for one hour. Thus, if you calculate, it will not even be ten minutes of concentration a day. So it is clear that you are not engaged in attempting to destroy the vasanas constantly. Furthermore, my son, previously you were constantly engaged in enjoying and indulging while you lived in this world. Now tell Mother whether there is any meaning in your argument?

The *brahmacharin* was tongue-tied. He turned pale as he sat with his head hung down. The Holy Mother put him on her lap and consoled him, saying,

Amma: Don't worry, son. Mother just wanted to make you aware that it requires long-term practice and patience. At least you are aware that those *vasanas* exist and that they need to be eliminated. That in itself shows that you have evolved. This awareness itself is a great accomplishment. People in the world do not even know that there are terrible *vasanas* in them. They are totally drowned in them. Compared to those people you children are much more evolved. Be happy. Why do you worry so much when Mother is here to take care of you? Mother is here for you, isn't she?

The Mother came to the hut by ten-thirty and the *darshan* began. One of the devotees asked a question about performing worship to different *devatas*. The Holy Mother replied,

Amma: Although *devatas* are superior to human beings, they depend on humans for their food. That is why in the *puranas* and epics we find stories of *devas* who obstruct those who are doing penance. Once a human being reaches the state of non-action, these *devas* will not get their share, which is mainly gained through various rituals and oblations. When a human being evolves to the state of *sannyasa*, he renounces all actions, even rituals and oblations. Thus the *devas* lose what they had been getting from that particular individual. Action is meant only for mortal humans, not for one who rises to the state of immortality. That means actions cannot bind such a person. He too works but he renounces the fruit of it, which also means renouncing the action itself. Detachment from an action that you do means you are not doing it, that is, your mind is not identified with the action. Therefore, there is nobody to give and take, so this results in the *devas* losing their share. They do not want that to happen; that is why they create obstacles for a person who does penance to realize the Self.

There are different aspects of divinity which are potent within us. When we do good and wise actions, the goodness in us will be invoked and will lead us to progress and prosperity. But then, as we continue our striving, when we try to concentrate all our attention on the Supreme Self, this goodness itself will become an obstacle because, in order to attain the Ultimate Reality, i.e., Self-Realization, we have to transcend everything, even goodness. Goodness is also a bondage. These great ideals also exist as thoughts. To reach the state of non-action, the state of complete renunciation, all thoughts must go. The mind must disappear. If the mind has to disappear, all thoughts must disappear because the mind is nothing but thoughts. When we try to obtain that thoughtless state, the same good thoughts will also create impediments. Even good thoughts will try to pull you back to the same old state of action. They cannot exist without your cooperation, without your acting. Actions, doing good things, performing sacred ceremonies are food for these good thoughts; that is what makes them exist.

Rituals and other ceremonies will help to cleanse and purify the mind. Through rituals and other religious observances, the mind, filled with all kinds of evil thoughts, will become good and virtuous. When that is gained, don't stop; proceed and transcend that as well. If you attach yourself to the good and virtuous, these again will become habits and consequently *vasanas*. Whether good or bad, a *vasana* is an obstacle in the path towards attainment of the state of Perfection. Therefore, do not halt for a long time with good thoughts; go beyond them. Only if you go beyond all goodness and badness will you reach the state where there is neither good nor bad, neither sorrow nor happiness, neither success nor failure, the state where you always remain as That, That alone. It does not matter whether you are bound with a golden chain or an iron one. Bondage is bondage, no matter with what one is bound. Therefore, to make the mind completely still, goodness also should be transcended. Good or bad thoughts will always create waves in the mind, which will disturb its stillness.

Devotee: It is all a question of renouncing all ego-centric thoughts and actions, isn't it, Mother?

Amma: You are right, Son. Thoughts and actions which would feed the ego in any way should not be done. Good actions and good thoughts also will bind you if they are performed or thought with an attitude of "I" and "mine." This is why it is said that one should approach a Perfect Master. He alone can help you get rid of the feelings of "I" and "mine." It is very subtle but strong. Subtle *vasanas* are more powerful than the gross ones. Things that are subtle have more pervasiveness also. When ice melts, it becomes water which is more subtle and powerful and more pervasive. Water, when heated up or boiled, becomes vapor, which is still more subtle, powerful and pervasive. It has such power that this steam is used to run huge machines. Again, water power, when it is converted into electrical energy, becomes much more subtle, powerful and pervasive. In the same way, the mind and the thoughts with which it is constituted will become stronger and more pervasive when the subtlety increases. Human effort alone will not be sufficient enough to remove the deep-rooted subtle tendencies. God's or the Guru's Grace is a must. That alone can take the mind to the subtlest state where there are no thoughts and no mind. In that state of supreme subtlety, the mind transforms into the most powerful source of inexhaustible energy. In that state it becomes all-pervasive energy itself. That is the final death of the ego, which will no longer return.

Everyone sat amazed for a long time, looking at the Mother with all humility and reverence. It seemed that

they all became aware of her greater dimension and omniscience. The most scientific explanations about the
highest philosophical truths told in a very simple and lu-
cid language by the Mother filled their hearts with immense bliss and inspiration. Her simplicity and innocence are fully reflected in her talk as well.

A simple looking village girl who had not even completed her formal education in school, who had not
studied even the preliminary texts of spirituality, who
was not at all in the habit of reading anything, was talking like an eminent scholar and has become the master
of scholars and of highly educated men and women! Is
this not an extraordinary phenomena? Those who have
eyes will see it. Those who have ears will hear it. Those
who have a heart will know it.

The Mother paused for a while. She closed her eyes
and was transported to another world of her own for a
few moments. Uttering "Shiva, Shiva," and whirling her
right index finger in the air, the Mother opened her
eyes.

Devotee: Brahmacharin Balu told me of an incident
that showed how disobedience and egoism in front of
the Guru can bring about one's ruin.
Amma: (with the curiosity of a child) What is that?
What did he say?
Devotee: He told me about a boy named Hari who often used to visit the Ashram and who did *sadhana* as
you instructed. One day he didn't eat because he was
upset with you for not taking him with you on one of

your trips. In order to console him and to make him eat, you offered a banana to him. He would not accept it. Again and again with the love and affection of a mother, you expressed the wish that he accept the banana and eat it. But each time when you offered it, he rejected it, saying, "No, I don't want it." All of a sudden your facial expression changed and you became very serious. You threw the banana away saying, "Here goes your last fruit. Son, this was your last fruit." Brahmacharin Balu told me that from then on that boy could never meditate even for a second. So he wanders here and there simply wasting his time and energy. He left spiritual life and now leads a worldly life with all kinds of problems.

Amma: Mother usually doesn't say such things. Yet no matter how much Mother humbled herself before him, he would not obey on that day, and the words just came out. Even Mother herself could not stop them. Maybe that was his fate. God will not tolerate the ego. Children, the ego can cause great disasters.

It was four o'clock in the afternoon. The Holy Mother wanted to listen to a particular song titled *Saranagati* (Give Refuge, O' Mother). A tape recorder was brought and the song was played. It had been sung by a resident with accompaniments. The Mother was completely absorbed in the song. The hut was filled with devotees.

O Mother Immortal, Who is Shakti,
The very Embodiment of Power,
Who dwells in the essence of all beings,
Who is the Personification of Auspiciousness,
And who is Purity in the exalted sense,
I bow to Thy Holy Feet.

After some time, the Mother got up and went out. She roamed around for a while in the coconut grove. Later she related, "Mother could not listen to that song and give her heart completely to it. Had she done so she would have lost all control, which Mother did not want to do at that time since there were many people in the hut who know nothing about these matters. That is why Mother got up and left." The song was over. It was time for the ensuing *bhajan*.

One by one the residents and the devotees from the outside came and sat in front of the temple. One devotee still sat in the hut and meditated. Suddenly the Mother stepped in asking, "Oh, son, haven't you gone?" She sat on the cot. The devotee made a full prostration in front of the Mother. He took the Mother's feet and placed them on his head. His eyes filled with tears, he prayed to the Mother thus: "Mother, these feet of yours are enough for me. I don't want anything else. O Mother, please don't make me play games in this world of plurality."

The Mother carefully listened to him. Casting a compassionate glance at him, the Mother caressed her son with all love and affection. "Come, son, it is time for the *bhajan,*" she said as she went out and walked towards the temple.

The *bhajan* began as usual at six-thirty. The Mother was playing the *ganjira* (a small hand drum with only one head). In a few minutes she put it down and picked up the cymbals and began playing. It seemed that the Mother was struggling to keep her mind down. Now she also put the cymbals down and sang, creating waves of unconditional bliss which radiated all around with *Manase Nin Svantamayi...*

> Remember, O mind, this supreme truth:
> Nobody is your own!
>
> Because of doing meaningless actions,
> You are wandering in the ocean of this world.
>
> Even though people honor you,
> Calling you, "Lord, Lord,"
> It will be for a short time only.
>
> Your body, which has been honored for so long,
> Must be cast off when life departs.
>
> For which sweetheart have you been struggling
> All this time, not even caring for your life?
>
> Even she will be frightened by your dead body
> And will not accompany you.

Trapped in the subtle snare of Maya as you are,
Do not forget the Sacred Name
Of the Divine Mother.

The Lord will attract devotion-soaked souls
Like a magnet attracts iron.

Position, prestige and wealth are impermanent;
The only Reality is the Universal Mother.

Renouncing all desires,
Let us dance in that bliss
Singing the Name of Mother Kali!

Singing with the Mother, especially in the evenings, is a joyous experience which opens the heart to a much more elevated plane of devotion. Sitting on the powerful spiritual wings of the Mother, the devotees and residents fly high every evening at *bhajans*, drinking in the nectarous bliss of Supreme Devotion. Each moment is an experience, exposing the heart to another spiritual treasure chest. Today also it happened. Everyone sang forgetting themselves.

4 April 1984

Nobody knows when the Mother will come out or when she will go back to her room. No one can predict what the Mother will do or say. We may be quite convinced that she will do a certain thing at a certain time, but instead of doing that, she will do something quite unexpected and in an entirely different manner, one we would never have even dreamt of.

Day and night are the same to her. If she wants to do something, whatever it is, the Mother does it, irrespective of time and place. She is unpredictable and irresistible. Nobody can tell how the Mother will handle a particular situation. We may have ideas and calculations, but such ideas will all crumble into pieces as we watch the way she handles things. We see only the present, just the things that happen right now in this moment; but the Mother sees through everything. Her eyes penetrate into everything, into all experiences, all happenings, going beyond into the far distant future. While we see only the gross aspects of a thing, her eyes pierce and penetrate into its recesses and draw out all the subtle, nay, even the subtlest, aspects of it.

Today a family of five from northern Kerala came to see the Mother. The Mother had not yet come to the hut. Understanding that they were newcomers and wanting to have some information, one of the residents went to them, greeted them with palms joined and politely inquired, "Where are you from? Is this the first time that you have visited the Ashram?"

The man who seemed to be the head of the family spoke. "We come from the northern part of Kerala. This is our first visit; therefore, we don't know much about the ways of the Ashram. Is it possible to meet the Mother?"

"Of course, you can. But the Mother has not yet come out. She will definitely come, but we can't say when." The resident spread a mat in front of the temple and requested them to be seated till the Mother came. It was only nine in the morning. The head of the family, not quite convinced, once again turned to the resident and asked, "Excuse me, are you sure that the Mother will come today?" "Don't worry, she will come," reassured the resident.

By nine-thirty the Mother came directly over to where they were sitting instead of going to the hut. She walked towards the temple as if she knew that the new visitors were there. They all got up and stood reverently when the Mother stepped onto the temple verandah. The resident, who was still standing there, offered his prostrations to the Mother. Seeing him doing that, all four of them, who had wondered how to honor the Mother, also did the same. The Mother said, "Actually, Mother had intended to come down in the afternoon to see the devotees. But all of a sudden she changed her mind and decided to come now."

The head of the family expressed, "We are fortunate." They were all still standing. The Mother asked them to sit. Introducing the others to the Mother, the head of the family spoke. "The others with me are my wife, son, daughter and daughter-in-law. We have been thinking about coming to see Mother for the last two months, but it always got postponed due to different reasons. Even though we could not come until now, we have all been thinking about you almost every day."

The Mother closed her eyes for a few moments. Then she called the young girl, who was their youngest daughter, and had her lie down on her lap. The girl started crying. The other family members silently shed tears.

The Mother now lifted the young girl from her lap and wiped her tears, and once again made her lie down on her lap. She gently continued patting her back. The others also wiped their tears. The Mother, in a soft voice told the father, "It was quite unfortunate for her to see the results of the test and find out that she had leukemia." There was an obvious shock which shook all three of them. They were already surprised when the Mother called the girl without their having given any hint about the terrible disease she had. Unable to restrain his feelings as was revealed by his quivering voice, the father exclaimed, "But we didn't disclose to you the fact that she had leukemia nor about how she found out about it. So you know everything." The whole family felt as he did, so once more there was an emotional upheaval.

The Mother very calmly said, "Forget about all this. Wipe your tears. It is not fair to become uncontrollably emotional in front of her. What she needs now is strength and courage to confront the situation. If you become too emotional in front of her, she will become mentally and physically weak."

They regained their mental control and discussed with the Mother what to do with their only daughter, whose name was Salini. She was still lying on the Mother's lap and the Mother continued to rub her back. Salini's mother said, "Although she is a medical student, Salini is very God-fearing. Every morning she does a *puja* to Mother Durga. Even in this condition she does it without fail. But Mother, look at her fate. God has given her this terrible disease. Most unfortunately, as you have predicted, she happened to see the results of the test which we wanted to hide from her. Mother, imagine the mental agony of a girl who knows that she is afflicted with leukemia."

At this point, the girl lifted her head from the Mother's lap, and looking at her face, Salini remarked, "Mother, I am not in mental agony as they say. I cry because I am in Mother's presence, something which I have been thirsting for."

The Holy Mother soothed her forehead and expressed her love and affection for Salini.

Amma: In fact, it is due to her *sankalpa* that she is here today. God will never forsake His sincere devotees.

The father: Amma, even without our saying anything about the disease, you disclosed it. Amma, you know everything. I believe that it is her devotion to Durga that brought us here today, and without even the least exaggeration, I believe that it is Mother Durga's lap that she is lying on now. Amma, please save her; you alone can do it.

After his plea, he fell in full prostration in front of the Mother and wept. All the while the girl was comfortably lying on the Mother's lap. When she heard her father crying, she lifted her head and said,

Salini: Father, we are at the Mother's feet. Let her do what she likes. Please don't say, "Do this, or, don't do that."

The Holy Mother looked at Salini's face in appreciation of her attitude. She asked one of the *brahmacharins* who was standing nearby to bring some sacred ash. When it was brought, the Mother held it right below her own nose, imbuing her pure, vital energy into it. Having applied some of the ash on the girl's forehead, the Mother gave the rest to her mother, instructing her to apply a little of it on her daughter's chest every day. She told Salini that she could also eat a little bit of it every morning and evening. The Mother once again consoled the family, telling them not to worry and that Mother would take care of their daughter. Salini then got up from her seat to go. Before they left, the Mother once again called all five of them to her and each one was duly attended to.

Leaving them, the Mother went and sat in the front of the meditation hall. The *brahmacharins* and a few householder devotees surrounded her.

One brahmacharin: Mother, is that girl going to be cured? Did you make a *sankalpa* to save her?"

Amma: It is not your job to think about that. Your job is to do *sadhana*. Why do you worry about such things? Everything will happen as it should happen. (Turning to the householder devotees) Anyhow, Mother liked that daughter's attitude. Death is right in front of her, yet she advises her father, "Let Mother do what She likes. Please don't say 'Do this, don't do that'." Her faith is very firm. She is one who has known the real principle of spirituality. Children, this is a good lesson for you. This is how one should take refuge in God. One should pray, "O Lord, do as You will; don't let me suggest. Let Your will be done." Anyhow, Mother feels that her disease will be cured owing to her pure *sankalpa* and right attitude.

[Note: This statement came true, as the tests done after they visited the Mother proved that the leukemia cells in her blood had completely disappeared. Slowly she regained her health and became normal. The next time they visited the Ashram they told the Mother that after meeting her, this daughter gave up all medicines except the sacred ash given by the Mother, which she strongly believed was the best to cure her disease. Salini's father said, "Even we became terribly scared thinking about what would happen to her if she stopped all her medicines, which had been sustaining her body and her life. But her determination was very strong. Finally Amma saved her."]

Brahmacharin: Amma, what happens in *samadhi?*
Amma: Nothing happens. All happenings stop in *samadhi*. That is what happens in that state.

At twelve o'clock the Mother went up to her room. By the time she reached the room, an old relative of the Mother's family arrived just for a visit. He was a middle-aged man. He knew nothing about spirituality. He considered Mother to be just an ordinary girl who belonged to his family. He had been very antagonistic about the Mother's Divine Moods before. Now, he doesn't protest, that is all. He followed the Mother and went into her room. Posing himself as one of the eldest members of the family, he walked into the room looking around with an air of pride. Then, pulling a stool toward him, he proudly sat on it, keeping one leg on the other, i.e., his right foot was placed on his left knee. This was a very disrespectful and egotistical way of sitting. Those who were present could not bear it. But as Mother was present, they could not say anything.

It is quite effortless for the Mother to adjust to any circumstance, any situation. Whatever be the circumstance, she could easily adjust it, placing herself at the level where she could be understood by the other person. Here the same thing happened. The Mother began conversing with the man, giving him a feeling that she was only an ordinary girl, a relative who was very much interested in the family affairs. It was very interesting to watch how diplomatically and, at the same time, naturally, the Mother had woven in the activities of the Ashram and the principles for which it stands. He was so caught up in *maya* that he simply shook his head for whatever Mother said and still remained seated in the same posture, putting on airs. However, this attitude did not last long. He slowly put his leg down and started massaging it with his own hands. There were also signs on his own face which made it clear that he was undergoing some severe pain in one leg. The massaging went on. The Holy Mother asked, "What happened, Uncle?"

Through the pain he replied, "I don't know why, but all of a sudden my leg started hurting without any particular reason." The Mother sincerely expressed sympathy, but the pain did not stop. It continued to increase. Unable to bear the pain, he who had walked in with an air of pride had to leave the room limping, supported by two people on either side. It seemed that it was the mental pain of the devotees who were present which got transmitted into his leg.

The Mother rose from the cot to take a shower as if she did not know anything about the things that had happened. It was two-thirty in the afternoon and until now, the Mother had not even had a glass of water to drink. Yet this was not a new experience. She always gives the least importance to her own needs. Sometimes she does not eat even if food is served at the correct time, which usually does not happen since her schedule for meals is always different. Breakfast is just one or two sips of tea. On most days it turns out that what normally is lunch and supper would become supper and breakfast and these terms are just for namesake. Then there are occasions when she is stubborn like an innocent little child and refuses to eat when the food is served a little late. But that is only to teach the brahmacharins a lesson about sraddha (faithful deliverance of one's duty, understanding the need of the situation).

In the evening the Mother went to the seashore. Two college professors, two children and a few brahmacharins accompanied her. There on the seashore the Mother sat still, facing the ocean. The blue vast ocean, the symbol of infinity, with its unending waves of different sizes, was a magnificent sight which invoked peace and tranquility in a *sadhak's* mind. Although the nature of the ocean is never-ending waves, its mere sight can somehow help to sublimate the thought-waves of the mind.

The setting evening sun, radiating golden rays all around, shone on the western horizon. Its rays reflected on the waters of the ocean and colored that part of the sea a brilliant reddish gold. As if they were desirous of adorning the Mother's already radiant countenance, the rays showered themselves upon her face as well, accentuating her eternally blissful smile. There was the setting sun on the western horizon, and there was the Mother, the ever glowing Sun of Knowledge on the horizon of spirituality.

The Mother instructed the others who were with her,

Amma: You should meditate, imagining either a rock or a fully-blossomed lotus in the sea; then install your Beloved Deity sitting on it. Or you can consider the ocean as the world. In it vibrates the *jivatman* of the waves. Even beyond that, imagine the form of Devi sitting silently on a lotus, making everything still as the witness-consciousness and meditate on that.

After meditation, the Mother became childlike. She started playing, digging holes on the seashore with her hands. Then she called one of the two children to her and covered the child's feet with sand. After that, she drew a triangle, symbolizing *Shakti* (power, serpent power), on the sand and placed a small piece of stone in the middle, representing the *bindu* (central point). Then the Mother began performing *archana* to it, using the sand to represent the flower petals that are normally offered from the heart. One of the girls also joined her.

After a while the Mother began playing with the waves in the sea. She took water in her cupped hands and splashed it on the children, who screamed in alarm and ran back to the shore. Seeing their plight, the Mother laughed. At one point, she took water in her cupped hands and poured it over her own head. As she repeated this a few times, she called out loud, "Hey...Shivane..."

One may wonder, is this person who sports like a small child the same one who protects thousands of people who throng to her for solace and succor? Is she the head of a spiritual institution? Is this the person who is the spiritual Guru and Mother of thousands of people who come from all around the world? These different faces of the Holy Mother are unbelievable and incomprehensible, even when one sees them with one's own eyes.

Returning from the seashore, the Mother went directly to the vegetable garden where she started plucking "country greens" (a term commonly used for many varieties of amaranthus and chenopodium). Now she looked exactly like a housewife who is keen about the things that are needed in the kitchen.

CHAKKA KALI

The day was getting closer to dusk. From the vegetable garden, the Holy Mother slowly walked towards the front of the temple just as Harshan, son of Sugunanandan's sister, was approaching. He was lame. Since this cousin had been the Mother's fond childhood playmate, she was very excited when she saw him. Immediately her mood again changed to that of a little girl and right at that moment she wanted to play *Chakka Kali* (a children's game similar to Hop-Scotch).

The rectangular drawing was made on the sand and the game began. All the residents of the Ashram and a few outside devotees gathered around to see the Mother playing. They felt tremendous joy while watching her and the way she played. The Mother played just like a child who became identified with the game which she played, using all the different tricks that would be used by an expert. It also appeared that the Mother engaged in a bit of foul play.

She threw a stone, which is part of the game, into one of the divisions, praying, "Oh, Shiva, may I win the game." But the stone did not fall into the division which she wanted. The Mother humorously remarked, "Oh, Shiva did not cooperate!" (All burst into laughter). It bounced and fell at a distance. "Alas," the Mother said, and with a desperate look on her face, she stood aside. Continuously jumping on one foot, the Mother started panting. But she did not want to give up easily. Like a determined, adamant little girl she went on playing.

Just then the sound of the harmonium and a *mridan-gam* (a double headed drum) were heard from the temple. The Mother ran towards the water tank to wash her hands, legs and face, saying, "It is time for the *bhajan*."

What is this state of *jivanmukti*! How can we understand it? How can we comprehend the different moods? What interpretation can one give for these seemingly strange moods of such great souls? It is all a mystery until we reach that state of Realization. Utterly complex is the Mother outwardly but fully and perfectly integrated is her inner personality. She uses this external complexity as a veil to cover her inner Perfection. Not that she does not want to reveal her real nature to us, but it is to make our minds fully one-pointed on her so that she can work on us. The sportings of a *Mahatma* are only to draw and bind his devotees towards him. When they have fallen in love with him and are completely attached to him, the *Mahatma* starts disciplining them to make them know and realize the non-dual Self with which he is one. Otherwise, we would not be able to imbibe or appreciate him even if he did fully manifest his real nature. In one verse of the Mother's own compositions, *Omkara Divya Porule*, she says, *Piccha nadakkunnu makkal...*

> Toddling you are, my darling children,
> Mother walks beside you
> In order to develop the consciousness
> Of Eternity in you.

What was the meaning of Krishna's sporting in Vrindavan? What was all that stealing of butter from the houses of *Gopis*, playing with *Gopis* and *Gopas*, grazing the cows? What was that all about? Were all those childhood pranks and merriment insignificant and meaningless like the play of an ordinary child? No, they were not. They were all different methods to bind the devotees to Him and ultimately carry them to the highest realm of Absolute Awareness where He was established. But that would not have been possible if He remained in that state of bliss, without speaking, playing, mingling and moving along with the people of Vrindavan. Surely they would not have appreciated Him as they did. In the same way, the Mother comes down to our level of understanding and acts like one of us, manifesting little by little her glory to make us feel and appreciate her. She will slowly become dear to us, and then in due course, the dearest. Thus it will culminate in a very strong inseparable relationship from where she can easily lead us to the state of Realization. The Mother says, "In order to catch a thief sometimes the policemen will disguise themselves as thieves and will act in the same way. Once the thieves are caught, the policemen will reveal their real identity. In the same way, Mother acts like one of you so that she can catch the thief of your mind and direct you to God."

The *bhajan* began. The Mother was transported to a rapturous mood. She raised both her hands and called aloud, "Amme, hey...Devi, my Mother." Soaring to the highest peak of spiritual bliss, the Mother sang, *Amme Bhagavati Kali Mate...*

> O Mother, Supreme Goddess Kali,
> Today I will catch hold of You and devour You.
> Hear what I say!
> I was born under the star of death.
>
> A child born
> Under such a planetary conjunction
> Devours its own mother.
> So either You eat me
> Or I will eat You this very day itself!
>
> I am not going to keep quiet
> Unless I know of Your choice.
> Since you are black
> That blackness will rub off all over my body.
>
> When Kala, Lord of Death, comes
> With rope and rod
> And tries to catch me with His noose,
> I will smear the black ash
> From my body onto His face!
>
> How can I, who have contained Kali within me,
> Be caught in the hand of Death?
> Chanting the Name, "Kali,"
> I will mock at Kala!

The Holy Mother continued singing the refrain (first verse above). The tempo reached its heights. All of a sudden the Mother got up from her seat and began dancing blissfully and rhythmically. This continued for some time. Then she moved toward the coconut groves and slowly disappeared in the darkness. Everyone got up to watch her but continued singing the same song in the same tempo a little while longer. Nobody went near the Mother as everyone felt that it was better to leave her alone when she was in this kind of ecstatic state. Through the darkness everyone could see the white clothes of the Mother. She now walked like one who was in oblivion. Her steps faltered. The fear that she might hit herself against a coconut tree made Gayatri and a few *brahmacharins* move toward her and keep a watchful eye on her. At one point she threw herself on the ground, which was wet from the rain, and started rolling around. Her infinite inner bliss manifested itself as continuous joyful laughter. Sometimes she clapped her hands and raised them skyward. The fingers of both her hands held two different divine *mudras*. The Mother made a noise with her tongue which sounded like the peculiar sound of satisfaction and contentment which one makes after having tasted something very delicious. She was completely lost to this world. The Mother remained in this enchanted spiritual mood for a very long time.

One would wonder if it were the same person, who sported like a small little child on the seashore and later in the game *Chakka Kali*, who now became so immensely intoxicated with Divine Bliss.

Slowly the Mother's body became still. She remained lying for a while longer. Gayatri went near her and made sure that she had returned to her normal mood. She then sat down near the Holy Mother. The *brahmacharins* also got closer and sat on either side of her. In a few minutes the Mother sat up and remained seated.

The time was nine-forty-five. The residents and the other devotees had their supper of *kanji*. The Mother came to the kitchen and sat down on the bare floor. She had a few balls of rice from the food sent by a woman devotee. It looked as if it were only to fulfill the devotee's wish that she ate. The Mother fed all the children who were there at that time with the remaining rice. Immediately after that, the Mother lay down with her head on the lap of a girl who sat next to her.

Markus, the devotee from Germany, was also sitting close by. The Mother asked him, "Markus, chirp like a pigeon." Being a good mimic, Markus did so. Then the Mother said, "Next like a crow." He did that as well, followed by other different sounds like the barking of a dog, howling of a jackal, meowing of a cat, etc. The Mother and the others enjoyed this and continuously burst into laughter. Hearing Markus imitating these different sounds, Harshan also was inspired. He too started making some sounds. There was a chain of laughter for a long time.

Leaving the kitchen, the Mother once again went to the coconut groves where she lay on the wet sand till ten thirty. It seemed that the Mother was struggling to keep her mind in this world. That unknown world, where nobody else had access, and where she was all alone at all times, lay far beyond this plural world of happenings.

Through the impregnable silence of the night flowed the sweet melody which emerged out of Markus' flute. When it was eleven o'clock the Mother went to her room followed by Gayatri and Kunjumol. Thus, one more day with the Mother had passed.

5 April 1984

Another day begins. Each day with the Holy Mother has its own charm and resplendence. A new, unique chapter begins; it is never boring. An ever-fresh feeling of enchantment and serenity surrounds the Mother irrespective of time and place. Whoever comes to that Presence can drink in as much as he or she wants. This ocean of beatified splendor, its holiness, its depth, its vastness and infinitude are for us to enjoy and experience. The Mother invites us most lovingly with overflowing compassion, stretching her arms to each one of us. Let us go running and lock ourselves in that heart-soothing embrace of Divine Love and Beauty.

At nine o'clock in the morning the Mother summoned all of the *brahmacharins* upstairs into her room. Once in a while she calls all of them together and gives them some general instructions concerning their *sadhana*, their work (each one has a definite work prescribed), their behavior toward others, principles of spirituality in their lives at the Ashram, and other pertinent matters. Sometimes she would point out a resident's error during this time, if it was repeatedly committed.

To the assembled group of *brahmacharins*, the Mother spoke,

Amma: Children, you have all the proper circumstances to do your *sadhana* and pursue your spiritual practices without any hindrance. Everyone will not have such an opportunity. There are many who really want to dedicate their lives to spirituality yet cannot do it. Whereas, you have plenty of time to do it. Utilize this opportunity provided by the Lord to the utmost. If you do not, you will be cheating the great tradition of spirituality. This Ashram is the best place for you to fight and test your strength. If you win the struggle here, you can go anywhere in this world and you will not have to fear anything at all. However, you must strive hard to attain that state. You may feel that these rules and regulations are a bit difficult to follow, but remember that this bondage which you experience now is to make you completely free in the future. If you had remained in the world, you would have been bound by the objects of the world. That bondage would lead you to more and more slavery and sorrow. But the bondage you feel here will help free you from all bondages in the future. Those who have real love for God and who are intent on the goal *(lakshya bodha)* will not feel this bondage. For them, this is the most suitable place to lead a happy and blissful life in doing their *sadhana* and performing selfless service to society and ailing humanity.

Look, children, Mother does not insist that any one of you stays here. The choice is yours. Therefore, the question is whether you want to minimize your enjoyments for some time in order to experience everlasting happiness. Or perhaps you not only want to minimize your external pleasures but you still want to indulge to the maximum and suffer. You are free to do both.

There are some people who say, "Let me enjoy the pleasures and then when it is time I will take up spirituality." Children, there is no such particular time to turn to spiritual life. A person's determination is the deciding factor. If you are waiting for old age to come after you have finished enjoying all the worldly pleasures, that is the worst period of time to do anything spiritual. In old age, you may want to think of God, but it will be too late as the mind will have lost all its flexibility. The mind will become a storehouse of the past, filled with all kinds of thoughts. At that time, you can do nothing except simply lie down and recall past events, chewing the cud like a cow does, so to speak. You will simply lie down, watching the past on the screen of the mind. You will not be able to see the Lord's form as your eyes will lose their power of seeing. You will not be able to sing the Lord's glory properly. Old age will damage the throat. You will not have any teeth to correctly pronounce the words of the hymns or chants. You will not even be able to hear *bhajans* or other hymns or chants clearly, for your power of hearing will fail. Even to offer a few flower petals in front of the Lord's picture will become difficult because your hands will be trembling due to old age. Above all, the mind will become like a trash can. Even if you want to do any of these things, the

mind will not let you do it. Even if you do manage to do
something in this period of your life, it will only be me-
chanical. The mind will not cooperate at all. That
means that there will not be any concentration. What is
the use if you do spiritual practices without concentration?

Some say that *sannyasa* is to be taken after *grahasthashrama*. Who is a real *grahasthashrami?* A real *grahasthashrami* is one who leads an ashram life while living in
his home, that is, one who leads a well-disciplined life
even while leading a family life. Most people are mere
grahasthas, not *grahasthashramis*. The latter is equal to a
real *sannyasin* if he or she leads a life of self-sacrifice and
love. He is not selfish. He is not one who is totally en-
meshed in the net of attachments and aversions. All of
his or her attachment is to God, not to the world. For
him the world is a means to attain God. The world is
not a problem for him at all. If someone leads such a
life, even if he or she is a *grahasthashrami*, one can attain
God-Realization. But how many of those who live in the
world lead such a life? It is difficult to find such
grahasthashramis in this age.

Therefore, children, this is a God-given opportunity
for you. You are fortunate to turn towards spiritual life
at such a young age. Above all, you have Mother with
you. Do your *sadhana* as best as you can and leave the
rest in the hands of God. Try to observe and find out
how competent you are. If you feel that it is difficult for
you to continue here, children, you have all the freedom
to quit the Ashram. But Mother will not allow anyone

to act and behave against the principles of spirituality while staying here. A true spiritual life cannot be achieved by leading a life of pleasure. It solely depends on renunciation and penance.

There was utter silence for some time. Each person's eyes were fixed on the Mother. She looked at her children and gave a compassionate smile which soothed their hearts and souls. The Holy Mother got up from her seat and went up to each of the *brahmacharins*, who were all standing now. Fondly patting each of her children on the shoulder, she also lovingly caressed and gently rubbed the forehead of each one. Her smile and this most affectionate touch made each of them feel very blissful. This inner feeling of joy was quite evident on their faces. Afterwards she called Gayatri and asked her to bring something to distribute as *prasadam* to her children. Gayatri brought some bananas. She gave a piece of *prasadam* to each person. She washed her hands with the water which Gayatri brought and proceeded to walk out of the room. As she went through the doorway, the Mother said in a very humble tone, "Forgive Mother if she has inadvertently said something which hurt her children."

This humility of the Mother always keeps her children aware of the need to be humble in spirituality. This is how she teaches her children. After saying something, she simply does not walk away. The Mother sets an example by doing what she says. She not only talks about self-sacrifice and love, but the Mother herself lives it.

This is a great source of inspiration for those who come into contact with her.

Although the Mother expressed her humility through the humble statement above, the truth is that even the most severe scolding of the Mother has a sweetness of its own. Moreover, the so-called "scoldings" are not mere scoldings but real *satsang* (spiritual teaching). If somebody feels a little pain at all, by the mere touch and compassionate look from the Mother, the pain will melt away like an ice cube in the sun. She sometimes scolds someone for making a mistake repeatedly. Through her words and manner she will make him feel that she is very angry with him so that that person will always remember and not make the mistake ever again. But the person who has received the scoldings will sometimes feel a little pain for being scolded by the Mother. In this case too, the Mother's medicine has an incredible power to heal his hurt mind. It is so simple. A few moments later, maybe a few hours later (but rarely days later), she will walk up to that person and smile at him, graciously touching him on the shoulder or patting his back. She will lovingly say, "My son," "My daughter," or "My child." Lo and behold! His mental pain and heavy-heartedness will disappear. Not only that, he or she will become immensely blissful.

A well-known *sannyasin* once came to the Ashram. His intention was just to see the Mother, spend a couple of hours in the Ashram and leave. But once he had the Mother's darshan, he could not go. He postponed going until the next day. The next day came and again he postponed it until the following day. He behaved like a two-year-old child when he was in front of the Mother. Strongly attracted to her, he became inordinately attached. If she did not look at him, he would not eat. He would sit alone and cry like a baby if the Mother did not say at least one word to him. He acted like one who had lost his senses, like one gone "mad." Such was his love for the Holy Mother.

One day the Mother was conversing with some of the *brahmacharins* about certain matters concerning the Ashram. The *sannyasin* entered without asking permission. He had done the same on several previous occasions, but the Mother had kept quiet. This time, however, in a serious and very strict tone, she said, "Swami-mon, please go out. Don't you know that it is impolite to enter without permission?" The *swami* turned pale. Immediately he went out. Later the Mother found him sitting in front of the temple verandah; he was crying. The Mother approached him and again spoke to him without showing any love,

Amma: Swami-mon, look here, you are a *sannyasin*. You should not become weak-minded like this. It is people like you who should set an example to these *brahmacharins* through your words and deeds. The whole world might shout at you, speak ill of you, abuse you, fabricate tales about you and criticize you, but a real *sannyasin* will stand still. There will not even be a ripple in the mind of a real *sannyasin*. He would be unshakable. All criticism and insults should crumble into pieces as they hit against his strong mind. Look at the ochre clothes you are wearing. This means that you have gone beyond body-consciousness. Even if you have not attained that state, in order to set an example for others, a *sannyasin* should not express such weak-mindedness outwardly. He should be like a lion, not like a sheep.

The Mother's voice was very powerful. She was serious too. Having said this to him, she walked away without uttering another word. The swami became totally upset. He could not contain himself sufficiently to withstand the Mother's words. He wept like a child. The *brahmacharin* who translated the Mother's words tried to console him but failed.

An hour passed. The swami still sat in the same place in front of the temple verandah. The Mother once again passed by. This time she approached the swami, smiled at him, rubbed his chest and said just one sentence, "Son, after all, it's your Amma, isn't it?" Without another word, she went to her room.

The *brahmacharin* who was present observed the swami's face, which revealed that he was in total bliss, in ecstasy. Due to overwhelming inner joy he could not even speak. A big smile beamed on his face and as he faithfully kept his hand on his heart, cherishing that spot where the Mother had bestowed her magic touch, he said, "What is this? What has happened? All the heaviness has gone. I feel very light and relaxed. I want that touch once more. I want that touch once more." He repeated this again and again. One could clearly see that his heart was filled to the brim. This one-touch-cure for mental agony is a familiar "miracle" among the Mother's devotees.

After the meeting with the *brahmacharins*, the Mother came down the steps. Now it was nearly ten-thirty in the morning and she went to the front verandah of the temple where a householder devotee was performing the reading of the *Srimad Bhagavatam*. She sat there for some time. Acchamma, the grandmother, sat in a corner making garlands and listening to the reading simultaneously. The devotee was reading the part where the childhood sports of Sri Krishna were depicted. Acchamma seemed to be enjoying it very much. Hearing the stories of how Krishna stole milk and butter from the houses of the *Gopis*, Acchamma laughed loudly, showing her toothless gums, and commented, "Little thief." The Mother threw an appreciating glance at her innocent faith and devotion.

At this time a group of nearly twenty young men came to visit the Ashram and to meet the Holy Mother. They were all taken to the small hall which was situated on the south side of the temple. This was the classroom in which the *brahmacharins* were taught the scriptures. Mats were spread and they all waited for the Mother to come. The whole group of young men was undergoing a training about how to extract cooking gas from cowdung.

The Holy Mother came and sat in front of them on another mat. Then she found that some of them were sitting on the bare floor. She exclaimed, "Oh, my children, don't you have a mat to sit? Don't sit on the cold cement floor. It is not good." The Mother stood up and took the mat on which she was sitting. She herself went with the mat in her hands to that spot where they were sitting. The young men were perplexed and at the same time amazed to see her humility and her natural way of treating them. They got up from their seat and said, "No, Mother, no. We will sit on the floor. You please sit on that."

The Mother replied, "No, children, Mother is used to it. She can sit and be anywhere." By that time, another mat was brought for the young men. The Mother asked the *brahmacharins* to spread that one for her. The *brahmacharin* showed a little hesitation to do that as the mat which he brought was not a very good one. He wanted to give it to the visitors and get the Mother's mat back as it was a special one particularly meant for her. The Mother understood his mind and said strictly, "Don't you hear me? Spread that mat for me." The *brahmacharin* helplessly did so. The Mother made the young men sit on her mat and she sat on the other one.

When everyone was seated, the Mother asked, "Children, are all of you interested in spirituality?" Several of them gave positive answers. The Mother described the Ashram and the principles for which it stands. In conclusion, she explained,

Amma: It is not to make them stay here permanently that Mother brings up these children. One day or other they will have to go out and serve the world without expecting anything. Mother's wish is to provide some real servants to the world. Now they cannot be sent out. They need to be molded. They need mental strength and balance to confront the different situations which they will have to face in the world. Mother thinks that these children will love and selflessly serve the people who are in the scorching heat of worldly problems; that is why she loves them.

One of the young men: Isn't there *grahasthashrama* (the second stage of life as a householder) and *vana-prastha* (the third stage of life, going to the forest for penance) before *sannyasa?* Isn't *sannyasa* the final stage of life? Why should these young men renounce everything now at this age?

Amma: Children, in the olden days whatever was the path chosen by an individual, it was only a means to attain God. Even married life was considered as another path to God. They maintained that purity throughout their life. Before getting married, most people spent ten to twelve years with a Guru learning and practicing spirituality. Then after coming out of the *gurukula* (the Guru's hermitage) they entered the next stage of life. Some continued as *brahmacharins* and became *sannyasins,* and others who desired to have a family got married and became *grahasthashramis.* It all depends on one's mental maturity and spiritual disposition inherited from the previous birth.

Suppose many people study music in a music college. They all learn the same lessons under the same teacher. The time they get is also the same. But you can see that some of them become real masters in that field. Some others don't. Why? It all depends on the predominant nature or innate tendency that one has. Just a push is sufficient for such people to become that. A mere touch is enough for them, and they will be on the right track.

Using force, external force, will stunt spontaneous growth of a person. Of course, one should be corrected if he or she happens to swerve from the right path. Mother talks about those who have certain talents in and inclinations towards a particular field. Such people should be provided with the necessary circumstances for their inner growth. For example, if somebody shows great interest in painting, he should be encouraged to pursue painting. The parents or teachers should not force him to become a musician. If he is forcibly enrolled in a music college, he will be a failure. He cannot become a good musician because his innate tendency is to become a painter. Each person's *vasana* is different. That is how one person becomes an engineer, another a doctor, someone else an actor or a musician, etc. In the same way, those who have a spiritual inclination will become a seeker of truth. If you force such a person to become a lawyer or something for which he has no inclination, he will not be able to do it. It is unnatural for him.

Just as everything is not over when you are enrolled as a student in a music college, spiritual life is not completed just because you come and stay in the Ashram.

Constant practice, always keeping the enthusiasm and interest at its peak, will only help to reach the goal. Therefore, son, it is not you or Mother who decides what people should become, the deciding factor is their accumulated tendencies.

Mother has tried several times to send them back to their houses and to find a job, but they wouldn't go. Therefore, Mother thinks that it is predestined for them to be renunciates. Once they take refuge and surrender, it is Mother's duty to take care of them. In the olden days, *grahasthashramis* would have one or two children. Once the children were capable of standing on their own feet, the husband and wife would enter the third stage of life, *vanaprastha*, after having entrusted all the family responsibilities or official responsibilities in an appropriate manner to their children. During this period, they did severe penance and attained the fourth stage of life, *sannyasa*, the state of desirelessness. All that they had done previously while living in the world was only for the attainment of this goal. Their whole life was a preparation for this goal. Children, is this how people live today? Is it possible to attain this state while living at home? We all live our individual lives, but the attitude in which we approach our goal is the determining factor.

Is there selfless love in worldly life? What benefit does the world get from selfish people? How many times more is the benefit that the world gets from a real *brahmacharin* whose life is dedicated to selfless service than from a selfish person who is concerned only with him-

self. If you really look with an impartial and discerning
eye, you can see that it is people who are established in
brahmacharya who do real benefit to the world.

If there is a good ashram, the people who live in the
world, that is, the grahasthas, will get solace and succor
from it. Tapasvis and brahmacharins are always benefac-
tors of the world.

Children, you ask why they should renounce everything now. Spirituality is not something that should be
begun when you are old and weak. You will not be able
to do any kind of spiritual practices at that time as you
will become weak mentally, physically and intellectually.
It should be commenced when you are young and your
sense organs are strong. Old age is the most disorderly
part of life when nobody can do anything creative.

Question: Don't the children have a duty towards their
father and mother?

Amma: What duty, son? Doing good to the world is the
biggest and greatest duty. This world is the biggest family. God is our real Father and Mother. Our real duty towards Him is serving and loving the poor and needy
selflessly. The family consisting of a husband, wife and
two children is the smallest fraction of this big family.
Looking after the smallest fraction is nothing. That is
narrowing down. On the other hand, by loving and
serving the world family, the so-called "family" will also
get a share of our selfless service. If we are only looking
after the immediate family, neither they nor the world
will be benefited. What Mother means is that regardless
of how much we serve or love our family there will be

only dissatisfaction and discontent. Whereas, it is through real service to the world that the family also gets real benefit. The *sannyasins* perform this duty much better than the *grahasthas*.

Not only that, the families of the *brahmacharins* who stay here have enough money to live. There are also other brothers and sisters to look after the parents. So is it necessary for them to stay in the house only to make money? It has never been known that anybody has ever taken their worldly achievements with them when they died.

Children, look here, two days ago somebody who visited the Ashram was telling Mother about his life. He was a very wealthy man, a millionaire. He was afflicted by a severe ulcer on his foot. It was badly infected. Pus and blood were oozing out all the time. He was not even able to get up from his bed. There was nobody to look after him. Even his own children and wife had abandoned him. Therefore, he decided to give some of his property to a charitable institution as a gift. Hearing this news, his children gathered together and got a doctor's statement certifying that their father was insane. They forcefully seized him and committed him to a lunatic asylum after having beaten him up severely. This man, who was a millionaire, has nothing now. He is completely broken down. In tears he narrated this to Mother. This is the kind of love that worldly people have. The *brahmacharins* who stay here are trying to know the Self without taking up this worldly path.

It seemed that the young men were all happy. They all got up to leave. All of a sudden, the Holy Mother walked towards the row in the rear. She approached a young man. The Mother caught hold of his hand and asked, "Do you have something to tell Mother?"

The young man was very surprised. In front of all the others he replied in a surprised tone, "Mother, it is really surprising to know that you understood my heart's wish. I am going through a very hard time. I wanted to confide all those problems to you and get some instructions about how to confront them. Mother, please allow me a few minutes to talk to you."

The Mother took him to the coconut grove and conversed with him, sitting in a shady place. While he was talking with the Mother, one of his friends had a talk with Brahmacharin Pai to whom he revealed, "Actually, on our way to the Ashram, he told me that he would like to have a talk with the Mother if it was possible. He has many problems. It is quite surprising that the Mother clearly understood him. I don't understand how it happened."

Pai replied, "It cannot be otherwise; that is the answer. The Mother is like a mirror. Our sincere prayers will simply reflect in her." The young man said, "Anyhow, we are all very impressed by her."

The Mother finished talking with him. He joined the group with a smiling face. Just then three Christian women came to see the Mother. One of them had visited the Ashram several times before and had several experiences. Today she brought two others with her. The other two newcomers were mother and daughter. The older of the newcomers (the mother) told her tale of woe to the Holy Mother. She had four children, including the one who came with her. Her husband had left her and was living with another woman. Sobbing and shedding copious tears, the lady prayed that the Mother straighten out her family problems. "Otherwise, I will commit suicide," she said.

The young men who were about to leave saw this scene. The Mother had talked to them about the nature of family life only a few moments ago. Now they witnessed an example with their own eyes. It seemed as if it had been especially arranged for them.

Amma: Daughter, does he ever come home?

Woman devotee: Yes, he came yesterday, but I didn't speak to him.

Amma: No, no, daughter, that should not be your attitude. You should speak to him. You should be loving to him. Otherwise, his enmity will increase.

The Mother consoled her and wiped her tears with her own hands. Her daughter was also crying. The Mother lovingly caressed the daughter's head and said, "Child, don't cry. If you cry, your mother will become very sad and mentally weak. You should try to console her." The Mother entered the temple and returned with *prasadam* for them. Giving that to the lady she once again consoled her. The lady's daughter had a burn on her foot. It was infected. The Mother soothed the wound with her hands and put some medicine on it.

A few minutes before they left, some fishermen arrived. They waited for the Mother to finish with the lady and her daughter. The Mother turned to the fishermen. Since they had not been able to catch any fish for many, many days, they came to seek the Mother's blessing. The Mother gave them some tulasi leaves after having imbued it with her pure vital energy. They left happily. From experience they knew what to do with it.

The Mother literally lives within her own saying, "Mother is the servant of all." She always serves everyone who comes to her without any difference. She expects nothing. Neither can we repay her. The debt to the Guru always remains as a debt. No one can repay it. The most one can do is to sincerely follow in the footsteps of the Guru, to apply in one's own life those principles by which she lives. The Mother says,

Amma: One can say that God and I are One, but one cannot say I and my Guru are One. The Guru is far beyond everything, even the Trinity. The Mother makes her children lead a life based on spiritual principles by inspiring them to remember God and thereby lead a life of selfless service and love.

How many people, who had previously lived an utterly selfish life, have beautified their own lives with the fragrance of selflessness and love for humanity through the Mother's touch of Grace?

The Mother says,

Amma: Mother wants people to work hard to attain spiritual bliss. She does not want people to idle away their time in the name of spirituality. While people come to Mother for varied reasons, she will somehow make them remember God. She doesn't want her children to chant the Lord's Name simply with their lips. Mother wants them to chant it with their hearts and live in the Lord's Name. Devotion is not simply doing *pradakshina* (circumambulation) around the temple, chanting "Krishna, Krishna" and then kicking the destitute beggar who asks for alms as you come out. The compassion and love that you show to the beggar is the real devotion to God. This is what the Mother wants her children to do.

The bell rang. It was time for lunch. The Holy Mother's elder sister Kasturi arrived with her two children, Shivan and Vishnu. Kasturi wanted the Mother to perform the first feeding to her second son, Vishnu. An oil lamp was lit. In a few minutes the Mother was sitting on the front verandah of the temple with Vishnu on her lap. She applied sacred ash on the forehead, chest and upper arms of the child. The Mother offered a few flower petals on the child's head. She waved camphor in front of the child. All the while she kept the child on her lap. The Mother then fed the child with her own hands. The child had a big smile on his face. He happily smacked and swallowed the few grains of rice which the Mother gave him. Raising one of his hands, the child caught hold of the Mother's *rudraksha* rosary and tightly held it up for a while, gazing at the Mother's face with the same big smile on his face.

Amma: Hey, little boy, what do you want, *rudraksha* or rice, or do you want both?

Everyone present felt that the Mother asked the child if he wanted spiritual life or worldly life or did he want to become a *grahasthashrami*. It seemed that she was ready to give any of the aforesaid if the child asked. In a subtle sense, the child might have responded to her question and the Mother might have given it as well. Who knows?

6 April 1984

This morning one *brahmacharin* narrated an experience he had the morning of the previous day. The Holy Mother had asked him to make his *sadhana* more intense. She instructed him to get up at two a.m. and perform his meditation and other practices until six o'clock. He was happy to do it.

Amma: In the beginning you may find it a little difficult to get up at that odd hour of the night. It will become easy for you to do so once it becomes a habit.

The *brahmacharin* had doubts about whether he could do it or not. Therefore, he looked at the Mother's face and in a prayerful tone begged, "Mother, I have no power to do it. Please shower your Grace upon me so that I can sincerely follow your instructions without fail." The Mother encouraged him and furthermore said, "Son, don't worry about getting up at two. Tomorrow Mother will call you at two o'clock." He thought that the Mother would come to his room at two in the morning and call him. But suddenly he realized that it was a Thursday when Mother spent the whole night in *Devi Bhava*. He ran different thoughts through his mind about how the Mother was going to call him. "Is she going to come to my room in *Devi Bhava*? Or is she going to send someone to call me? Or would the Mother finish *Devi Bhava* before two and come to call me?" Since it was a crowded day with so many people who came to behold the Mother as the Divine Mother, the *brahmacharin* did not get another chance to talk to the Mother to clarify this detail.

Though his faith in the Mother and her words were unshakable, yielding to human nature and its doubting tendencies, the *brahmacharin* borrowed an alarm clock from another resident and set it at two before he went to bed at eleven o'clock. The *Devi Bhava* was still going on. Judging from the big crowd awaiting to receive *darshan* from the Holy Mother, he estimated that it would easily go till three-thirty or four. Once again he sincerely prayed to the Mother and slept peacefully.

The *brahmacharin* was awakened by the sudden sensation of something falling on his face. Simultaneously, the alarm went off, which startled him. He turned on the light and searched for the thing which fell on his face. He was wonderstruck to see the object. It was a

small, framed picture of the Holy Mother which was
kept inserted between the thatched coconut leaves which
formed the walls of the hut. The *brahmacharin* slept with
his head towards the wall, almost touching it. The time
was exactly two. Thus the first day of his two o'clock
sadhana started as instructed by the Holy Mother. He
became more and more amazed when he remembered
the way she woke him up at two. She had kept her
promise. It was quite obvious that it was none other
than the Mother who woke him up by making her own
picture fall on his face. The *Devi Bhava* was still going
on.

He was very anxious to share this experience with
others. But he felt a bit sad later when Mother told him,
"Son, if you had believed Mother's words and not set
the alarm, Mother would have come to you in person,
getting up in the middle of *Devi Bhava*. By setting the
alarm, you proved that you were double-minded, that
your faith was incomplete."

Today the Holy Mother once again summoned all
the residents, this time to the meditation hall. The
Mother talked about different things. The meeting was
mainly meant to fix a timetable for performing the daily
routine of the residents.

Amma: Children, to derive the full benefit of any action, whatever it may be, love for that particular action is
absolutely necessary. Without this factor of love, your actions will be found lacking. Meditation should be performed with love. Chanting of the *Gita* also should be

done with love. Performance of an action without love is a sin. In the same way, it is equally a sin to do a work hesitantly. Whether it is meditation or some other action, if work is performed with a negative attitude, misfortunes will occur in the Ashram. It is the duty of each one of you to do it. The amount of interest and intensity that you put forth will show the sincerity and love that you have towards the Ashram and Mother.

Even to enjoy smoking one must have love. If one does not have love for it, he will not enjoy smoking at all. We can see some people holding their noses and running away from places where people smoke. There are others who will cough and vomit if they happen to smell the smoke of cigarettes. Whereas, those who like it enjoy smoking and they will take in the aroma as much as they can. Love for an object or action is the most important factor which inspires you to act. Dislike or lack of love makes you refrain from acting or show less interest in performing an action.

Children, you should try to develop this attitude of love for your *sadhana*. Your attitude should be, "Not enough, this is not enough. I should do more." The attitude, "if only circumstances could be better," should be given up. Don't waste your time walking around and talking unnecessarily. Do your *sadhana* punctually and sincerely. That is your duty now. Have the readiness to undertake any work which is for the common good with love. Don't say, "I will do only this work, not that one. I like to do this work and dislike to do the other one." This is not a good attitude, as far as a seeker is concerned. Undertaking or doing a work which you like is not at all a big thing. Anyone can work on something which he or she likes. There is no greatness in it. For example, you like to do gardening but you don't like to remove the cowdung and clean the cowshed. You like to cook but you don't like to wash the dishes. You like to serve food but you dislike removing the leftovers. A worldly man can have this attitude, but a spiritual seeker should not. A spiritual seeker should perform any action with equanimity of mind, rising above personal preferences. You love and caress a charming, good-looking child but you feel aversion towards an ugly-looking child who is born in a low caste. These distinctions are common among worldly people, for they dwell in the world of likes and dislikes. Remember that the sole purpose of your life is to transcend these distinctions, all likes and dislikes.

Readiness and willingness to do any work at any time in any circumstance is the hallmark of spirituality. Spiritual people do it with love and sincerity, without expecting anything. That is why there is always a charm and beauty in whatever spiritual people do. They love to do the work because the work itself gives them infinite happiness. Whereas, we are concerned more about the result, and in that worry about the result, the work loses all its beauty. The factor of love is absent in our actions.

Now the Mother concentrated on figuring out a timetable for the daily routine of the residents. At this time she noticed one *brahmacharin* shaking his legs unnecessarily. She said,

Amma: This is a sign of mental restlessness and impatience. A *sadhak* should learn to sit without moving his hands and legs unnecessarily. It is a habit. He should also not look here and there unnecessarily. Such movements are done by people who have no concentration. You might have seen people who constantly bite their nails and those who simply sit, turning around and around the button on their shirt. These are cases of mental restlessness or impatience. It is also a kind of mental disease. Spiritual aspirants will try to overcome the mind and its habits. They should not be enslaved by such base habits.

Almost all worldly people have the habit of shaking their legs unnecessarily while seated on a chair. A *sadhak* should not do this. As much as possible, a seeker should sit in an *asana* (a sitting yogic posture) on the floor. Sit in an *asana* even if the opportunity arises for you to sit in a chair.

Before making the mind still, try hard to still the body. It does not mean that you should spend your time idling without doing anything. No, that is not what is meant. Unnecessary movement of your hands and legs and other parts of the body should be avoided.

THE BLISS-INTOXICATED DIVINE MOOD

At six-thirty in the evening the residents began the singing of *bhajans*. After a few songs, Brahmacharin Balu started singing *Saranagati* (O Mother, Give Refuge). By the time the Holy Mother came to join in, the same song was still being sung since it was a long *bhajan*. She took over the lead singing.

> O Light that illumines the whole Universe
> And even the sun, moon and the stars;
> O Primordial Nature,
> Governess of the entire Universe,
> O Universal Mother, who is the Incarnation
> Of pure and selfless Love,
> This destitute cries for Thy vision
> With a heart endowed with intense yearning.

The Mother was unusually enraptured with the bliss of Divine Love. She swayed vigorously from side to side, back and forth. An inexpressible and indescribably beautiful blending of the diverse aspects of supreme devotion and love slowly manifested in the Mother. It enveloped each and every person present. Through the Divine voice of the Holy Mother the song attained wings. It soared up and flowed like a never-ending stream as the song continued,

> O Mother, the ocean sings Thy Glory
> Through the resounding of the Sacred Syllable,
> Aum...one after the other,
> Each and every wave dances gleefully
> In time with the Pranava, the Primordial Sound,
> Aum...

With a voice full of feeling and a heart full of longing, the Mother called out, "Amme...Amme..." Her eyes were fixed on the sky above and her hands were out-stretched. The Mother's call was so full of love and au-thenticity that it gave the feeling to everyone that the Divine Mother Herself was standing in front of the Holy Mother. The Mother sang out,

> O Mother Divine, Thou art beyond
> The scriptural verses of Purushasuktha
> (Scriptural text which glorifies the
> Universal Being).
> O Mother, Thou art beyond the Brahmasutra
> (Scriptural text which describes the
> Absolute Brahman).
> O Mother, even transcending all the four Vedas,
> O Mother, Thou alone knowest Thee indeed.

At this point the Mother started laughing, an exter-nal expression of her inner bliss. This mysterious laugh-ter persisted as the *brahmacharins* continued singing. The Mother clapped her hands like a little child and im-mediately raised both hands above her head. Now the laughter stopped, but her hands remained in the up-lifted position for a while. The fingers of each hand dis-played two different divine *mudras*. A beatific glow illu-mined her face. Bringing her hands down, the Mother again sang,

> O Mother, seeking Thee, this child will cry,
> Wandering along the shores of many seas;
> O Mother, to each and every particle of sand
> This child inquires about Thee.

O stars, glittering in the vast blue sky,
Did any one of you see my Mother
Passing through this way?

The Mother sang these lines repeatedly, over and
over again. The shawl which covered her head had
fallen down as Gayatri tried to place it back into position. Strands of her hair fell loose around her neck and
gently swirled around as her head swayed with the
rhythm of the music. Tears trickled down her cheeks.
Raising her hands up, the Mother went on calling,
"Amma...Amma...Amma..." This went on until finally
she burst into a flood of tears, but the next moment the
Mother took a long, deep breath and became still. Her
hands still manifested divine *mudras*. The *brahmacharins*
went on singing,

O my Mother Bhairavi, there is no shore
Where I have not searched for Thee,
O Mother, my darling Mother,
Bliss-embodied One,
No time exists when I have not sought for Thee,
O my Beloved Mother, for aeons and aeons
Hast Thou hid from me,
This poor child of Thine.
O Compassionate One, why dost Thou delay
To shower Thy Grace upon this child?

In the light of the burning oil lamp everyone could
see the radiant face of the Holy Mother. No sign of external consciousness was evident. Saturated with divin-

ity, the atmosphere evoked spontaneous meditation in the minds of all who were present, devotees and residents alike. One could easily discern that they were all singing with their minds fully fixed on the object of their meditation. Some sang with their minds totally focused on their Beloved Deity, shedding tears of bliss, while others sat unmoving, deeply absorbed in profound meditation. Struggling to bring her mind down to the physical plane of consciousness, the Holy Mother once again sang,

> O Mother,
> On Thy fingertips revolve hundreds,
> Nay, millions of universes;
> How is it justified if Thou makest me,
> This poor child, also revolve
> On the same fingertips of Thine?

Again the Mother was transported to her own world of infinite bliss. She lost her control to stay in this physical plane and stood up. As she walked towards the coconut grove in her ecstatic rapture, she allowed herself to drown completely in the ocean of love and supreme devotion. Such was her God-intoxicated state. Spell-bound, the *brahmacharins* and devotees continued to glorify the Divine Mother as they sang,

> O Mother, come to me,
> Stand in front of me today;
> I wish to inundate Thy Holy Feet with my tears.
> O Mother, the sound that rings in my heart,

The emergent tune from my heart
Is the call of loving devotion unto Thee.
O Mother, other than that,
I need nothing...

The *bhajan* ended with these lines. Enjoying the experience of bliss and the fervor of pure devotion and
love, everyone sat immersed in meditation. Total silence
prevailed, the silence of inner peace. This hallowed atmosphere hung suspended in a sacred stillness as the
cool, gentle breeze floated the beckoning call of the
ocean from the west.

After the *arati*, everyone's eyes and hearts reached
out in search of the Holy Mother. Standing at a respectful distance, they all watched the Mother dancing in
pure bliss. It felt as if the Mother was dancing all
around the entire Ashram even though she was only en-
circling that one particular spot in the coconut grove.
Completely lost to this external world in which we were
standing, she reveled in her own mystical inundation of
splendor.

We can only observe from the outside. But what can
we say, and how can we say anything about this utterly
incomprehensible and mysterious plane of consciousness?

Yatô-vacô-nivaṛttantê-aprâpya-manasâ-saha

From where speech along with the mind
returns, unable to reach There.

[TAITTARIYA UPANISHAD]

How many commentaries, how many interpretations have already been written about that "undiscovered country" by different scholars and philosophers and how many are yet to come? Still it remains a mystery, unexplained and unrevealed.

Supper was being served. Some left for the dining hall, leaving behind the others who stood there drinking in the nectar of this most rare and wonderful scene, forgetting themselves. The time was ten o'clock as nearly two hours had passed. The Mother was still in the Divine Mood, but her physical movements gradually slowed down. By now the devotees and residents were all sitting down. Some meditated while others steadily gazed at the figure in the coconut grove. The Holy Mother lay down on the sand among the palm trees. Moments of abated breath passed in utter silence. As if to espy this unearthly, enchanted scene, the glittering stars peeped through the canopy of coconut leaves. Another half hour passed and the Mother's voice again filled the air and the hearts of devotees with *Anandamayi Brahmamayi...*

O Blissful One, O Absolute One,
O Blissful One, O Absolute One,
Whose form is of unsurpassed beauty
O Blissful One, O Absolute One.

Devotees have always found this particular composition of the Mother's especially enchanting and were overjoyed to hear her continue, *A ra dharangal...*

Crossing the six mystical centers,
The yogis come to know Thee,
The Invaluable Treasure.
Thy Glory, O Infinite Power,
Is only slightly known to them.

The song echoed in the atmosphere. It seemed that the Mother, who had gone beyond, transcending all the six *adharas* (mystical centers), was struggling hard to bring her mind down to this world of plurality. From wherever she operated, every action and every word of the Mother's embodied a teaching. So too were her songs, as her children imbibed the lyrics of *Tripudiyum podiyayidum...*

O Mother, Who constantly dances blissfully,
I salute Thee.
The Chidakasa,
Where sits the thousand-petalled Lotus,
Wherein lies the Eternal Union of Shiva-Shakti,
Shines forth like a million suns shedding light,
At the same time in which the state of Tripudi
(The experiencer, experienced and experiencing)
Ceases to exist completely There,
At that Sahasrara, the thousand-petalled Lotus,
O Mother, Who constantly dances blissfully,
I salute Thee.

7 April 1984

It was three in the afternoon. The Mother was seated on the cot in the hut. The fragrance of incense permeated the entire atmosphere. Behind the Mother, on the wall of the hut, hung a large golden-yellow curtain on which the *Gitopadesha* (famous illustration of Krishna standing next to the chariot as He instructs a kneeling Arjuna) was beautifully portrayed in embroidery. There were a few devotees, both men and women, sitting on the floor close to the cot. They wanted to sit as close as they could to the Mother. The Holy Mother was conversing with them, with the never-fading smile on her face. One of them asked,

Question: Mother, can one do *sadhana* by repeating the *mantra* which was given in a dream?

Amma: Children, it is generally not good to do *sadhana* by repeating a *mantra* which one received in a dream. That *mantra* can possibly be just a feeling of the mind. It may not really help you progress spiritually. Since you have not attained the state of Perfection, whatever you feel or think may not come true. However, you may chant it after checking it with a Perfect Guru and having gotten permission from him. If *mantras* obtained through dreams are recommended, many people might proceed in that manner which will then increase the possibilities to err and fall. Therefore, it is better not to depend on *mantras* received in dreams.

Question: Mother, what is the significance of *bijaksharas* (seed letters)?

Amma: Children, *bijaksharas* symbolize the spiritual powers that are imminent in us. They have immense power. The great saints and sages, our forefathers, received them through spiritual revelations. They did not create them; they were already there in existence. Just as pearls and other precious things were there on the bottom of the ocean even before human beings found them, these *mantras* and the *bijaksharas* were already there in nature. The *rishis* through penance tuned their minds to that plane of consciousness. That is how these *mantras* and seed letters were revealed to them. Their minds became pure and clear like a crystal. In that pure mind dawned all knowledge. When we chant those *mantras* with concentration, that power will be awakened in us also. Each seed letter has a presiding deity. That deity or that aspect of spiritual power will be invoked in us when we repeat it with one-pointedness.

SELFLESS ACTION

Question: Mother, what is selfless action?

Amma: Action performed with concentration without the thought about its fruit is selfless action. Such actions are possible only when the fruits are surrendered to a higher ideal. We call that higher ideal God because only in Him can we see the perfection and balance of all the essential principles of life. We cannot see that in a limited human being. Therefore, when we sincerely do something for God, in reality, we are inspired by those higher values. Mother is not talking about people who worship God only to fulfill their desires. On the contrary, it is about people who sincerely seek God, just out of love for Him, not to gain anything from Him. Such people work inspired by the ideal. They work simply because working for that ideal gives them tremendous happiness. Similarly, when we are really devoted to a *Mahatma* or a spiritual master we work for him and his spiritual institution forgetting ourselves. We don't expect anything from that work. Why? Because we are inspired by the spiritual ideals in which the Guru constantly lives. That too is selfless action. One who selflessly acts does not grieve about the past. He does not become worried about the future. In a very relaxed mood, he works with concentration, love and dedication. His mind is not split, but is one-pointed. From such a mental attitude of one-pointedness, he derives a tremendous amount of energy. Only such people can uplift and transform society as a whole.

Remember that when we worship a *Mahatma*, it is not his body that we worship or adore, but the higher principles which are manifested through him. He himself is an embodiment of those ideals; that is what we worship. The body is only secondary.

Again, remember that Mother is not talking about people who work for the success of a particular cult, creed, class, sect, community or nation. Their vision is still limited compared to the highest Ideal. Genuine workers are beyond and untouched by such limitations and are utterly selfless. They work solely out of love for everyone.

Question: Mother, why do you say that the body of a *Mahatma* is only secondary? Does that mean that it does not have much importance?

Amma: No, children, no. After all, the medium of the body is needed for the higher qualities to manifest. They do not have a form of their own. In reality love has no form. Only when love constantly flows through a person does it assume a form that we will be able to experience; otherwise, we cannot. Even when the *Mahatma* leaves the body people still worship the form for ages. It is just because it was through that body that all those great ideals manifested and helped us to experience it. That is the greatness of the body of a *Mahatma*. His body is also pure because it undergoes transformation and purification through his penance. His whole being is pure. It is not like the body of an ordinary human being.

Suppose there are twin brothers. They look alike. Each and every part of their body is so identical that it is very difficult to tell them apart. Their height, weight, everything is the same. Now, one of them becomes a great saint by doing severe penance and the other becomes wicked and crooked, influenced by malevolent company. People will worship and adore the saintly brother and hate the other one even though their bodies look the same. Even if the latter were a normal human being, people would not worship him like they would the brother who became a saint, although they might respect him since he was the twin brother of the saint. Their bodies look alike. Still, why do they adore the saintly brother and not the other one? It is because people feel God and experience Godly qualities such as love, equal vision, compassion, and renunciation in the saintly brother, but they do not feel those qualities in the other brother. Therefore, the qualities come first and only secondarily the body. Not that the body is insignificant. There is no doubt that a saint's body is divine too. His body is equally powerful since it is through that body that the Infinite Energy manifests with all Its glory and splendor. That body which *Mahatmas* themselves choose by their own will must have tremendous power to withstand the constant stream of *Shakti* which manifests through it.

A thousand watt bulb must have enough power to manifest that much of electricity through it. We cannot simply say, "After all, it is electricity which makes it shine." That is meaningless. Without the medium of the bulb, electricity cannot be experienced. So the medium, the body, is equally important.

Question: Mother, what is the significance of meditation?

Amma: Children, meditation alone is beneficial. Do you know what is the position of those scholars who walk around without doing any *sadhana*? Haven't you seen people who stand as guards for somebody else's property like a paddy field or a wealthy man's estate? When these guards talk to someone, they will pose and speak as if the whole thing belongs to them. Scholars are just like that. They just walk around babbling, having heard or read the things that somebody else has said and experienced. They do not understand nor do they try to understand that those who said those things were not mere gate keepers or guards but real owners of it.

The real owners are ones who have realized the inner wealth through meditation, not through mere intellectual knowledge. Whereas, those scholars, whose status is nothing more than a parrot or tape recorder, are like mere gate-keepers who pretend to be the real owner. A parrot will repeat whatever it is taught. In fact, it doesn't even know anything about the words that it repeats. Similarly, whatever is recorded in a tape-recorder will be played back when it is turned on. Such is the case with these book scholars.

In worldly life it is also the same; a peon or gate-keeper displays much more pride and arrogance than the managing director or the real owner of the company. In most cases the real owners are relatively humble and simple.

Therefore, children, those who want to make this knowledge their own must practice meditation. Meditation is not only good for spiritual aspirants but also for people in all walks of life. In a way, meditation is the only selfless action. Some kind of desire will cling to any other type of action. While doing meditation there is no such thought that somebody else should respect us and so on. As far as a true *sadhak* is concerned, meditation is only to purify his mind. That is his only thought.

People may interpret this thought of purifying the mind as a desire as well. But this desire for purification is to eliminate all other desires and thereby do selfless service to the world. The intention behind this desire is high and pure. Whereas, the intention behind almost all other desires is not so. While the desire to purify the mind destroys all other thoughts and desires, the desire to enjoy worldly pleasures redoubles the thoughts and desires, the end result of which will be sorrow and suffering.

Question: Mother, why does complete faith not come, even when human beings get various experiences?

Amma: Complete faith means Liberation. He who has complete faith is a Liberated Being. He has the full faith that God alone is, *Paramatman* alone is. Everything else is changing, momentary. He who has complete faith will experience that each and every object is pervaded by Supreme Consciousness. Others, who have not experienced this, say that every object is pervaded by Supreme Consciousness simply because somebody else whom they respect has said so. Their words and deeds will not go together. They might say that God alone is and that one should have unconditional faith in Him. But if you watch them, you can see that they believe and take refuge in many other things and ideas. This is not complete faith. This is divided faith, having faith in the many and not in the One. Believing in many things is not faith. In fact, that is faithlessness. Faith is one-pointed, having faith in one and the same Reality. In that sense only a Self-Realized soul has real faith. All other faiths are incomplete and unreal. They have incomplete faith while attempting to attain complete faith.

Our faith is divided. It is in many, not in one. It is not one-pointed. We have faith in our body, our husband, wife, children, father, mother, car, house, etc. We believe that the body will live long, that all these people

and objects are mine, mine forever. That is not faith.
This kind of faith is unsteady as the objects we believe
in are unsteady. This again shows the unsteady nature of
our mind. A spiritual person's faith is steady and one-
pointed; therefore, his mind is also steady. He does not
believe in the body. His faith is in the one, changeless
Atman, not in the changing, plural bodies. Only this
kind of faith will help. But in the Kali Yuga it is difficult
to have such faith. Even then, we should try hard to attain it.

Perfect faith comes only when there are no more
doubts, no more doubts in the existence of God, the
Paramatman. At present we are full of doubts. Doubts
are the cause of our lack of complete faith. All uncer-
tainty should die. All beliefs in plurality should die and
real faith should take its place. All arguments and conflicts should end to allow complete faith to take place.
Until then, we will go on with our incomplete, little beliefs.

Mayyâvesya-mano-ye-mâm-nitya-yuktâ-upâsate |
Sraddhayâ-parayo-petâs-te-me-yuktatamâ-matâh ||

Those who have fixed their minds on Me,
And who, ever-steadfast and endowed
With Supreme faith, worship Me...
Them do I consider Perfect in Yoga

[BHAGAVAD GITA, XII-2]

While listening to the conversations of the Holy Mother, both those who asked questions and those who sat and listened clearly experienced the most subtle aspects of the *Upanishads* and *Vedas* slowly blooming forth through her simple explanations. It was a unique experience for the visitors as well as the residents who were present.

Om jñāna-svarūpinyai-namah

Salutations to the Mother Who is the Embodiment of True Knowledge.

FALLING DOWN FOR HER SON

9 April 1984

The Holy Mother was sitting on the northern end of the front verandah of the meditation hall at ten o'clock in the morning. Most of the *brahmacharins* sat in front of her. Gayatri and Kunjumol and a few women devotees sat behind the Mother. A few male householder devotees were also present.

Householder devotee: Amma, there is a letter from my younger son who is in Dubai. How should I reply?

Amma: When he left for Dubai this last time, Mother felt that there was going to be some problem with his job there.

Householder devotee: Your feeling was correct, Mother. He has had some serious problems with his job. He mentioned it in the letter he wrote to me. He says that it was Mother's Grace alone which helped him to straighten up the situation. It was very complicated. They even threatened him in many different ways. Mother has saved him.

Amma: This last time when he visited the Ashram, Mother wanted to give him a hint about it, but he left soon after the evening *bhajan*. Even then, Mother went with Gayatri searching for him in the dark, hoping to find him at the ferry on this side of the *kayal* (backwaters). By the time we reached the ferry he was gone. However, while walking towards the ferry in the dark, Mother stumbled on something and fell into a ditch. This might have been another sign for the possible danger that he was going to confront. By falling into the ditch, Mother felt that the possible danger that he would have confronted was averted. God might have let him avoid it by making Mother fall down. When you write to him next time, ask him to think of God more constantly.

Question: Mother, several people have experienced the state of *nirvikalpa samadhi* (natural state of abidance). Are all of them in the same identical state or is there a difference from person to person?

Amma: Children, the state of *samadhi* is Perfection. One completely merges. There is no one to say even *Aham Brahmasmi* (I Am Brahman) in that state. Though it is said that people have the experience of Brahman, there is a difference in the power which they manifest. Krishna was not like Rama and Buddha was not like

Krishna. Yet within them they will have the awareness of "I am That." Externally, however, they will show a certain amount of limitations and differences. Two people are not needed to express one and the same *bhava*, for God manifests different *bhavas* through different forms.

Question: What about those who have attained *nirvikalpa samadhi* by doing *sadhana*?

Amma: There are people who suddenly attain that state, losing all control during the time of *nirvikalpa samadhi* without any *sankalpa* to come back. They merge in the Absolute Brahman forever, just like the gas in a sodawater bottle goes up and merges in the atmosphere with the sound "pop" when it is opened. They wanted to attain that *samadhi*; that is why they sat in penance. Such people proceed wishing for that, and thereafter will not came back to earth since they have no individuality. Whereas, there are others, *nityamuktas* (eternally liberated ones), who will certainly keep some kind of *sankalpa* in their mind to return before leaving their body. They have an individuality of their own which they themselves have created with the help of the *sankalpa*. Even if they leave the body through *samadhi* and merge in the Absolute Consciousness, they can come back to earth again, if they want, for the benefit of the world. They can assume a form whenever they want.

One *brahmacharin* did not come for meditation at the correct time. The Mother said,

Amma: Children, you should not fail to do your daily

routine. No matter how tired or sick you are, you should try to sit and meditate. That is what a really determined person does. Lying down and saying that I am sick even when only a headache comes shows your weak will. It is not fitting for an aspirant to be such. In the beginning you should develop a love for your daily routine. It should become a part of your life. If you are not able to do it at the set time, you should feel the pain of having missed it and the longing to do it. If she ever forgot to remember God even for a moment, Mother, during her *sadhana* days, used to feel intense pain and cry to the Lord. To make up for that lost time, Mother used to do more severe and intense penance. That is the feeling you should develop.

Worldly tendencies will rise up if there happens to be a break in your *sadhana* in the beginning stages. If you want to stay in the Ashram, you should proceed towards the goal by doing *sadhana*. Children, time will not wait for you. You will not get the lost time back.

Question: Mother, many people commit suicide. Is it right to do so?

Amma: Children, people commit suicide for different reasons. Some do it because of family problems. There are many who commit suicide owing to disappointment caused by frustrated expectations. Failure in a love affair is a common reason which causes people to kill themselves. There are people who give up their lives for the sake of a common cause, for their community, class, creed or sect. This is no shortage of people who commit suicide due to love for their country. There were great warriors, valiant soldiers and rulers who committed suicide because they did not want to be captured or killed by their enemies. Thus there are different situations and circumstances in life when people make a decision to take their own life. Each one who commits suicide, no matter what category he falls in, will think that it is quite reasonable to commit such an act. He will think that it is the only way to escape from the problems which he confronts at that particular time; therefore, he will go ahead and do it.

In most cases it is fear which makes one commit suicide, fear that their dignity or status in society will be lost, fear to confront the situation, fear that one might be killed by the enemy. In other words, it is mental weakness which develops the suicidal tendency in a person. Fear arises when the mind becomes weak and helpless to confront a threatening situation in life.

In any case, committing suicide is not correct. We must try our level best to confront every situation in life, using all our might and strength. Failure cannot be avoided; it is just another aspect of life. Life cannot be without success and failure. It is unavoidable, inevitable. Even if you commit suicide, the situation is not going to change. It is the nature of the sun to shine and illumine. It is the nature of the ocean to have waves. It is the nature of the river to flow. Each object has its own nature without which it would lose its very existence. This innate nature cannot be separated from the object. In the same way, it is the nature of life to have happiness and sorrow. The two are inseparable from life. Now think, why do you cry and worry about something which will not change at all? Is it not meaningless to do so?

Suppose there is a cut on your finger. Will the cut get healed if you keep looking at it and cry? No, it won't. The only way to heal it is to apply medicine and wait patiently. Again, if your hand is injured or if your leg is crippled, you do not cut off the whole hand or leg. Nobody will do this. You will be ready to lie down on a bed for several weeks or months for the injury to be healed. You undergo the treatment, taking the prescribed medicines and wait patiently. This is what is needed in any circumstance. Putting an end to your life is not at all a solution to life's problems. You should sit somewhere, be relaxed and think properly. There is a solution to everything. You must try to find it. That needs patience. Do not lose patience; that will lead you to ruin. Patience is precious. If you think patiently, you can see many of your problems straightening up.

After all, committing suicide is not a solution for any of your problems. Remember that you are creating more problems for your family by committing suicide. Think of the trouble that they have to undergo. By killing yourself you push them into the midst of misery. Again, do you think that once you commit suicide everything ends there? No. By doing so you are creating a chain, a chain of misery. You go on extending and postponing your own evolution towards the Supreme.

Children, the life force is given by God. We have no right to put an end to it. It is against nature's law. Knowing this, if we do it, we will have to suffer for doing an unlawful act, a sin. From his treasury a good king will give gifts in cash or kind to his subjects. To misuse such a gift is improper. It is arrogance to misuse such a gift, isn't it? We have no right to use it incorrectly. We must utilize it to accomplish good and righteous goals; otherwise, we will have to suffer. Punishment will follow any wrongdoing. In the same way, life is the gift of God. He wants us to use it to know Him, to do good and righteous actions. Instead, if we decide to put an end to it for silly and trivial reasons, this would be questioning His power. It would be misusing His gift to us. It would be arrogance on our part. He is the one who gave, He alone has the right to take it back. He alone is the one who has the right to decide when and how life should be taken. We have no power to create; therefore, we are not supposed to destroy life in any way we like.

Question: Some people commit suicide when their leader dies. Some others love their country so much that they do so when their country is in a crisis. Is this justified?

Amma: The best way to express one's love for one's leader after his death, provided that the leader had many good qualities, is by following in his footsteps and by serving society selflessly as he did, not by committing suicide. There is no meaning in committing suicide for a leader who was wicked and selfish. If somebody does that, it is just out of blind attachment to that person. That again means nothing.

Some people may commit suicide in the name of love for their country. But real patriots will not do that. They will try to contribute their part to overcome the crisis. They will try to renounce their happiness for the sake of the country. Loving the country means loving the people who live there. Otherwise, there is no meaning in the saying, "I love my country." If you really love your country, love the people, serve them. Do something to eradicate their suffering. Instead, if you commit suicide, that means you do not want to do anything to solve the situation but only want to escape from it. Thus, if you analyze properly, you can find that you are more concerned about your own happiness than about your country's welfare. You don't want to be unhappy; that is why you commit suicide. By your doing so, the country loses your service.

Mahatmas leave their body in different ways. It is said that some of them left their body by consuming poison knowing that it was poison. This cannot be called suicide. They are the ones who have realized the Self. As far as they are concerned, the body is just a tool for them to use according to their wish and will. They can take it or give it up whenever they want. The body depends on them; they do not depend on the body at all. Whereas, our case is not so. We depend on the body. They control the body, and we are controlled by the body; that is the difference. They take a body for a certain purpose and leave it when the purpose is fulfilled. For them, living in the body is almost like living without a body because they are not at all attached to it. For them, the changes and sufferings of the body are the changes and sufferings of the body only. Their minds are not affected. *Mahatmas* are totally detached from the body. Their body is for the world, for the people, for the devotees and disciples, but not for themselves. To cast the body off, they may choose any means. That is just like a bird flying away from its nest or cage. But for others this is not true. This human birth is very precious. Try to live this life, which is a gift from God, with intent on the goal *(lakshya bodha)*. You should strive to know God.

One brahmacharin: Mother, I always have a fear of failure.

Amma: Son, Self-confidence is an important aspect that a *sadhak* should have. By "Self-confidence" we mean confidence in the Self, faith in the Self; hence, that I am the Self, everything is in this Self. In essence, having faith in the Self is having faith in God or the Guru, for the Guru is the *Atman*, the Self. With this kind of confidence or strong conviction that the Guru will guide you along the path most befitting your innate nature, the Guru will take you to the highest goal, and by the Guru's Grace, you will come out victorious. Thus the victory will be the Self's.

Faith and obedience in the *Satguru* will give us Self-confidence. Obedience to the Guru is very important. The Guru is the All-Pervading *Parabrahman* (Absolute Self) in human form; therefore, he is immanent. He is the Self of you and of the whole creation. Having faith in him is equal to having faith in your Self. Faith is utter obedience to the Guru. If you have that, son, then there is nothing to fear. On the other hand, disobedience to the Guru will cause the worst to happen.

There was a spiritual master who knew how to make pure gold out of certain leaves. His disciple had a desire to learn that art. He expressed his wish to the master. The master said, "No, I won't teach that to you. A true seeker's goal is to get rid of all desires." The disciple's mind became very restless. Due to this intense desire to learn the art, he could not even do his *sadhana* properly. Again and again he approached the master and requested him to teach him the art of making gold. At last, due to his insistence, the Guru taught him the art, having made him take an oath that he would never teach it to others or do it himself. After some years, the Guru left his body. The disciple stuck to his oath for some time and did not practice the art of making gold, but he could not stick to the oath for long. He finally decided to make gold. The disciple started collecting the necessary ingredients and got everything except one leaf. He searched for it everywhere but failed to find that particular leaf. Days and months went by; still he could not find it. His whole mind was fixed on finding the leaf. Finally his obsession drove him insane. From that day until his death, the poor fellow went on smelling all the leaves that he saw, wherever he was. He continued searching for the leaf. That was the result of the disobedience that he showed to his Guru.

A householder devotee came with his family to see the Mother. Their youngest son, a boy of eight or nine years, was very close to the Mother. She caressed and played with him for a long time, making him sit on her lap. Beholding this sight, some of the residents smiled, looking at each other meaningfully. It always happened that if the Mother ever showed a special love or attention to a certain person, that person either became an ardent devotee, or in some cases, they left their hearth and home and came to stay at the Ashram permanently. Whenever such an occasion arose that the Mother showed a special affection to a particular person, the residents would say to each other, "One more hut," which meant that he or she would abandon worldly life and come to stay in the Ashram where the residents dwell in huts.

During one such occasion, the Mother said, "Mother doesn't look at children very intently. If she does, then one day or another, they will change their lives and come to spiritual life. Latent tendencies are yet to be manifested in young children. They have the ability to capture our minds. Then, if Mother's mind somehow gets fixed on them, they will change and come to spiritual life. Mother has a special feeling when she sees some people. It must be because of their inherited spiritual merits from the past birth."

Once the Mother went to the house of Mavelikara Valyammachi, a woman devotee who lives in a nearby town known as Mavelikara, about twenty-four kilometers from the Mother's Ashram. Her name is Saraswathi Amma, but everyone, including the Holy Mother, calls her Valyammachi (elder mother). The *Gita* class was going on. Nearly a hundred children were present. The Mother felt so much love and affection for all the chil-

dren. But every now and then the Mother glanced at
two children. Both of them were sitting behind her, but
even then the Mother would turn around and look at
them. She felt a spontaneous attraction towards them.
Later Valyammachi related that they were the children of
a musician who was a good *sadhak* and a true devotee.
As they were born to a devotee, his virtues and qualities
were seen in them also.

Question: What is more important for one's spiritual
growth, spiritual disposition inherited from the previous
birth or the Guru's Grace?

Amma: Nothing is possible without Grace. Whether in
this birth or in the previous birth or in the births yet to
come, one cannot acquire a spiritual disposition without
Guru's Grace. If you have any spiritual disposition inherited from the previous birth, that was also acquired
through the Guru's Grace. This does not mean that self-
effort is not needed. That, of course, is important. But
effort is human; Grace is divine. Effort is limited; Grace
is unlimited. The limited human effort can take you
only to a certain extent. From that point it is the vehicle
of the Guru's Grace which carries you to the goal. Do
your *sadhana* sincerely with an attitude of self-surrender
and love, and then patiently wait for the Grace to come.
Nobody knows how or when that will happen. Through
humility one can easily gain the Guru's Grace.

The time was half past twelve in the afternoon. The
Mother stood up and walked towards the coconut grove.
A few children from the neighboring houses were stand-

ing there, and the Holy Mother went near them. She was talking to them for quite a while, and both the Mother and the children conversed with each other laughingly. At one point the children burst into laughter, and the Mother did too. The others who remained in front of the meditation hall could not figure out the topic of their conversation as they were standing quite a distance away. The Mother was always very friendly and loving to the children and the adults who lived near and around the Ashram.

Leaving the children, the Mother went by the side of the backwaters. She stood in between two coconut trees looking at the vast sky and swinging her body slowly to either side. Her hands were clasped behind her. The children slowly walked towards her, not making any noise. They stopped when they reached a few steps behind the Mother. They simply remained there gazing at her. The Mother was oblivious to the circumstances. She did not move from that place for quite some time. Her eyes were still fixed at the sky. The children also stood there unmoving until at last the Mother looked back and smiled at them.

All these children, who were under ten, were used to seeing the Mother almost every day. Even then, this spontaneous attraction and love which they felt towards her was something extraordinary. Even they called her "Ammachi."

Turning around, the Mother looked at them and smilingly caressed their heads. The children looked very happy. The Mother then went to her room. The time was a few minutes past one.

At three o'clock a young man came to the Ashram. He seemed very distressed. Brahmacharin Balu was standing in front of the temple. The young man approached him and spoke, "I am Chandra Kumar from Bombay." He spoke in Malayalam; therefore Balu asked, "But you speak Malayalam." "Yes, I am originally from Kerala but I was brought up in Bombay," he explained. Balu inquired, "Have you had your lunch?" and the young man affirmed, "Yes, in Kayamkulam" (a town about twelve kilometers from the Ashram).

He continued, "I would like to see the Mother. It is just to see her and talk to her that I especially came all the way from Bombay. Will I be able to meet her?" There was an anxiety in his voice.

Balu replied, "You know, it is difficult to say when she will come and when she will go. Not only that, today the Mother was here till about quarter past one." Balu took him to the front verandah of the temple and spread a mat on the floor for him to sit down.

"It will be my bad luck if I don't see her and talk to her today," Chandra Kumar expressed worriedly.

Balu reassured him, "Don't worry. You will certainly get her *darshan* if you really long for it. By the way, how did you come to know about the Mother?"

Young man: I was going to tell you about that. It was quite accidental. Last week as I was returning home after work, I met a man traveling in the same train with me. He was between thirty-five and forty years of age. He was also from Kerala, so we easily began a conversation.

When we stopped talking, he took a small book from his pocket and started reading it. There was a picture of the Mother inside the book. The picture attracted me very much, particularly the love and compassion which I felt in her smile and on her whole countenance. I asked him about her and he told me everything he knew about the Mother. I heard from him how his life was completely transformed after seeing the Mother. He had been addicted to drinking, smoking ganja and other bad habits. His wife and children suffered a lot because of his habits. They endured much distress. His elder brother forcibly took him to the Mother. He said that his meeting with the Mother marked the beginning of a new life. He told me that it was the Mother who saved him and his family from utter ruin. He completely gave up all his bad habits after meeting the Mother. Now he leads a happy and devoted life. He concluded the conversation saying, "Though I was taken to the Mother by force at first, now thinking and cherishing her form are so spontaneous to me." I got the inspiration to see the Mother from him. In fact I believe that it was God who made me meet him, because, dear brother, my family is also facing a big problem.

He paused for a while. Again looking at Balu's face he asked, "Will I be able to see the Mother?" The young man seemed very sad and restless.

Balu was touched by the young man's mental predicament. He said, "Let me try to find out whether the Mother will come down again or not."

Just as he was about to get up and go, he suddenly saw the Mother coming down the stairs. He softly told the young man, "Look, the Mother is coming." He added, "Sincere prayers always will be answered."

The Mother, as if she knew that he was there, walked towards the young man, who was now standing in the front yard of the temple. Her white clothes danced in the cool, gentle ocean breeze. The Mother's heart-softening and compassionate glance fell on the young man. She lovingly smiled at him, and he responded by bursting into tears. The young man fell at the Mother's feet. As she bent down to lift him up, she wiped his tears with her own hands. The Mother took Chandra Kumar to the southern side of the temple.

He told the Mother everything he had explained to Balu. He continued as the Holy Mother listened keenly, "Mother, my father and mother are in Bombay where I also live with them. My father is a business man and I help him in his business. I have an elder sister. She was in her final year of studies for a Home Science degree." He stopped and seemed as if gathering strength to complete the story.

The Holy Mother lovingly stretched her right hand and affectionately caressed his left upper arm. He continued, "Six months ago we began to notice a small change in her character. She had always been intelligent, cheerful and very polite in her behavior toward others. Slowly in a few weeks time, she became completely isolated, living in her own mind. Her cheerfulness and happy moods totally disappeared. She stopped talking to every-one, even to my parents and myself. At first we thought that it was only a temporary change. But we soon real-ized the gravity of the situation.

"She would neither eat nor drink nor could she get any sleep at night. Within two weeks she became a com-pletely changed person. Mother, you can imagine how worried my parents were. We took her to different psy-chiatrists and psychologists, hoping that they could cure her. All their treatments were futile. Some people said that she was possessed by evil spirits; others gave the opinion that she was an hysteric. In any case, there was no improvement in my sister's condition. Her health has deteriorated fast. She has become gaunt like a skel-eton. She always sits in her room, staring at something or other. The only thing that sustains her body is the liquid food that we forcibly pour into her mouth. Some-times she drinks it; at other times it just spills out of her mouth.

"Amma, my sister's condition has been like this for the past six months. Nobody can figure out the cause or the cure for her disease. My parents are heartbroken. I am unable to console them as I myself am in distress thinking about her. I am very much concerned about my parents too. Looking after my sister and attending to her, they have neither slept or eaten very much since this illness began.

"Amma, please save my sister, please save my par-ents, please save our family from this crisis." Supplicating in this manner, the young man covered his face with both palms and sobbed like one who had lost everything in life.

The Holy Mother sat closer to him, placed his head on her shoulder and gently rubbed his back. She consoled him saying, "Son, don't worry, everything will be all right. Don't lose your mind; give strength to it. Don't worry, Mother is here." Her soothing and loving words calmed him. He regained control of his emotions. The Mother lifted his head from her shoulder and wiped his tears, reassuring him, "Son, don't worry. Mother feels that daughter (the sister) will be all right."

The Mother then asked Balu to bring some sacred ash from the temple. When it was brought, the Mother imbued it with her pure and concentrated vital energy. She sat in meditation with the ash in her hands for some time and then gave it to the young man.

The Holy Mother then instructed the young man in how to use the ash and then got up to go. Chandra Kumar prostrated to the Mother and took leave of her. The Mother went to her room as the time was nearing four forty-five.

There were no more new visitors at the Ashram. The brahmacharins were meditating. The atmosphere was very calm and quiet. All of a sudden Gayatri came running down and asked if the young man from Bombay was gone. "Why?" inquired Balu. She handed over some sugar candies to him and said that it was prasad from the Mother for his sick sister. It was only five minutes after he had left. Hoping that he could meet him at the ferry, Balu ran to the boat jetty. By the time Balu reached there, Chandra Kumar had already gotten into a boat and was halfway across the backwaters. Balu waved his hand from the shore and shouted to him to wait on the other side of the backwaters. He took another boat across and handed the *prasadam* to Chandra Kumar.

[Note: Three weeks later, the whole family visited the Ashram. It was then that we came to know about the remaining portion of the divine drama which had occurred.

Three days after his visit to the Ashram, Chandra Kumar reached Bombay in the evening by train. It was a great surprise for him when his sister asked immediately when he stepped into her room, "Where is the sugar candy?" He could not believe his ears because after six months time when all hope had been given up, he heard his sister speaking for the first time. He was more amazed when he heard what she asked for; it was the sugar candy which the Mother was sending to her as *prasadam.* How did she come to know about it? He could not speak for some time. When he regained his composure, he could not wait to ask her all about it.

From his sister's narration, Chandra Kumar learned that for three continuous nights, starting from the day he visited the Ashram, she had the same dream about the Mother. After each consecutive dream, she felt a special awakening, as if she were coming back to normal. Her parents also began to notice a change in her. On all three nights she dreamed that the Mother said to her,

"Your brother came to see Mother. Mother will send some sugar candy to you as *prasadam*. Ask for it when he steps into the room. Take it from him and eat it. You will be all right." After eating the sugar candy, she recovered both mentally and physically.]

10 April 1984

The blissful song of the fishermen pushing their boats into the ocean came flowing into the Ashram atmosphere. The mother sea happily received her children, the fishermen, into the cradle of waves and lovingly carried them into her heart, the mid-ocean, singing her never-ending lullaby and affectionately caressing them with the arms of the splashing ocean waters.

The *Vedanta* class for the *brahmacharins* was being held in the meditation hall at eleven o'clock in the morning. The Holy Mother was sitting on the front verandah of the temple facing east. A few devotees from the outside sat near her. Some more arrived and took their seats, after having offered their respects to the Mother. Each one of them had his own problems. The Mother called the devotees one by one and listened to them. The conversation changed to other topics.

One devotee: Mother, a *soma yaga* (Vedic sacrifice for restoring the lost harmony of nature and atmospheric purification) is going on in Trivandrum. *Yaga* (ritual) is not the *dharma* of the age, is it?

Amma: Son, whether *yaga* is the *dharma* of the age or not, there is one thing which nobody can deny. That is, there exists a high degree of atmospheric pollution, and the performance of *yagas* is very good to purify the atmosphere. They offer many things which have very good medicinal power in the sacrificial fire coupled with the chanting of *mantras*. They are all very good for nature. Is it possible to do meditation or other spiritual practices in a polluted atmosphere? Even to do worldly things we need a certain amount of atmospheric purity.

Human beings, through their ego-centered thoughts and actions, have polluted the atmosphere. The atmosphere is completely filled with poisonous smoke and gases from cars, buses, and factories. The worst poison which pollutes the atmosphere is the selfish and wicked thoughts of human beings. Nature's balance is gone. To restore and build up this lost harmony, *yagas* and *yajnas* will help. This is also another way to protect, preserve and spread the *Vedic* tradition.

Moral and spiritual values are the factors which give strength, integrity and unity to a nation. When that is gone, the nation also falls apart.

India's culture is spirituality. The origin of spirituality, though it is beginningless, to speak in empirical terms, is the *Vedas*. Therefore, to preserve, protect and spread the *Vedic dharma* is equal to preserving, protecting and spreading the moral and spiritual values of the country which will help to uplift and unify its people. This alone will protect the country from a great downfall.

Mother does not say that the performers of such *ya-gas* and *yajnas* should only do the external rituals. It is very important to understand the inner principles and live up to them. The goal is to transcend such rituals and oblations and to live constantly in its principles. How many can transcend them? There are still millions who do not know anything about them. How can those millions be ignored just because of a few who have transcended them? While doing them, try to explain what they really mean. Tell them the spiritual significance of the rituals, the science behind these performances.

Son, the atmosphere becomes purified even when we light an oil lamp. Whatever the *rishis* said has meaning and significance. There is nothing to ignore. Look with a subtle eye and you can find the real benefit of such religious performances. There is no sense in criticizing something without studying it properly.

Devotee: Amma, isn't the performance of *yagas* and *yajnas* like taking the people five or six thousand years back? It is primitive.

Amma: How do you determine that? Are you trying to say that human beings have evolved? Mother doesn't think so. In fact, they have gone backwards. The criterion to determine whether one is evolved or not is one's mental maturity and broad-mindedness. If this is the norm, people who lived five or six thousand years ago were more evolved than we are. We are the ones who are primitive mentally, physically and intellectually. They were far superior than we in every field, in every word and deed. Try to see and evaluate things impartially without having any prejudice. Try to have a more intellectual approach and evaluation. The disintegration and destruction of those ancient societies were caused by people like Duryodhana, Dussasana, Sakuni or Dhritharasthra (wicked characters in the *Mahabharata* epic). They represent wickedness, selfishness and egoism. In those days there was only one Duryodhana, one Dussasana and one Dhritharashthra; whereas today, each person is a Duryodhana, a Sakuni or Dussasana. We are mad after name, fame and position. We want to possess everything. Those individuals caused the destruction of an entire race. We are going to cause the destruction of the whole nation, nay, the whole world. Children, who is better, they or us?

The ancient wise men have told us and shown to us the terrible outcome of selfishness and egocentricity. They have also told us how to overcome these traits. Still, we do not want to listen to them. We do not want even to test or experiment with their advice. We just want to criticize what they have said. But who are we to say anything about it? There are those who have studied it properly and scientifically; let them be the ones to evaluate it. Anyhow, if these *yagas* and *yajnas* are performed as prescribed by the *Vedas*, definitely they must bear fruit.

Devotee: In the *Srimad Bhagavad Gita* Lord Krishna says, "Yajnanam-japayajnosmi" (Amongst *yajnas*, I am *japa yajna). Japa yajna* is the simplest and the most accessible to everyone. It is the *Kali Yuga dharma* (that which must be observed as right conduct in the dark age of materialism). Lord Krishna also tells Arjuna, "*Trigunya-vishaya-veda nistraigunyo-bhavarjuna.*" (The *Vedas* are constituted of the three qualities. Therefore, O Arjuna, go beyond them, i.e., the three qualities.) The limit of the *Vedas* is only up to the heaven.

Amma: It is possible for people to go beyond if they could go up to heaven, isn't it? It is also possible for people to go beyond the three qualities if they can go up to heaven, isn't it? The discriminative person will definitely do that. That is why Mother said that they should not become attached to the act of just doing rituals. The performer himself should become the offering. The attitude should be, "O Lord, here, by offering this ingredient, I offer all my attachments to you. O Lord, now by offering this ingredient, I offer all my aversions to you. I burn all these in this fire of knowledge. Take this and purify me." This is the right attitude. But even to attain this state of mind one should either have a lot of inherited spiritual merit accumulated from the previous birth or a lot of *abhyasa* (practice) endowed with *vairagya*.

We cannot expect this attitude from everyone. This can be seen only in very few people. The others also will slowly reach this state through the performance of *yajnas* and *yagas*. But at present they want to fulfill their desires; therefore, they cling to the *yajnas* and *yagas* as prescribed in the *Vedas*. Through performance of these rituals, in due course their minds will become more and more subtle. They will realize that desires are a burden, that they cannot be exhausted completely and that they will only cause sorrow. As their minds become more and more subtle, they will find that renunciation of desires is the only way to get rid of all sorrow and suffering. Thus they will understand and imbibe the real meaning of *yajna*, that is, renunciation, and then they will also live in the *yagna* attitude.

Therefore, do not say that *yajas* are *mithya*. People have different tastes and are of different mental constitutions. Let each one of them choose what he wants. There is benefit in the leaves and branches of a tree even if you do not get the fruit. (The Mother indicates that the *Karma Kanda* of the *Vedas* are the leaves and branches; the fruit is *Atma Jnana*). People have turned their attention to spirituality due to the performance of *yaga*, haven't they? Therefore, there is benefit, isn't there?

Another devotee: Mother's answer is perfect. Even Veda Vyasa wrote the *Bhagavatam** after the *Mahabharata*. Devotion to the Lord which is followed by *jnana* can be gained only after performing actions, such as fighting negative tendencies and dealing with conflicts or other agitations within oneself.

Amma: Who can live without doing anything? Children, without performing any actions no one can live in this world. Isn't *karma* needed to reach *nishkama*? When all the *karmas* are directed to God that is *nishkama*.

---

* The *Bhagavatam* was written after the *Mahabharata*. Here the *Bhagavatam* is presented as devotion and the *Mahabharata* as the fight between the good qualities and the vicious tendencies or the fight between the higher nature and the lower nature in man. When all bad tendencies are annihilated, goodness preponderates. In such a mind, devotion arises.

When it is directed to acquire objects, it is *karma*. When all actions are directed to God, that is *yoga*. When all actions are directed to the world, it is *kama*. Acting in the world, seeing objects as they are and expecting the fruit of action, is *kamya karma*. Acting in the world, seeing the Lord in all objects without expecting the fruit of it, is *nishkama karma*. *Karma* should become *nishkama* first. Out of *nishkama karma* arises one-pointed devotion. From devotion arises *jnana*.

Once Narada saw a strong effulgence. He went near it and found that it was Jnana Devata performing penance. He asked upon whom She was meditating. She replied that She was meditating on the Lotus Feet of the Lord. Here also, the importance is stressed for *bhakti*. *Jnana* will not be received by a person who has no devotion. In that sense, one can say that both *bhakti* and *jnana* are one and the same.

Moreover, attenuation of *vasanas* will happen only if *karma* becomes selfless.

It is not enough if you simply sing *kirtans*, you should sing by involving all your body, mind and intellect in the *kirtans*.

Pointing to a laborer who was turning the soil with a spade (a primitive way of plowing), the Mother said,

Amma: Children, have you seen him turning the soil with his spade? He is a hired laborer. He does the work on a contract basis. He just has to put on a show that he is doing the work. He will just turn the soil on the surface, using the spade. He won't dig it properly, removing the weeds and the roots of coconut trees that have been cut down. How will the seeds germinate and sprout if those are not removed? If it is his own land or field, he will dig it deeply and remove the weeds and the roots of coconut trees that have been cut down and other extraneous growths. He doesn't have any love towards the action that he does. He thinks only about the money, not about the work. Such a person, who loves only money and not the work, who works only because he is forced to, does not have any sincerity. There is no love in his work. He only wants to earn money. This is not the way to perform an action. Any action should be performed with love, and this should be your attitude when you call God. Calling and praying to God is also an action which should be done with love.

In some houses we can see the children singing *kirtans* at dusk. They are not doing it out of love and devotion for God. They do it just out of fear of their parents. They are forced to do it; they are helpless. There is no other way for them; therefore they sit and chant. But as they are chanting they will be fighting or snatching a toy or a doll from another child's hand, desperately scratching their heads, yawning and dozing off, breathing in and delighting in the aroma of the food that comes from the kitchen, and doing other distracting things while singing the Divine Name. This is not *bhakti*. They do it simply out of fear or helplessness. There is not even one iota of love in it. If this is the kind of *bhakti* that we have, the dirt within us will not go. Only if lust, anger and other negative tendencies are uprooted from within through sincere effort, will God dwell within one. How can seeds sprout if they are sown without removing the weeds? In the same way, when there are the weeds of lust and anger in us, the seed of *bhakti* will not sprout in us and God will not dwell in us.

Question: Mother, it seems that here the *brahmacharins* undergo a lot of disciplining; is that much discipline necessary?

Amma: The ancient masters have thoroughly studied the human mind. They have pierced the mind, penetrated into it and understood all its subtleties. They knew very well the tricky nature of the mind. It is only after such exhaustive study that they have written down all the disciplines that a spiritual aspirant should observe. Today everyone writes a book. But Mother wonders about what study they have done about life and their mind. The *rishis* were not superficial; they spent days and nights, foregoing food and sleep to study their mind. The result was the attainment of Ultimate Knowledge. They knew well about the obstacles that a *sadhak* will have to confront during his spiritual journey because they themselves had faced them. They found methods to overcome the obstacles and this is what they instruct us to follow. It is from their own experience that they speak; it is not a borrowed idea.

Controlling the mind is the most difficult task; therefore, the disciplines are extremely arduous. They are not at all too much. Mother does not give the same kind of discipline to everyone. It depends on each person's power to withstand the disciplining. All of the *brahma-charins* do not have the same mental strength to withstand it. Anyhow, discipline is not the first thing that should be done. Love and affection are the first thing to be given. Through the experience of pure love, when they come closer, we can then discipline them. That is what Mother does. Mother did not start disciplining any of them immediately after they came except for a few. Those few had the strength and maturity to undergo such discipline.

More detergent is needed if the cloth is very dirty with too many stains on it. In the same way, the mind is full of stains from different habits and worldly experiences. They can be removed only through proper disciplining.

Mahapurushas (great souls) and *avatars* (divine incarnations) will make rules. There is no way for ordinary people to escape without these rules. But the *Mahatmas* cannot wait for rules. They will make the rules, but they are beyond them. Great souls are beyond all rules. They will move away, having created the rules. God moved away, having created the world. He said that He was not at all related to this. We cannot question Him.

We will become good only if there is somebody to give us rules and discipline us. Aren't there superior officers in offices and in the army to discipline and make workers and soldiers obey? Without them and without the rules, proper disciplining cannot be carried out.

It is not possible to make a *brahmacharin* do *sadhana*
later if he is not made to do it with discipline immediately after he comes. Therefore, very good discipline is
needed from the beginning itself.

Question: Discipline under a *Satguru* is very hard, isn't
it, Mother?

Amma: Oh that! Children, Mother will tell you. A real
Guru will test the disciple in different ways. After some
years of staying with the Guru, sometimes the disciple
might feel that now he is perfect and that he has controlled his mind fully. He may think that nothing ad-
verse can happen to him in any circumstance. In order
to make him recognize his mistake and understand his
own ignorance and to help him traverse that obstacle,
the Guru will again test him.

Once there was a Guru who told his disciple, "Look
here, my child, go to this particular place. There is a
woman living there from whom you are to obtain certain things that I will indicate." After the disciple left to
go on this errand, the Guru himself assumed the form
of a woman and arrived at that particular place before
the disciple. Upon meeting the woman, the disciple lost
his self-control and became enslaved by her. The poor
fellow did whatever she asked. When her demands were
accomplished, the woman disappeared, but not after her
having given a severe thrashing on the disciple's back.
An ashamed disciple returned to the ashram, but he
walked in as if nothing had happened. As soon as the
Guru saw him, he asked the disciple, "Hey fellow, what
is that on your back? He stood perplexed, not knowing

what to say. He didn't say anything due to fear and shame. The Guru then disclosed everything that had happened, revealing that he himself had played the role of the woman. Thus by exposing the disciple's mental state, the Guru made him understand his own weaknesses. He gave the necessary instructions for deepening his *sadhana* and let him go.

The Guru will test the disciple in every way. He will lock the disciple in a room where there are naked women standing. Sometimes the Guru will ask the disciple to apologize ten thousand times in a peculiar way for a silly mistake that he has committed, for example, to apologize on bended knees, with arms crossed over the chest, the right hand holding the left ear and the left hand holding the right ear.

"Please teach me the Ultimate Knowledge, O Master, if I am competent enough to be your disciple." Praying thus, the disciple should approach the Guru with an attitude of complete self-surrender. The Guru, if he accepts him, will put him through many trials and tribulations as he teaches the disciple whatever he himself knows. Finally, if the disciple comes out victorious in all his tests, the Guru will teach the *Brahma Sutra* to him, not only the intellectual material but the experience as well. Only if the disciple surrenders to the Guru will he be meritorious.

My children, what about today? If a person gets ten rupees, he will go to a bookstore, buy a *Brahma Sutra* text and finish reading it in one sitting. There ends the study of the *Brahma Sutra*. Thereafter, he thinks that he is *Brahman*. A person like this once came to the Ashram, claiming, "I am *Brahman*." Mother replied, "If you are *Brahman*, then that fish, dog and cat are all *Brahman*." What reply could he give? He simply said, "Yes, yes."

One brahmacharin: (Indicating another person) That swami doesn't do any *sadhana*, but he is very interested in getting disciples.

Amma: Why should you comment on others? Do not do that. Try to make your path clear. Please, my children, none of you should go in search of disciples. Whatever time you get, do *sadhana* and try to attain Self-Realization. Once you attain that goal, everything will come to you automatically. Do you know what you need now? You should try to meditate even while sitting in the toilet.

Son, it is foolishness to destroy this life without attaining that which should be attained. This body is like a business concern. *Atman* is what should be gained as profit from this business. The very purpose of human birth is Self-Realization, but that is the one thing that we forget. We forget the most important thing.

Another brahmacharin: Amma, I cannot control hatred and anger.

Amma: Son, no hatred or anger will come if you consider others as your own. A mother will not consider the odor from the excreta of her own children as foul-smelling, bad or harmful. An infected, putrid smelling wound full of pus on our own body is not a problem for us because it is our own body. We can bear the smell.

But if it is on somebody else's body, we cannot stand it. We don't feel any anger or hatred towards our son or daughter even if they scold or hit us. Why? Because of the feeling that they are our own. Thus, if we hold the attitude that all beings are "my own," hatred and anger will go. We can overcome these negative traits if we become aware of their terrible consequences. Anger will make us do all kinds of evil deeds. It will dissipate all our good energies. It will take away our discriminative power and make us bitter, mad and even insane. Consider anger as your first and foremost enemy. If you become aware that you are going to get angry, leave that place immediately and try to contemplate in solitude.

All of a sudden the Mother turned to look at one young man who was a newcomer and said,

Amma: Children, before marriage a person will dream many things, such as, "My wife shall be of 'such and such' a nature; she shall be very beautiful and she shall love me like her own life," and so on. Such a dreamer will have a hundred different kinds of thoughts and imaginations. He may not find even one of these qualities in his wife after the marriage. Then disappointment arises and soon quarrels and fighting will begin. This will be followed by mental agitation and eventually the man and wife will end up in the divorce court. What a life this is! Sorrow alone is the result of one who lives in this non-eternal world.

Upon hearing these words of the Mother, the young man fell at her feet and cried. What Mother had just said was his own experience. He had had such imaginations and dreams about his wife and married life. But after the marriage, they always fought with each other and their whole life together was in sorrow. Now he was thinking about divorce.

There was a short pause after which the Mother asked Brahmacharin Pai to sing a bhajan. He sang *Bandhamilla*.

> No one is ours
> And there is nothing to call our own.
> In our last days
> Only the True Self will remain as ours.
>
> We can take nothing with us
> During the last journey.
> Why then this madness
> For earthly possessions?
>
> That which truly exists is within us.
> To see That, we must go within.
> There is not even a trace of sorrow there.
> There the True Self shines in Its own glory.
>
> The awakening of the Inner Self
> And True Knowledge
> Comes only when egotism is completely gone.
> We go from untruth to Truth
> When we love and serve all living beings.

Entering into a rapturous mood, the Mother was sitting with eyes closed with tears rolling down her cheeks. She uttered a laugh in that state of sweet bliss. When she came back down to the plane of normal awareness, the Mother said,

Amma: The bliss of singing the Divine Name is something unique. It is inexpressible. Mother is not at all hesitant to take any number of births to sing the Name of the Lord. There is no question of gaining total and complete satisfaction in singing the Lord's Name. That is why even those who have reached that State will come down and sing the glories of the Lord with the attitude of a devotee. That is something which one will not feel fed up with at all.

At this point Brahmacharin Nealu came and prostrated to the Mother. He sat with the other devotees. One of the devotees asked the Mother about another devotee who was his friend.

Question: Amma, did he receive a *mantra* from you?
Amma: No. But it is not necessary to receive a *mantra* from Mother externally. It is enough if Mother's *sankalpa* is present. This power can also be transmitted through a glance or touch. Even then, *sadhana* is needed.
Question: Devotees who live in distant places say that they have seen Mother in surprisingly strange circumstances. What do you say about that, Amma?

Amma: That happens due to their strong faith and innocent love.

The Mother did not utter even one word more about it.

One devotee: The Mother has a body made of pure effulgence beyond this gross body that we see. Using that, she reaches as many places as she wants to at the same time. She is omnipresent.

Again the Mother kept quiet.

Question: Amma, it is said that the dangers of pitfalls are many while one pursues the spiritual path.
Amma: That is right. A *sadhak* should be very careful and constantly alert. One moment's carelessness can pull a person down.

Children, the dangers of pitfalls are there, even while standing one step below the state of *jivanmukti* (liberated state). A pitfall is possible even the night before *jivanmukti*. Recall the story about the churning of the *Milk Ocean*. Ambrosia emerged while the *Milk Ocean* was being churned. Snatching the ambrosia, the demons ran away before the celestial beings could retrieve it. It was taken due to a moment's carelessness. How hard they strived to get it back. A *sadhak* should always be alert. A moment's carelessness can cost you Ambrosial Bliss.

Sita desired to have the golden deer. She was the incarnation of the Goddess Lakshmi and was very wise.

Still she was attracted by the golden deer.* Although Rama advised her not to crave for the it, she begged him to capture it. What followed was a whole chain of calamities. When the deer was shot by Rama's arrow, it (being the demon Maricha) gave out a cry, imitating Rama's voice. Sita then urged Lakshmana to go help Rama. Lakshmana tried to convince her that there was deceit behind this cry and that nothing bad could possibly happen to Sri Rama. But Sita was adamant. She lost her wisdom, her discrimination and all other virtues for a moment. She became angry with Lakshmana and even uttered insulting and crude words at him. This incident in the *Ramayana* symbolizes how a person, even one highly evolved, can err and fall at any moment, if one is not alert.

Question: Mother, how do we develop alertness when the mind is more attached to worldly pleasures?

Amma: Children, it is true that mental control is a difficult task while living in this world. It is like standing on the seashore. Even if we do not go into the water, the saline mist will stick to our body. It is just like taking a bath in a room where coal is kept. However much we try to clean our body, there will be coal particles all over us.

---

*While Rama, Sita and Lakshmana were in the forest during the years of banishment from the Kingdom of Ayodhya, Ravana, King of Sri Lanka, desired to have Sita. He plotted to abduct her through trickery by enlisting the help of the demon Maricha, who adopted the guise of a beautiful golden deer which evoked Sita's desire. The deer lures Rama away from Sita, and the demon's deceitful cry, imitating Rama's voice, causes Sita to send Lakshmana away to save Rama. Through her own indiscriminative actions, Sita is left unprotected as Ravana forcibly takes her away.

Children, even then, those who are really determined to attain the goal can score a victory over the mind. Even to achieve worldly ends, we will renounce many things. For example, a businessman who travels a lot will sometimes have to forsake many of the comforts he has at home. He may not be able to eat or sleep at the usual time. He will get only very little time to be with his wife, children and other family members. He will not be able to have his favorite dishes everyday. Still he works hard. In fact, in his desire to make money and to make his business flourish, he forgets all about such comforts. Think of the people who go to the Gulf countries to make money. They have to work hard. Most of them have very difficult jobs. They have only the minimum living facilities, a small room with five or six people squeezed in it. They have to cook for themselves and have to undergo very hard times. Once they go, these poor people cannot come back to see their wives, children, parents or friends for two years or more. Still they work, renouncing many pleasures and comforts, undergoing all kinds of hardships. Why? Because they need money. They want more comforts, so they endure these discomforts. They feel the need to endure, and thus they do not feel the burden of these sufferings or hardships. They are happy to do it.

In the same way, children, we should feel a similar need and urgency to attain this inner wealth. Once that arises in us, then alertness will come, followed by renunciation and determination.

A businessman or a banker who deals with huge amounts of money will always be alert and vigilant.

Why? Because a little bit of carelessness may culminate in a big loss. He does not want that to happen; therefore, he is alert. The Prime Minister's or the President's bodyguards need to be very alert and vigilant, because one moment's inadvertence can cause the death of the Prime Minister or the President. They do not want that to happen; therefore, they are very keen.

Similarly, one moment's lack of alertness can cause a pitfall in a *sadhak's* spiritual life. While being attached to an object or while in a particular circumstance, a *sadhak* might feel, "Oh, after all, it is only a small thing, not very significant. Nothing is going to happen if I do it." So he does it. Then a chain of reactions will follow. Be aware and alert that this can happen to you at any moment and then fix all your attention on the goal and work hard to reach it. Definitely you will get it.

Nealu, who was present, asked,

Nealu: Amma, as you said that in the beginning, controlling the mind is not an easy job, especially while living in the midst of worldly pleasures. This is still more difficult for the people who live in the West. Their materialism is much stronger than here in India. What advice do you have to give them concerning this?

Amma: Mother is very happy to see the enthusiasm and spirit of the children in the West in wanting to lead a spiritual life.

Whoever it may be, *vasanas* will exist, except in one who has reached the state of perfection. To control the mind means to eliminate the *vasanas*. Actually what one should do is to try to remove the previously created tendencies and to block the entrance of new ones into the mind. This cannot be achieved in a short period of time. Mother will not ask you to stop indulging completely and devote all your time to doing spiritual practices. There are people who are interested in doing that, but the majority do not want to nor can they do it right away. They want both. They want to lead a worldly life and simultaneously lead a spiritual life. For them the best way is to slowly and steadily control the habits, one by one. During this process, one might fail many times. Let failures happen. After all, failure comes only to a person who tries for success. Therefore, do not get worried or agitated if failure happens. Again and again it might occur. But do not lose your enthusiasm and interest. Try again and again. Declare an open war with your mind. The mind might pull you and push you into the same old habits. Understand that it is only a trick of the greatest trickster, the mind, to divert you from the path. Do not give up. There will come a point when the *vasanas* will lose all their strength and give way for the Lord to come in and rule. Till then try and keep trying. Let the failures "fail" to stop you from continuing your practice.

Children, this world is created by the Lord for you to enjoy. No spiritual master or scriptural text has ever said that everyone should give up all kinds of worldly enjoyments and engage in constant remembrance of God. No one has said that everyone change their residences and live in ashrams and become *sannyasins*. As Mother said before, there are people who can do it and who are determined to do it. Let them follow their path. But there is a way for others also to become closer to God. That is possible by slowly preparing the mind for that final leap while leading a normal life in this world.

While driving one must obey traffic rules and regulations. If not, accidents will occur. Not only you, but others will suffer if an accident happens. Likewise, while driving the vehicle of life along the road of this world, you have to adhere to certain laws, certain do's and don'ts. It is these rules and regulations that the Gurus and the scriptures talk about. If you follow them, you can avoid danger and will be safe both in your personal life and social life. However, conflicts and calamities will arise in both areas of your life if you break these rules and regulations through over-indulgence and other undisciplined ways.

Children, negative thoughts might arise in your mind while you proceed in your *sadhana*. Don't worry. Don't give them too much importance. Giving too much importance to negativity will make your mind weak. Once the mind becomes weak, you will not be able to do anything. It will become impossible even to put forth the mental strength or the capacity we already have in order to do our *sadhana*. Ignore them and continue your *sadhana*.

Therefore, children, do not worry. Mistakes might happen. Do not bother your head thinking about them. Remember, by worrying about them you are losing the mental energy and strength to confront and correct them. Do not waste your time worrying. Proceed and pursue your practice.

Children, remember food is for us to eat. Do not let the food eat us. This world is for us to enjoy. Do not let the world toss you up and down with attractions and aversions. This body, mind and intellect are tools for us to use according to our wish and will. Let us have perfect control over them. Do not let them control us.

The Mother then asked Sreekumar to bring the harmonium. She sang *Martyare Samsara*.

> O Mother, Thou art the Redeemer of mankind
> Taking us across the ocean of the world.
> Thou art the Primal Cause of the world,
> The Power behind the Universe.
>
> Thou dost manifest as the three gunas
> And as the Supreme Life Force.
> I know, O Mother, that Thy love for us
> Makes the fulfillment of human life possible.
>
> The moonlight of Thy smile gives light
> And peace to this world of misery and darkness.
>
> Out of the five elements the Universe
> Is made to manifest Thy Gracious Glory.
> Thou art the Holy Waters,
> The Elements and the Root Cause.

Thou fillest the whole Universe,
Manifesting them with and without form.
If, for even a moment, Thou abandonest me,
Tell me then, O Mother,
What is the use of this life on earth?

AUM

GLOSSARY

{Certain words are the same or similar in Malayalam and Sanskrit. Thus *Abhyasa* and *Brahmacharin* are Sanskrit whereas *Abhyasam* and *Brahmachari* are Malayalam}

ABHYASA(M): Constant effort

ADHARA(M): Substratum

ADVAITA(M): Non-dualism

AHAM BRAHMASMI: 'I am the Absolute' (Whole).

AMBROSIA: The elixir of eternal life (Amrit).

AMMACHI: The Mother. *Chi* is a word indicating respect.

AMRITATTVA(M): Immortality.

ARATI: Waving the burning camphor, which leaves no residue, with ringing of bells at the end of *puja* (worship) indicating total annihilation of ego.

ARCHANA: A mode of worship by repetition of one hundred, three hundred or a thousand names of the chosen deity.

ARJUNA: The third among the Pandavas and a great archer

ASANA: Steady position for meditation

ATMA(N): The Self

AVADHUT(A): An advanced wandering ascetic.

AVATAR: Incarnation. Great Souls who are fully aware of their identity with God right from birth.

BHADRA KALI: See Kali

BHAGAVAD GITA: The teachings of Lord Krishna to Arjuna at the beginning of the Mahabharata War. It is a practical guide for common man for every day life and is the essence of Vedic wisdom. *Bhagavad* means 'that of the Lord' and *Gita* means 'Song', particularly, an advice.

BHAGAVATA(M): The book on the incarnations of Lord Vishnu, especially Krishna and his childhood sportings. It upholds the supremacy of devotion.

BHAGAVATI: The Goddess of six virtues, viz, prosperity, valor, auspiciousness, knowledge and dispassion

BHAJAN: Devotional singing

BHAIRAVI: Consort of Bhairava (Siva).

BHAKTI: Devotion.

BHAVA DARSHAN: The occasion when Amma receives devotees in the exalted state of Universal Mother.

BHAVANA: Creative imagination.

BHAVA SAMADHI: Absorption into the Self through devotion.

BHOGI: A pleasure seeker.

BIJAKSHARA(S): Seed letters in a *mantra*.

BINDU: Point.

BRAHMAN(M): The Absolute, Whole.

BRAHMANANDA: The incomparable bliss of Realization.

BRAHMACHARI(N): A celibate student under training of a Guru.

BRAHMACHARYA: Celibacy

BRAHMAMAYI: Who is nothing but *Brahman* .

BRAHMANANDA(M): The bliss of Realization.

BRAHMANISHTATTVAM: Establishment in *Brahma*.

BRAHMASUTRA: Aphorisms on Vedanta composed by Vyasa.

CHAKKA KALI: A game played by children. The word "Kali" (with a short 'a') in Malayalam means play and (with a long 'a') Universal Mother.

CHAKORA(M): Cacabis Partridge. It is believed that seeing this bird at the commencement of a journey is an auspicious omen.

CHAMUNDA: An aspect of the Universal Mother.

CHANDA: A demon killed by Kali.

DAKSHINA: Offerings made to the Guru or the priest.

DARIKA: Another demon beheaded by Kali.

DARSHAN: Audience of a Holy Person or deity.

DEVA(TA): Demi-god, celestial being

DEVI: The Goddess.

DHARMA: Righteousness.

DHRITARASHTRA: Father of Kauravas and King of Hastinapuri. He was physically blind and blind with attachment towards his son,Duryodhana, which eventually led to the Mahabharata War.

DHYANA(M): Meditation

DURYODHANA: Eldest son of Dhritarastra and villain of Mahabharata epic.

DUSSASANA: Brother of Duryodhana.

EECHA: House fly

GANJIRA: A small hand-held drum

GITA: See *Bhagavad Gita*

GITOPADESA: Sri Krishna's instructions to Arjuna in the form of the *Bhagavad Gita* . (Famous illustration of Krishna in the chariot giving advice to a kneeling Arjuna in the Mahabarata epic.)

GOPA(S): Cowherd boy(s), companions of Sri Krishna

GOPI(S): Cowherd girl(s), known for their supreme devotion to Sri Krishna

GRAHASTA: Householder

GRAHASTAHSRAM(A): Householder who leads a righteous life.

GURU: Spiritual Master / Guide.

GURU DAKSHINA: Offering made to Guru as a token of respect.

GURUKULA(M): Residential school of a Guru

HANUMAN: A great servant devotee of Lord Rama who crossed the sea by jumping over it with the power of constant remembrance of the name of Rama.

HATHA YOGA: Gaining mastery over the body as a means of Self-Realization.

HOMA: Offering made to celestial beings by means of pouring clarified butter and other pure materials into the sacred fire.

ISWARA: God

JANMA(M): Birth

JAPA YAGNA: The vow of constant repetition of a *mantra*

JAPA: Repetition of a mystical formula (*mantra*)

JIVANMUKTA: A Liberated Soul

JIVANMUKTI: Liberation.

JIVA(N): Life force

JIVATMA(N): Individual Soul

JNANA: Spiritual or divine wisdom

KALI: The Divine Mother. She is depicted in many forms. Her auspicious form is called *Bhadra Kali.*

KALI YUGA: Present dark age of materialism.

KAMYA BHAKTI: Devotion motivated by desires.

KANYAKUMARI: The southern point of the Indian subcontinent where there is a temple of the Divine Mother as a virgin.

KARMA PHALA(M): Results of action.

KARMA: Action.

KARMA KANDA: Ritualistic portions in the *Vedas*

KASHAYA: The ochre color denoting the fire of Divine Knowledge.

KAURAVA(S): The hundred children of Dhritarashtra.

KAYAL: Backwaters

KIRTAN(AM): Hymns

KRISHNA: Principle incarnation of Lord Vishnu

KUNDALINI: Spiritual energy depicted as the serpent power coiled at the root of the spine which rises to the head by spiritual practices, leading one to Liberation.

LAKSHMANA: Brother of Lord Rama.

LAKSHMI: Consort of Lord Vishnu and Goddess of wealth.

LAKSHYA BODHA: Constant awareness of and intent on goal

LALITA SAHASRANAMA: Thousand names of the Universal Mother in the form of *Lalitambika*

LEELA: Divine play.

LOKA(M): World

MAHABHARATA(M): Great epic written by Vyasa.

MAHAPURUSHA(S): Great person

MAHA KALI: A form of the Universal Mother

MAHATMA: Great Soul

MAKKAL(E): Children. *Makkale* is the vocative form.

MANASA PUSHPAM: Offering of the mind (heart) as the flower in worship.

MANASA PUJA: Mental worship of God.

MANTRA: Sacred formula, the repetition of which can awaken the spiritual energies and bring the desired results.

MARGA: The path.

MAUNA(M): Vow of silence.

MAYA: Illusion.

MILK OCEAN: The abode of Vishnu, represents the pure mind.

MITHYA: Transient

MOL(E): Daughter. *Mole* is the vocative form.

MON(E): Son. *Mone* is the vocative form

MRIDANGAM: A type of drum widely used in Indian classical music.

MUDRA: A sign by hand indicating mystic spiritual truths.

MUKTA: The Liberated One

NARAYANA: Lord Vishnu

NISHKAMA KARMA: Action without expectation of results

NIRAKARA: Without form

NIRGUNA(M): Without attributes

NIRVIKALPA SAMADHI: The state of abidance in the Self.

NISHKARMA: Non action, detached action

NITYA MUKTA: The Ever-Liberated One

PADA PUJA: Worshipping the feet of the Guru. As the feet support the body, it is the Supreme Truth that supports the principle of Guru. Thus His feet are the symbolic representation of that Truth.

PANDAVA(S): The five children of King Pandu and heros of the epic *Mahabharata*

PARA SHAKTI: The Supreme Power, Universal Mother.

PARA BHAKTI: The supreme form of devotion devoid of desire, absolute love the Lord.

PARABRAHMAN(M): The Supreme Absolute.

PARAMATMA(N): Supreme Self.

PEETHAM: A high platform.

PUJA: Worship.

PRADAKSHINA(M): Circumnambulation.

PRASAD(AM): Consecrated offerings distributed after *puja*.

PREMA: Deep Love.

PURANA: Epic.

RAJA YOGA: The Royal Path of Union with the Supreme.

RAMA: Hero of the epic *Ramayana*. An incarnation of Vishnu and the ideal of Righteousness.

RAMAYANA(M): The epic about Lord *Rama* composed by the sage *Valmiki*

RAVANA: The villain of the *Ramayana*

RISHI: A great sage or seer.

RUDRAKSHA(M): A sacred seed (bead) having spiritual and medicinal value.

SADHAK(AN): One dedicated to attain the spiritual goal, one who practices *sadhana* (spiritual discipline).

SADHANA: Spiritual practices.

SADHU: Mendicant.

SAGUNA(M): With attributes.

SAIPPU: A Westerner.

SAKARA: With form.

SAKUNI: Maternal uncle of the Kauravas, a crooked intellect.

SAMADHI: State of absorption in the Self

SAMSARA: The world of plurality

SANKALPA: Creative, integral resolve

SANKARA: Siva. Amma sometimes uses it as a synonym for 'simpleton'.

SANNYASI(N): Ascetic who has renounced all worldly bondages.

SARI: A long piece of cloth worn by Indian ladies.

SATGURU: Realized Spiritual Master

SATCHIDANANDA: Existence, consciousness, bliss

SATSANG: Company of the wise and virtuous

SATTVIC: Of pure quality, goodness

SAUNDARYA LAHARI: Songs on the glories of the Universal Mother. The word means 'beauty' or 'intoxicating'.

SHAKTI: The dynamic aspect of *Brahman* as the Universal Mother.

SHIVA / SIVA: The static aspect of *Brahman* as the male principle.

SIDDHA VEDA: A school of *Yoga*

SITA: Wife of Rama

SOHAM: 'I am That'- the *mantra* that incessantly resonates within every person.

SOMA YAGA: A form of fire ceremony

SRADDHA: Faith. Amma uses it with a special emphasis on alertness coupled with loving care of the work in hand.

SREE RAMA: See *Rama. Sree, or Sri,* is a mark of respect

SRIMAD BHAGAVATAM: See *Bhagavatam. Srimad* means 'auspicious'

SUKA: Son of Vyasa who was perfect from birth.

TALAM: Beat, rhythm.

TAPAH: practicing spiritual austerities.

TAPASVI: One engaged in penance.

TAPOVAN(AM): Hermitage, a place conducive to meditation.

TATTVA: Principle.

TATTVATTILE BHAKTI: Devotion rooted in discriminative knowledge between the eternal and the ephemeral.

TYAGI: Renunciate.

UNNIKRISHNAN: The Child Krishna

UPANISHADS: The concluding portion of the Vedas dealing with the philosophy of Non-dualism.

VAIRAGYA(M): Dispassion, detachment

VANAPRASTA: The third phase of life devoted to austerities and a secluded life.

VASANA: Latent tendency.

VEDA: Lit. 'Knowledge', the authoritative Scriptures of the Hindus.

VEDA VYASA: See *Vyasa.* As he divided the one *Vedas* into four, he is also known by the name of *Veda Vyasa*

VEDANTA(M): The philosophy of the Upanishads which declare the Ultimate Truth as 'One without a Second'.

VEDIC DHARMA: Injunctions on the righteous way of living as prescribed by the Vedas.

VISHNU: All-pervading. The Lord of sustenance

VYASA: A sage who divided the one *Vedas* into four and composed 18 *puranas* and also the *Mahabharata* and *Bhagavatam.*

YAGNA: Sacrificial rites and rituals.

YOGA: Union with the Supreme. Popular used in the sense of a set of exercises to make the body and mind fit for spiritual practices.

YOGINI: A woman accomplished in *yoga*

YUGA: Aeon. The four ages are *Krita (Satya), Treta, Dvapara* and *Kali.* They represent the successive transition from a spiritual to material era. In Indian thought, the number '4' is associated with wholeness, hence, the 4 yugas. During each yuga, 25% of Dharma, or Truth, diminishes from the previous yuga.

INDEX

C

space made for 195
talking to 46, 47, 70
See also Form of God and
    Formless God.
gopa(s) 233
gopi(s) 80, 127, 233, 245
grace
    Mother's 254, 256, 278
    nothing possible without 288
    transforms mind, 93
    supports and protects 68
    versus effort 86, 122-123, 175,
        209-210, 215
grahasta 240, 250, 251
**grahastahsram 240, 247, 249,
    256**
guru
    and penance 177
    as Parabrahman 285
    beyond Trinity 254
    debt to 254
    definition of 172-174
    grace of 68, 122, 123, 210, 285,
        288
    guides 285
    following of 193, 254
    hearing xiv
    in awakening kundalini 199
    learning with in olden days 247
    necessity of 167, 170
    obedience to 83, 285, 286
    tests 96, 306, 307
guru dakshina 97
gurukula 247
Guru Vayur 47

H
habits
    as impediment 97
    controlling 316
    giving up 160
    goodness as 214

mind full of 30
    of arising for meditation 256
    of restlessness 261
    of devotee 291
    to talk 42
    versus bliss 48
hamsa 83, 88, 134
Hanuman, story of 68
happiness
    and laziness 165
    and remembrance of God 47
    and sorrow in life 281
    beyond 214
    giving up to attain bliss 48
    in loving God 7, 72
    nothing in world gives 33, 46
    of children as Mother's health
        130
    of Mother 36
    of spiritual realization 209
    of those at Ashram 160
    ours and welfare of country 284
    part of life 50
    people see life as 31
    through faith and self-control
        118
    versus God 72
    welcome equal to sorrow 48
Hari, story of egoism 216
Harshan 231
hate (hatred)
    from arguments 45
    makes mind ugly 197
    Mother feels none 196
    Mother instructs 308
    of evil not evil-doer 44
hatha yoga 101
homa, for purification, 78
humility
    for Realization 200
    gains guru's grace 288
    of god 71

S

sacrifice
of animals and animal tendencies 76-78
of ashram life at home 240
of Mother 38
of small for big things 77
sadhak
a devotee 288
and asanas 261
and food 84
and meditation 274
and photos 131
and self-confidence 285
as a bird 158
how they pray 54
like a student 67
mind on God 53
Mother speaks to xii, 41
needs patience 209
needs strong mind and equal-
heartedness 197
obstacles of 304
peace at ocean 229
places where lived 90
pitfalls to 312, 315
sadhana
after reading books 101
and discipline 306
and guru's test 307
and kundalini 102, 198
and mantra of dream 269
as compared to rishis 177
attitude for 122, 197, 199, 259,
288
before books 169, 273
do not worry 225
eliminates mind 27
instead of doubts 105
instructions from Mother 237,
238, 240, 280, 308, 317
intensifying 256-258

liberation through 156, 279
need for 30, 43, 82, 169, 311
of avatars 156
of brahmacharins 206
of devotee(s) 112, 113, 193,
209
of disciple 286
of Hari 216
of western children in ashram
160
place for 83, 88
separation of sexes in ashram
147
with Satguru 174
sadhu 41
sages: see rishis
saguna 15
See also Formless God.
saippu 161
sakara 106
See also Form of God.
Sakuni 299
**Salini, is cured of Leukemia
223-226**
samadhi
all happenings stop 226
bliss of 72
mahasamadhi 90
nirvikalpa 278, 279
of Mother xiii, 39
perfection 278
sahaja 60, 128, 157
samsara 68
sankalpa
and samadhi 279
Devi not a 103
of Miss D. 224, 226
of Mother 225, 311
of rishis 15
Sankara, Shiva 11
sannyasa
and devas 213